The Collected Yaps of the
WEE GINGER DUG

Volume 1

by

Paul Kavanagh

‖‖‖‖‖‖‖‖‖‖‖‖‖‖‖‖‖‖‖‖
D1426303

Best Wishes

Paul Kavanagh

WEE GINGER DUG BOOKS

Published in 2015 by Wee Ginger Dug Publishing

ISBN Paperback: 978-0-9934057-0-9
ISBN eBook: 978-0-9934057-2-3

Published with the help of Indie Authors World

Cover by Maurice Rapallini

Dedication

For Andy, and for all those who believed in Scotland but are no longer with us. We will carry them in our hearts and memories forever.

Introduction

I started this blog because I was trapped indoors caring for Andy, my partner of 25 years. He suffered from vascular dementia and could not be left unattended. His illness meant that he slowly lost all those parts of himself that had made me fall in love with him all those years ago. I never stopped loving him, but our relationship changed, I ceased to be his partner, and became his carer.

Eventually his illness took him, and he passed away just a few days before the Scottish independence referendum. One of his last acts was to sign his postal ballot paper, and he voted yes for Scottish independence. Andy wasn't Scottish, he was born and brought up in London, the son of an Irish immigrant. He spent his life in England and Spain, I brought him to Scotland in his final years as I knew I would need support to look after him as his illness progressed. In Scotland Andy found love, acceptance, compassion and care.

Dementia is a cruel illness. As I watched Andy slowly lose his personhood, his gifts and skills, and grieved for him while he still lived, I came to realise that I was losing myself too. Carers give everything, they give of themselves until there's nothing left. So I started the Wee Ginger Dug blog, named after our dog Ginger, a rescued Spanish mutt. Walking the dog was the only time I ever got to myself.

Writing gave me a wee island where I could be myself, and I'd sit on the sofa and type on the laptop while Andy sat beside me. Typing for my sanity, typing for myself, typing for a Scotland that lived only in dreams and hopes. What I never realised, lost as I was in the concern of a carer, and then lost in the grief of loss, was that this blog touches others.

One year on and Andy's loss still hurts, but the raw and bleeding edges of the hole in my heart have scarred and hardened. I miss him, I miss who I used to be be when we were together. But the loss has become a part of me, and I'm learning to live with it. As I wept during the days after his death, dazed and devastated, uncomprehending in the magnitude of grief, I slowly came to realise that there could still be hope, and that's what kept me going. I can live and love again. I can hope, and I can still dream.

And I have the readers of the blog to thank for that, the kind strangers who showed me that there was still a reason to hope, to fight, to go on. They gave me a reason to get up in the mornings, they gave me a purpose. They showed me that a country is a community, a community of care and compassion. With people like them in it, Scotland's future is assured.

And here we are, a year on, a referendum lost but a country gained. We're still here, still fighting, still persuading, still arguing, still being. With every word, with every day, we show that another Scotland is possible.

We don't all agree. After a year it's clear that the independence movement was always broad coalition of diverse views, distinct voices, and different opinions. We have disagreements, but that's a good and healthy thing. We are a nation not a political party, but we remain united in the belief that power rests with the people of Scotland, that the best people to decide on the future of this land are those who live here and love here. We remained united in the knowledge that our country's many problems and issues can only be tackled successfully when we as a nation take collective responsibility into our own hands and we stand before the world as an equal.

The referendum was not the end, it was only the beginning. But one thing is clearer now than it ever was, our day is coming, the confidence of a people grows, the realisation is made in more and more minds that Scotland unleashed and unchained can only grow and flourish.

Scotland is no longer submerged, we've come to the surface and we're breathing the fresh clean air again.

We do this for Andy, we do this for Margo MacDonald, we do for all those who believed in Scotland but are no longer here. We carry them in our memories and we will never forget. We'll carry them to the independent Scotland that they believed in and fought for. And we do this for our children, we do this for ourselves. It's happening. We are not afraid any more.

I'd like to thank Maurice Rapallini for the cover design of this book, and Sinclair and Kim Macleod of Indieauthorsworld.com for all their help and assistance in making this book a reality. And most of all I'd like to thank my mother Martha, my brother Tony, my nephew Steven and my good friends Frances and John for all the love and support they gave during the most difficult and painful period in my life.

October 2013

16th October 2013

Reasons a miserable auld git wants Scottish independence: Part 1

Positivity? Bah humbug. Being a miserable git is a vital part of my Scottish cultural heritage, along with swearing a lot, laughing at tourists who ask whether they should wait for the rain to go off, and the unshakeable belief that spaghetti hoops count towards your five a day. And it's because I'm a miserable git that I'll be voting Yes on September 18 next year.

Politicians are lying, conniving, self-serving basterts. I'll admit this doesn't hold for a tiny minority, the ones who practise socialism and don't just preach it. But that's a career killer, so all they can do is rant from the sidelines while eejits with expense accounts tell poor people they need to be poorer for the sake of rich people's bank accounts. Being one of those politicians is a bit like blogging, except their maw can assure her friends the wean really does have a proper job.

But for the rest of them, conniving self-service is the default position. Despite living rent free at 11 Downing Street, a certain Scottish MP and self-server claimed thousands in second-home payments on his constituency home while also renting out the London flat he'd designated as his 'main home'.

Alistair thinks his bank balance would be better together with payments from taxpayers. And he even got us to pay for his tax minimisation advice. No wonder he's so keen for Scotland stay with Westminster. He's currently leading the campaign to keep us all in the Union, so presumably his main home is the one in Edinburgh. At least for the time being.

There was a minor hoo, a bit of a ha, and a smidgeon of lip pursing when news of Alistair's freeform approach to expenses maximisation became public knowledge. But then Jim Devine and a handful of other sacrificial troughers were tossed to the polis, and a few others quietly stepped down from their political careers never to be seen again. (Remember poor David Marshall, former MP for Shettleston and his battle with depression? I'd be depressed too if I thought I might have to face a fraud investigation.)

Meanwhile Alistair skipped off behind the veil the Scottish media always draws over rank smells from the establishment. He's a respected elder statesman now. Must be the white hair.

Tories benefit too - this being the only context in which you'll see the words 'Tories' and 'benefits' in a sentence without the word 'cut'. Take Michael Forsyth (please, take Michael Forsyth, preferably somewhere far far away). Forsyth is the failure's failure. Even General Custer managed a last stand, Forsyth is the erectile dysfunction of politics.

Michael Forsyth, for those young enough not to remember and those old enough to have repressed the traumatic memory, was Thatcher's Scottish protege. He was going to convert Scotland to Thatcherism, he intended to foster a culture of free-marketeering amongst the populace of Freuchie, he'd convince the citizens of Prestonpans of the advantages of privatisation. Oh how we laughed.

Forsyth not only lost his own seat in the Commons, his strategy, insight and political nous was responsible for wiping the Tories off the electoral map in the 1997 General Election. That was when Scottish voters decided that conservationists aren't always right, and sometimes extinction really is the best thing for an endangered species.

This is the most comprehensive rejection a politician can possibly receive, short of actually putting him down a coalmine in Sverdlovsk and getting some Cossacks to shoot him. The message from the voters, thae folk that politicians are always telling us they're listening to, was resoundingly clear and simple: Get you tae fuck.

But Forsyth hasn't got tae fuck. He's still with us, still making our laws and deciding on our fates. He got bumped up to the House of Lords by his pals in the Tory party. Forsyth still enjoys a generous expense account for his time and the trouble he puts us to. He's spent most of the past 18 months trying to think up ways to screw the Scottish people out of their democratic right to self-determination.

Mere electoral rejection can't kill off a Westminster politician's career. And then they wonder why the public aren't interested in engaging in politics.

So whit dae ye dae with an untrustworthy useless bastert? You make damn sure they're somewhere you can keep a close eye on them, and where you can give them a well-deserved boot up the airse when they screw up, lie, or generally do a Darling. What you don't do is give them a career for life, along with your credit card, your bank details, and let them to pay you back a wee bit of your own earnings as pocket money. But that's what we're doing now.

You want to make sure that our political masters know that there is a severe penalty for failure, so that when they cock things up - as they always do - there will be a space waiting for them in the queue at the Job Centre where a twenty-something year old career advisor with a sad face can suggest they could consider a job where they could make a positive difference to people's lives. Like making party tricks out of balloons, instead of balloons making trick parties which is what happens just now.

With an independent Scottish Parliament and a written constitution we can tell the Forsyths of this world to get tae fuck, and we'll never see them blight our Parlie again. Vote Yes on 18 September 2014 and Forsyth and his ilk will never get their grasping paws on Scottish legislation ever again.

It's a no-brainer.

20 October 2013

Reasons a miserable auld git wants Scottish independence: Part 2

Unionist politicians feel the need to preface their every statement with "I'm a proud Scot ..." possibly because they realise that what's about to follow demonstrates no real pride at all. It's what psychologists call a compensation strategy. I could quote Wikipedia's entry on the topic, but Wikipedia is a by-word for inaccuracy, at least amongst people who've never seen a BetterTogether press release.

A compensation strategy is what happens when major failures are covered up by seeking gratification in another achievement, real or imaginary. Like prattling on about how the UK "punches above its weight, and Scotland's a part of that" while ignoring annoying wee facts like the UK being one of the most unequal states in Europe and inequality is projected to get worse. The growing numbers of people in poverty in Scotland, and in the UK as a whole, are not punching above their weight. They're being punched in the groin.

But what makes Unionist proud Scottery a behaviour in need of psychotheraputic remedy is that the claims made on Scotland's behalf usually fall into the "imaginary" category.

Saying that Scotland achieves a higher international stature due to its membership of the UK is frankly delusional, as anyone who has ever lived in furren pairts and learned the language can testify. Due to the economic policies of successive UK governments, Scotland probably has a larger population of furren dwelling furren speaking exiles than most. So it's doubly delusional to think that they're not going to tell folk back home. Especially after they've got home.

The Dug used to live in hot and dry Spain before discovering the joys of muddy puddles in Glesga pairks. In Spanish speaking furren pairts the colloquial term for the UK is *Inglaterra* and its inhabitants are *los ingleses*.

Ah but, the more pedantic minded Unionista might say, the proper Spanish word is *británico*. And if they mean "proper" as in "a word considered formal and literary and not widely current in colloquial speech, where it is in any case understood as a synonym for *inglés*" then they'd be correct. Because I can do pedantry too.

On the other hand, the colloquial term for "my Scottish friend", frequently heard when your Spanish speaking friends introduce you to other Spanish speaking people, is *mi amigo escocés-no-le-llames-inglés-porque-le-cabrea.* [my Scottish-don't-call-him-English-because-it-pisses-him-off friend] Very expressive language is Spanish.

So it's the *ejercito inglés* that is fighting in Afghanistan, it's *Inglaterra* that's falling out with everyone else in Brussels, it's *la reina inglesa* who's got her face on stamps, Davie Cameron is the head of *el gobierno inglés*, and a certain former secretary general of NATO was a *político inglés*.

Can you spot a wee theme here?

Scotland does not "punch above its weight" in the international sphere, Scotland isn't even in the game - not even as good natured losers who got put out in the qualifiers. The moral of this story is, if you want an international presence, you actually have to be an independent nation first.

It's true that in recent years, people in Spanish speaking countries have become far more aware of *Escocia* and *los escoceses*. But that's only because they know we are thinking about *independencia*, and we're giving the Catalans, Basques and Galicians ideas. They're following our debate very closely indeed. And we are giving them ideas.

There's almost as much coverage of the Scottish debate in the Spanish language media in Spain as there is in the UK media. Unfortunately it's of much the same quality, but you can't have everything. The Catalan language media is a whole lot better.

If just the possibility that Scotland could soon become an independent state is enough to create a very real Scottish influence in the wider world, just imagine what we could do if we really were an independent state. Sadly, Unionist politicians lack that imagination.

A case in point is George Robertson, the former secretary general of NATO who used to be a *político inglés*, who when appearing at an independence debate at Abertay University gave a long speil about what a proud Scot he was, before going on to tell the students that Scotland didn't really require independence, because we have no distinctive culture or language. Aye right. Gaun dook fur chips ya muppet, *agus pòg mo thòn* while ye're at it.

When Georgie and other soi-disant "proud Scots" are not being proud of imaginary things or confusing their own careers with the awareness of people in other countries of the existence of Scotland, they're invariably expressing pride in the achievements of those who are long dead. It's dead easy to be proud of the achievements of dead people. They've already done the hard work, so all that needs to be done is to mouth some platitudes while basking in the reflected glory.

But the best thing about being proud of dead people is that it doesn't even cost the two coins to pay the ferryman over the Styx. This is very handy when you're a Westminster politician, as they can only justify expense to the public purse if it's going to lead to a boost in the share price of ATOS. Or if they want to, ahem, "commemorate" the start of WW1 in George's Square in Glasgow with a red white and blue patriotfest the month before the referendum vote, entirely coincidentally of course. How very dare you imagine they're trying to influence the outcome.

The second best thing about being proud of dead people is that you don't have to consider what the dead people themselves actually believed or what their motives really were, you can safely hang any auld Unionjackery on their achievements. The dead are in no position to say: "It was for the right of small countries to decide their own fates." Which is exactly what Scotland is doing.

Proud Scots are also often proud of the achievements of professional sportspeople. Running about really fast or having a killer serve in tennis is all very well and good, but in the wider scheme of things it doesn't add any more to the sum total of human happiness than LOL kat pictures. LOL kat pictures at least have the advantage of not generating about half of what passes for news on Reporting Scotland. They only constitute about a quarter. Anyway, more people would complain if you tied a kitten into a sack and threw it into a canal than if you did that to a sports commentator.

I'm not a proud Scot. I'm not proud of being patronised and lied to by politicians who can't tell the difference between their own careers and Scotland's standing in the world. I'm not proud of a media that patronises and infantilises the country it claims to serve. I want something better.

I'm not at all proud that in a country which has energy resources coming out of its friggin ears there are people who can't heat their homes. I'm not proud that in one of the richest countries in the world there are people who depend upon food banks in order to fend off starvation.

And I'm positively sickened that one of those who caused the need for food banks in the first place posed for a photo-opportunity when a new food bank opened in his constituency.

Danny Alexander was very proud. If he was capable of normal human emotional responses he'd have realised the appropriate reaction should have been to hide his miserable face under a large rock, where he could atone for his sins by repeatedly ramming a tin of Morrison's own brand baked beans firmly up his Union-jacksie while repeating out loud: "Better Together with foodbanks, my arse."

I'm not a flag waver. I don't want to run around gushing about how proud I am of my country. But it would help not to be ashamed of it. It would be nice for people in other countries to know that it existed. It would be great if it was governed by people who had the well being of its citizens and residents as their sole concern and who weren't enthralled to the financial companies of the City of London. It would be fabby if we didn't have nuclear missiles just up the road from our biggest city.

It would be most fantastic of all if I was able to invite my Spanish speaking friends to visit the new tourist attraction in Nairn, the Screaming Rock of Alexander, but I don't realistically expect a Yes vote to bring that about. The rest, they're a very real possibility, and that's plenty to be going on with.

Then when people asked me if I was proud of my country I could say: Och, it's no bad.

21 October 2013

Nose pressed against the windae

Being a full time carer and so not getting out much, nor indeed having anything that might pass as a social life, I get a lot of time to peruse the online comments sections of newspapers. Although I rarely comment myself, you get to recognise the regulars. It's a bit like people watching in a public space, only you can have a comfy chair, a decent cup of tea, smoke a fag without getting disapproving looks, and you'll not get arrested for loitering.

The pro-indy posters are legion. Some are erudite, witty, and incisive. Most are informative, and the great majority demonstrate a positivity that demonstrates that Prozac manufacturers are in for a very tough sell in an independent Scotland. Some are just irritating. And a handful do appear to be certifiably batshit crazy. But possibly that's what comes of sitting on newspaper comments sections day after day, constantly rebutting the same auld pish from British nationalists who keep asking the same really dumb questions.

That's a national movement for ye, it includes old Scots and new Scots of all shapes, sizes, colours, and sanity ratings. What all have in common is that they have their own ideas about the sort of Scotland they'd like to see, and a belief that independence is the key that unlocks countless possibilities. It's an exciting time to be Scottish, and we don't get to say that very often. The Internet gives those of us who can't get out and participate in the debate in person a chance to press our noses against the windae and see what's going on.

But it's the regular No posters who are far more interesting to observe. Outside the zoo that passes for the comments section in the Hootsmon, regular No posters are far fewer in number. This is intriguing, for all that Project Fear carps on that a majority of Scots are proud to be British, damn few of them are proud enough to do something about it which doesn't involve a great deal of physical effort, nor even require much in the way of joined up thinking.

Most of those who can be arsed enough about saving the Union to post frequently online are strikingly deficient in any sort of vision for Scotland, and a noticeably higher percentage appear to fall into the batshit crazy category.

There are lots of dire warnings that we'll be evicted from the EU while at the same time having to adopt the Euro and sign up to Schengen. They've got unanswered questions up tae their oxters, and a lot of la-la-la-ing when they're given an answer. There's a positive joy in pointing out the supposed disadvantages of independence, which apparently will be as bad as experiencing the symptoms of dysentry while being forced to watch reruns of the Royal Wedding Party for

Our Great British Olympic Heroes on continuous loop. So not that unlike the BBC's telly output last year then.

But where we're actually going as a country and a society, and how we're going to get there. Nuhin, not a word.

The Scots-who-live-in-England category is also somewhat overrepresented amongst the valiant defenders of all that is good true and red white and blue. There's a bit of an overlap with the batshit crazy category, but that's probably coincidental. I'm sure regular readers of the Herald will know what I mean.

I met a lot Scots with low opinions of Scotland when I lived in London. They left Scotland, but now they're complaining that Scotland might leave them. For certain London Scots, it's important that Scotland remains a shit hole. It validates their reasons for leaving in the first place. Scotland needs to stay as it was when they moved away, because it gives them something to mark their own personal progress against.

Sadly this view is common amongst gay Scots in London, many of whom are convinced that Scotland is a sink of homophobia. This may very well have been true back in the 80s when the person concerned felt like the Small Town Boy in the Bronski Beat single, but times have changed and Scotland has changed. Now we can all find the love we need at home, gay or straight, no need to run away turn away run away. It's the London Scots who've stayed the same. Who's the cry boy cry boy cry noo?

(I came out as gay to my straight friends in the 1980s when I was living in Easterhouse. I never had any problems from anyone in Easterhouse because of my sexuality. I later moved to London where I got gay-bashed twice. Jist sayin, like.)

Scots-in-England also frequently post to express their displeasure that they're not allowed a vote in the referendum, like that's all the fault of Alex Salmond and the SNP. So let's break down the obvious for them.

You can't have a vote because Scotland isn't independent. That means there is as yet no such thing as a Scottish citizen with a right to vote in Scottish elections. There are only UK and EU citizens who are registered to vote in Scotland. If you're not registered to vote in Scotland, you can't vote.

Defining who is a Scottish citizen is something that only an independent Scottish constitution can determine. Since we do not as yet have an independent Scotland, granting the vote to "citizens of a hypothetically independent Scotland" resident in England, Wales and Northern Ireland must be administered and approved by the Westminster Parliament, and defining who those hypothetical citizens are means pre-negotiating Scottish independence. The Westminster Government has repeatedly said it's not going to pre-negotiate Scottish independence. There's yer problem right there.

So take it up with David Cameron, only you can't because he's refusing to debate the issue or provide any relevant answers. What was that about unanswered questions?

Oh aye, it was "la-la-la".

22 October 2013

Reasons a miserable auld git wants Scottish independence: Part 3

The telly's shite innit, and Scottish telly has always been a special tartan shade of shite. Those of us of a certain age will remember the BBC announcer informing us that we were about to be treated to a hauf daicent movie, before adding: "Except for viewers in Scotland." We'd be getting something involving Dougie Donnelly instead. Even now, many decades later, the phrase "indoor bowling from Coatbridge" still provokes an automatic wee sigh of bored resignation.

The telly is still shite, despite the fact there are now dozens of digital free to air channels catering to such niche markets as god-botherers, tarot card readers, devotees of badly acted Brazilian soap operas, people who make their own jewellery with offcuts from plumbing wholesalers which they bought on a shopping channel for their weight in credit cards, and a whole lot of sad gits who are turned on by disinterested sex workers squeezing their tits with the same degree of sexual arousal normally found in pensioners checking the freshness of vegetables in Asda. You can check out the courgettes, calls from a landline cost just £5.50 per minute.

Somewhere amongst the Pacific ocean sized soupbowl of pish which is being served up to us you'd think there might be a wee island of Scottish news and current affairs, what with us about to make the biggest decision in 300 years and everything. It doesn't even have to be the size of Arran, or even Millport. We're Scottish remember, and if our media is anything to go by we have very low standards. But they can't even be bothered to fob us off with one of the wee ones in the duckpond in the park.

On the Parliament and news channels, Scottish politics is either non-existent, or confined to a ghetto timeslot when normal people are either working, sleeping off the previous night's excess, or watching reruns of the Jerry Springer Show, which is easy to confuse with Johann Lamont at Furst Meenister's Questions. Same teeth and everything.

Every week it's "Jist haud me back, Jackie" as Johann screams that Eck is a durty lyin' dawg who's squandering the Scottish budget on crystal meth Forth road bridges and gambling on independence referendums, before yelling at the audience: "You don't know me." Which is true, what with her being unavailable for real questions, as opposed to the accusations of FMQs and occasionally granting an audience to a deferential worshipper on BBC Scotland, who takes her tortured syntax and garbled equivocations as gnomic utterances containing deep truths.

Then there's her deputy, Anas Sarwar hereditary MP - the title traditionally bestowed upon the heir to the Baron of Govan. His speciality is to harangue listeners about the undemocratic nature of the SNP. He'd know a lot about that then. In his spare time, which he has a lot of, he boors for Britain, inventing smears as he goes along. Anas debating is like compacted faecal matter being squeezed past a haemorrhoid.

If Anas was a crossword clue he'd be: Confounded Labour MP made a ran raw ass of himself (4, 6). By a peculiar quirk of fate a ran raw ass is a good description of what was handed to him on a plate by an angry audience of trade unionists in Clydebank.

But more commonly not being exposed to any wider media audience than stoned people who've forgotten where they put the TV remote, there's little pressure on either Johann or the Ran Raw Ass to up their game any. The media's job is to keep Scottish politics and current affairs boring, so they can be displayed in a wee box for 20 minutes after Jeremy Paxman where they can be protected by plastic and the Union won't suffer any lasting damage from exposure to the light.

And don't start me on Reporting bloody Scotland.

Normal countries have their own news channels. 24 hours a day of news which is, occasionally, relevant and/or of interest to the viewing audience. They have their own entertainment channels and sports channels. By way of comparison they get a three course meal of of arts, culture and current affairs, prepared by top chefs and tastefully served up with proper cutlery to allow you to cut it up and digest it properly. Scotland gets a fun sized Mars Bar, thickly coated in a batter of murrderr and deep fried in fitba, grumpily tossed at us by Gordon Brewer.

Countries don't even have to be independent to have better media than Scotland. Although admittedly we do set the bar pretty low.

Gagauzia has its own TV network. It's probably crap, but at least it exists. For those who don't know, which is most people, Gagauzia is a tiny scrap of self-governing territory in the poorest corner of Moldova, the poorest country in Europe. The Gagauz are Turkish speaking Orthodox Christians, a minority consisting of around 150,000 souls. Scotland isn't being denied its own national TV network because we're too wee or too poor. It's a political decision.

Catalunya does rather better. In the blink-and-you'd-miss-it coverage of the recent Rally for Independence, it was of course pointed out that the turnout didn't remotely compare to the 1.6 million who participated in the Via Catalana. What they didn't tell you that Catalunya has an active and lively media sector, with several of its own TV channels, including a 24 hour news channel, which actually reported on the preparations for the event and told people about it in advance. Because if there's going to be a high profile public event attended by a significant number of people who are significant in their fields, in order to kick off a national campaign in the run up to a national referendum, that sort of counts as national news, irrespective of what way you are currently inclined to vote.

Scottish broadcasters won't do that sort of thing because it might encourage ordinary people to challenge the status quo. Informing the public about the realities of the country they live in might make them demand change.

And this is in the wee bit of distinctively Scottish broadcasting we're actually allowed. In the so-called national news we get rank ignorance passing for erudition. We also get a whole lot of stuff which, while of passing interest, is not directly relevant to a Scottish viewing public. The upshot is that the average Scottish TV viewer is far better informed about what's going on in Sussex than they are about Scotland.

Broadcasting is one of those issues Westminster refuses to consider allowing Holyrood to get its paws on. It's hardly surprising really. Westminster has spent the last 3 decades privatising all the institutions that formerly represented "Britishness" on some level or other. British Rail, British Steel, British Coal, British Gas, they've all been broken up, closed down, and sold off to the highest bidder. The BBC is all they have left.

The irony is that it's Scottish independentistas who are accused of breaking up the Union, when really it's Westminster politicians who have been doing that job. We're just bayoneting the wounded for them, isn't that right Ian Davidson?

I don't expect Scottish telly to be hugely better after independence. We'll still get wall to wall soap operas, reality shows, X Factors, and people who insist on making their own jewellery out of overpriced dried macaroni will still be catered for. But people who do take an interest in the news and current affairs of Scotland will be catered for too, we will get a wee island of sanity amongst the dross. And that's got to be better than drowning in a sea of pish.

25 October 2013

Vote Yes for Kirriemuir Gingerbread

When you're a full time carer, managing to get out for an hour or so to the local branch of Morrisons to get the weekly shopping counts as 'quality me time'. It allows me to stock up on favourite munchies and comfort food. I like a wee slice of Kirriemuir Gingerbread, slathered with butter. The other half enjoys a thick slab of it in a bowl, covered in Devon Custard with a dollop of double cream. Bugger the cholesterol. But the other week there was none in the usual aisle, just a pile of Christmas cakes - and it was only bleedin October

I asked a guy stocking shelves where they'd moved it to. He apologised, and told me there wasn't any in stock. All the ordering is done by Head Office down in England he said, and they'd sent instructions that no more would be ordered until the New Year in order to make space for piles of Christmas cake. In October. Who eats Christmas cake in October anyway?

He added that the store manager had been on the phone to them, explaining that cholesterol laden grumpy auld gits throughout Scotland buy a lot of Kirriemuir Gingerbread, and they moan a lot when they can't get it. We sell a lot of it here, the shelf-stacking guy assured me. But Head Office in England was insistent that we really want to eat Christmas cake for the next 3 months. It's a Union benefit to shake us out of our provincial Kirriemuir Gingerbread munching ways.

The phrase "Head Office in England" got me thinking. Supermarkets account for a large chunk of weekly expenditure, especially in low income households, like those of the typical carer and cared for. Money spent in a Scottish supermarket belonging to one of the large UK chains - like Morrisons, Tesco, Asda, Sainsburys, or, if you're posh, M&S - generates VAT and other tax revenue for the UK Treasury that is identified as originating from the company's head office, which is most often in London or the South East of England.

Of course much of what we buy in supermarkets, like many foodstuffs, is zero-rated for VAT, but non-food items like deep clean skin cleanser and toilet duck are all liable for VAT at the standard rate of 20%, as are "luxury" food items like chocolate coated biscuits.

The same holds true for non-food retail chains. None of the VAT collected on the flat screen telly you bought from Currys before it closed down counted as Scottish revenue, despite the fact it was a tax paid on sales in Scotland. None of it could be used by a Scottish Government to protect Scottish workers against job losses.

Since it doesn't count as Scottish revenue, taxes generated by the money Scottish residents spend in most large retail outlets is not credited to Scotland in the UK Government's GERS (Government Expendture and Revenues Scotland) figures, the figures upon which much of the argument about Scotland's economic viability is based, and which Westminster uses to tell us how poor we are. Although on their own figures, Scotland generates 9.9% of UK tax revenues, with just 8.3% of the UK population.

Even on the UK's skew-you statistics, Scotland is doing better than Better Together would like to acknowledge, but an independent Scotland's finances would be even healthier, and by a considerable margin. The truth is that the GERS figures are about as realistic as the financial forecasts Craig Whyte made for the Gers.

As a furrinstance, the sales of toilet duck and choccie biccies in supermarkets mean that the revenues of an independent Scotland would be rather higher than the UK's GERS figures give us credit for.

In an independent Scotland, tax due on all sales or profits generated in Scotland would be paid to the Scottish Treasury. The 50p VAT on your toilet duck from Morrisons supermarket is an additional 50p that would go to the Scottish budget over and above the official statistics currently being bandied about by the UK Treasury. The 50p would no longer be tax income originating from a head office in London. It would be tax income originating from the company's offices in Scotland.

A bottle of toilet duck here and a packet of wet wipes there adds up. So just how much is Scotland being shortchanged? Finding out the exact figure would take a crack team of forensic accountants on speed, but we can get a rough idea. Let's have a wee look at the largest UK retail chain, Tesco.

During the last financial year, 2012/13, Tesco reported UK sales of £48,216,000,000. Much of this is food which is not liable for VAT. On my last trip to the supermarket, around 15% of the amount spent was on non-food items, and so liable for VAT. That's as good an estimate as any in order to work out some rough calculations.

I couldn't be bothered adding in the chocolate biscuits. In what universe is a McVities chocolate digestive a "luxury"? It could only be in a country where a spare room for the wheelchair, the walking frame and bathroom equipment is a luxury for people on benefits ... Oh.

But let's lean over backwards to give Georgie boy and the Treasury the benefit of any doubt. With a standard VAT rate of 20%, and assuming zero-rated food items make up 85% of Tesco's turnover, this means the company forwards roughly £1.44 billion annually in VAT to George Osborne's account books.

This figure does not include other taxes paid by Tesco to the UK Treasury, such as corporation tax. The company says that it paid a total of £1.5 billion in direct taxation to the Exchequer in 2012/13, a figure which includes corporation tax, property taxes etc., but doesn't include VAT payments.

All this money is counted by the UK Treasury as revenue originating from Cheshunt in Hertfordshire, just beyond the boundary of Greater London, where the company's head office is located and its tax returns are filed.

The revenues which the UK Treasury regards as originating from the company's head office were generated by the company's 3146 stores across the UK. Tesco traditionally has a smaller presence in Scotland than in England, where the bulk of its stores are located. However Tesco has many more "Express" and "Metro One Stop" outlets in England, these are much smaller than the company's main supermarkets and therefore do not generate the same amount of revenue for the company or the taxman.

According to the company's submission to the Scottish Government's consultation on alcohol, it has "over" 126 stores in Scotland. Let's say 128 then.

Getting out the back of a fag packet so we can make some rough calculations, and with the additional assumption that Tesco's Scottish stores each generate the same average revenue as stores elsewhere in the UK, this gives us a ballpark figure of £1.44 billion VAT + £1.5 billion direct taxation x (128 Scottish stores / 3146 UK stores) - working out at £119 million annually in tax payments to the UK Treasury from sales and profits generated by Tesco operations in Scotland.

Since a higher proportion of the Scottish stores are large supermarkets, and Tesco is also involved in non-food retailing such as financial services, this figure is probably a low estimate.

By way of comparison, Tesco Ireland has 137 stores in the Irish Republic. The Irish arm of the business is roughly the same size as Tesco in Scotland. Tesco Ireland generates a total of €3.07 billion (£2.64 billion) in sales annually. The standard rate of VAT in Ireland is 23%. Assuming the same 85% figure for zero rated food items, this means that Tesco Ireland forwards around €105 million (£90.3 million) annually to the Irish Government in VAT alone. At the 20% VAT rate in force in Scotland, Tesco's retail sales in Ireland would generate €92.1 million (£78.6 million) annually in VAT revenues for the Irish Government. This figure does not include the other taxes that the company pays to the Irish Treasury.

Our estimate of £119 million for the total potential Scottish revenues from Tesco is likely to considerably underestimate the true figure, it includes several other taxes as well as VAT. More realistically, the total due in VAT alone to an independent Scottish Treasury from Tesco operations in Scotland would be similar to the Irish figure, probably greater than £78.6 million annually.

Since the total in other taxes paid by Tesco to the UK Government is greater than our deliberately low estimates for VAT, the true figure for the taxes Tesco would pay in an independent Scotland is certainly well over the £140 million mark. At the moment, Scotland is not credited with a penny of this amount.

£140 million is a large sum of money, working out at 147 million packets of Kirriemuir Gingerbread at 95p per pack, or 582,758,206 tins of Tesco own brand baked beans at 29p per tin. The contents of the tins would be capable of producing more fart gas than a Better Together press release. But only by a tiny wee margin. If laid end to end a half billion tins of beans would wrap around the world almost one and a half times, or form a tower 34,600 miles tall stretching high into geostationary orbit. We could have our own space programme, and we could adapt Michelle Mone's bras to make a slingshot to get our astronauts to the Moon. Or possibly even Michelle herself as she's not keen on living in an independent Scotland.

But remember £140 million is only the hidden Scottish revenue from just one supermarket chain. What applies to Tesco applies equally to Morrisons, Asda and all the rest. It also applies to M&S, TopShop, John Lewis, and the other retail chains on our high streets and in our shopping centres. In these outlets the large majority of sales turnover is liable for VAT.

Few of these companies are headquartered in Scotland, yet together they make sales in Scotland worth billions of pounds annually, and the billions they generate for the UK Treasury are filed in tax returns from their head offices, which are usually in London. This is how London "subsidises" us.

There are other ways in which Scottish revenues are invisible in the official statistics. Much of the alcohol duty paid by our whisky industry is not counted as revenue from Scotland. Alcohol produced in the UK which is exported abroad becomes subject to UK alcohol duty at the point of export, and a large proportion of Scotland's multibillion whisky exports gets shipped out from ports in England. The UK Treasury counts the duty levied on this whisky as income from the tax region in which the port is situated.

Billions of pounds of Scottish revenue is magicked away in the official statistics, and doesn't count as Scottish revenue. It masquerades as revenue from other parts of the UK, most commonly as revenue from London. In total, the extra revenues which do not currently figure in the GERS statistics, but which would accrue to an independent Scottish Treasury, would be considerably larger than the entire annual income from the North Sea. Who needs the yle when you've got Tesco own brand baked beans eh?

This is why Project Fear is ramping up the hysteria. Scotland generates far more for the UK Government than it wants to admit to.

And so far I've not even mentioned how the expenditure part of the GERS statistics are likewise a skew-you to Scotland. That's a whole other rant.

Anyone who tells you Scotland cannae afford independence is farting verbally to the tune of half a billion tins of Tesco own brand baked beans. We would in fact be considerably better off than the GERS figures suggest. We could probably even afford the few extra pennies for the Kirriemuir Gingerbread with the icing topping.

No doubt in an independent Scotland the supermarkets would still insist on starting Christmas in September, but at least the revenues and taxation they generate would go to the Scottish budget, and count as income for the Scottish Government, to be spent in Scotland and on her population. And we'd be able to buy Kirriemuir Gingerbread all year round.

Vote Yes, for Kirriemuir Gingerbread.

27 October 2013

Dear Westminster: A divorce letter

I originally wrote this article during the lead up to the Holyrood elections, and it was first published in March 2011 in Newsnet Scotland. It was later published by the Scots Independent as their lead article in the edition published during election month. (My mammy was dead proud.)

Dear Westminster,

There was a time when you wooed me. Once you promised me the delights of India and the magic of Hong Kong, but these days all you do is sit on the sofa with your American pal playing war games. You've squandered all our money on expensive toys and presents for your mates in the City. Now you tell me you're cutting the housekeeping money but you're still buying two aircraft carriers, only there are no planes to put on them. You even had the cheek to tell me you were doing me a favour by letting me assemble the airfix kits. And don't start me on those bloody submarines.

You treat me like you're ashamed of me. You never let me leave the house alone. Are you afraid that I'll say something to embarrass you if I was to meet up with some other countries without you being there? I was really upset when you didn't let me go to Copenhagen to that workshop on climate change, especially because you know how much work I did installing wind turbines in the back garden and got all those books about tidal energy out the library. It was hurtful and unthinking. Does the term 'control freak' mean anything to you?

I always knew you were never faithful. I never mentioned your thing with Wales, you know, the other woman, your kidnap victim from a previous relationship. I was even your biggest supporter when you wanted to start that menage-a-trois with Ireland. You know as well as I do how much that particular little escapade ended up costing in therapy sessions and broken crockery. I can't believe how naive I was. It's all water under the bridge now, but I'll never have a proper relationship with my own family until you stop claiming the right to speak for me.

I bumped into Norway the other day, she's looking good and doing so well for herself. I remember her when she worked in the fish factory and didn't have two kroner to rub together, then she divorced Denmark and rushed into that rebound affair with Sweden which ended in tears. Well that's all changed. She was just popping off to some important do at the UN and was looking very stylish. And there was me in an auld coat and head-scarf like the depressive suicide risk in an Ingmar Bergman movie because you say I can't afford nice things.

I see the banks are Scottish again. That's nice. For years you've insisted on controlling all the pursestrings, and now the pursestrings are flapping around your ankles like snapped knicker elastic all of a sudden the empty banks are Scottish and a reason I could never look after myself. You're like a wean that breaks a toy then gives it back saying it was broken when you got it. Funny how you managed to play with the banks for years without noticing how broken they were.

You say the oil money is spent and gone, and you always said that it was never a significant sum anyway. Well now I've discovered the truth that you've been trying to keep from me for the past 30 years. For all that time you've known that I could be very wealthy, but you kept schtum so you could spend the money on things for yourself.

I don't know what's more hurtful, the fact that you kept secrets from me and stole from me, or that you didn't trust me enough to be honest with me in the first place. Just what other dirty little secrets are you keeping? You know what Oprah Winfrey said, when trust breaks down there can be no marriage. You've ripped up my trust, thrown it away, and trampled it in the gutter. You've only got yourself to blame for that.

Then there was thon weirdo Thatcherism cult you got seduced into joining. You gave away all the family silver and kept chanting that mantra about obeying the market. What a nightmare that was. You went all wild-eyed and starey and really scared me. Remember Jack Nicholson in the Shining? I was Shelley Duvall cowering in terror while you took an axe to everything. I'm still not entirely convinced you've got over that little episode, and there is no power on Earth that would force me to endure another bout of it. You've not done a great deal to boost my confidence on that score.

I'm under the doctor now. You don't care, you just mutter about Celts and alcoholism and tell me it's all my own fault because I'm feeble and useless. But the truth is I have cancer, the media and political parties that you support have turned against my body, poisoning my system. They make me weak and cause me to doubt myself and lose my self-confidence. They eat away at me from within. The doctors have diagnosed it as Unionosis, it's caused by a loveless and one-sided marriage.

What makes it worse is that it's you who is feeding the disease. I'm not saying you're doing it deliberately - that would imply you have a degree of self-awareness I don't think you're capable of - but I can't rid myself of the dark suspicion and you don't help by refusing to accept that there's a problem. It keeps me awake at nights and I've been drinking more than is good for a person.

All you do is to accuse me of having a chip on my shoulder. Well that's true, and guess what honey - you put it there. You aren't just a chip on my shoulder, you're a whole fish supper with extra sour vinegar all wrapped up in a copy of the Hootsmon. And frankly the fish smells pretty rank. Chip. I'll gie ye bloody chip.

Anyway, the only cure for Unionosis is to root out the problem at source, and that means leaving you.

We don't have any reason to stay together. The children are all grown up. Australia and Canada are doing so well for themselves. I used to worry about Canada living in that bad neighbourhood, but he managed to avoid getting led astray by that neighbour of his. Such a sensible and level-headed child. He gets that from me you know. Even little New Zealand has done us proud, and you know how I used to fret about him being so far away with nothing but sheep for company. It's worked out well for him, and I've learned not to judge who the children choose to spend their lives with.

I know you're angry. No one likes to be told they're a failure, and it's hard for you to hear you've been a failure as a parliament and a partner. But you react either by screaming abuse at me or by telling me I'm worthless and would fall apart without you. I don't believe you any more. You're acting every bit the spurned lover. You're acting exactly like you're always accusing France of behaving, and I only broke off my engagement with him because you convinced me he was possessive and jealous.

We'll always be close, we still share so much and I want us to be friends. But until you can learn to have adult relationships with the other nations in these islands, and treat us like equals and not as your harem, there's no hope for us and there's no hope for the people of England. People in England deserve a proper parliament and not the pretendy wee excuse for patronage, privilege and dressing up in fancy costumes that you've become. It's time you got your fat lazy arse up from resting on your Mother of Parliament laurels and went and took a long hard look at yourself in the mirror. You're very good at looking after your own interests, In time you'll realise that this is in your best interests too.

Meanwhile I'm taking a leaf out of your book and putting my own interests first. So I want a divorce. There, I've said it. There's not much love anymore, I think you know that as well as I do, and it's time we learned to live our own lives before what's left of our feelings for one another turn into hate. Being in this marriage has made both of us lose sight of who we are, and we need to find ourselves again. I'll still stand beside you to defend what we have in common, but I won't be under your thumb.

xx

Scotland

28 October 2013
Lessons in conversational Lamontese

I wasn't really paying attention to the Sunday Politics show on BBC Scotland. There are far more important things in the world than listening to Labour politicians attempting to justify themselves. But adrift amidst a mountain of washing and tripping over the hoover, I caught Johann Lamont declare that she had never said that people in Scotland get "something for nothing".

Aware that her something for nothing comments had been received like a deep fried cockroach in a bucket of chicken nuggets, Johann has spent the last year alternately back-tracking and being unavailable for comment. Now she's trying to pretend that they never happened at all, and it's all our fault for misunderstanding her.

Johann Lamont has a grasp of fact that's worse than a Young Earth creationist's grasp of evolutionary theory. The crazed creationist at least possesses the virtue of being consistently selective in their treatment of data, Johann just makes it up as she goes along.

In the speech she delivered in September 2012, her exact words were: "Scotland cannot be the only something for nothing country in the world," before going on to promise that her new commission would leave no stone unturned in its search for 'affordable' policies, and left no doubt that free education and free prescriptions would be amongst those things the commission might throw some stones at.

This wasn't an off the cuff remark either, Johann had herself called a press conference to let us all know that "Scotland cannot be the only something for nothing country in the world." She had invited telly crews and people who know how to take shorthand and use audio recorders. We heard her say it and we saw her lips moving.

At times like this we should always be kind, and try to think of an innocent explanation first. Maybe Johann just forgot, what with her being scared shitless that some of the blame for the Grangemouth debacle is going to rebound on the Labour party and the Unite union for allowing their petty internal politicking to put thousands of Scottish jobs at risk, and her only having her job because she got the Unite vote in the Labour leadership campaign. She's struggling to find a way to shift the blame onto Alex Salmond for that one. So the whole something for nothing stuff just slipped her mind.

Admittedly there are heroin addicts with head injuries who have better recall of events, but this is the Labour party in Scotland we're talking about here. They don't have high standards. Even so, the only way that Johann would be unable to remember making the statement would be for her actually to be in a vegetative coma. So come to think of it, it is a plausible excuse after all.

Perhaps it's also our fault for misunderstanding, what with us being Scottish and struggling to articulate sentences that make any sense, as Johann consistently demonstrates in solidarity with us ordinary folk. We can't put it down to linguistic differences though, since another Labour luminary has already told us we can't have independence because we have no language of our own. It's only Johann Lamont who has a language of her own.

So the sentence "Scotland cannot be the only something for nothing country in the world" was not a rehashed Tory slogan from a hash of a Labour politician who's adopting Tory policies so her party can get elected south of the Border and make a hash of social provision in the process. It must really mean something entirely different to what it looks like it means to us stupid people who don't speak Lamontese.

What she actually said was : "Scotland can obey the only summons for nuke gantries in a whirl," which was really coded advice to tell us to vote yes in the indy referendum so we can get rid of Trident. Johann's a closet Yes supporting nuclear unilateralist, who knew?

But that's about as plausible as the BBC interviewer challenging Johann when she tells a blatant lie.

31 October 2013

Gordon Brown tells the truth

According to one theory, there is an infinite number of universes, which in turn means that all possible things which can potentially happen do in fact happen somewhere in the infinite multiverse, no matter how implausible or unlikely. There is a universe where there are actually more Tory MPs in Scotland than pandas, it's one of the Hell Dimensions. There's also a universe where Reporting Scotland is a really good news programme, although quantum physicists consider this less plausible than the universe where the Daily Mail publishes an editorial begging the UK Government to allow in more asylum seekers from countries which Westminster has invaded.

However yesterday we discovered we reside in perhaps the most singular universe of all, the blessed land where Gordon Brown actually tells the truth for once. Gord has now admitted that he's an ex-politician, something the rest of us have known for quite some time. You have to phase these things out gradually you know, so he's still drawing his MP's salary, and his expenses, and gaining contributions to his pension pot and pay offs. He gave up doing any work himself a long time ago.

But we must not be harsh on him, he's really just practising the message that he preached while in high office. He's privatised his constituency work by farming it out to office staff he pays for out of expenses. So he's really a job creator and not a parasite.

Gord has lied for years on just about everything, mostly to himself, but also to the rest of us. He was the Labour Chancellor who proudly stuck to Tory spending plans and Tory attitudes to the jobless. He had a moral compass but it was really a device for telling the direction in which to sling some mud. He was the man with a plan who was going to put the Labour back into New Labour, but it turned out the only plan was how to get his paws on Tony Blair's job. Gord approached politics like an obsessive Monroe bagger, once he'd reached the highest peak he didn't know what to do with himself.

The blessed land where this miraculous truth telling occurred was not Scotland, that's too ridiculous for any universe in which we're not yet independent. It was Qatar. Gordie was doing what he does best when he's not got a book to plug or an after-dinner speech to make for nothing more than his food, travel, lodgings and a very fat cheque. He does it all for charidee you know. He was punching above the weight of the constituents of Kirkaldy at an international summit on something terribly important, held at a posh and lavishly appointed conference and hotel centre. Conveniently somewhere warm where people think he's the former prime minister ingliziya.

Removing themselves from being subject to difficult questions is the only demonstrable skill possessed by Scotland's Labour politicians. They are experts in disappearing, world class in fact. It's surprising that they didn't demand hide and seek to be added to the list of Olympic sports when the games were held in London. Between Gordie Broon, Johann Lamont and Jim Murphy they'd have snapped up gold, silver and bronze. It would have given them an excuse to wrap themselves in Union flags and pose on the front of United with Labour leaflets. Only there aren't any leaflets.

United with Labour is the invisible campaign for invisible politicians. Despite being launched with a fanfare of "that'll show thae nats a thing or three" puffery from media hacks, Labour's own campaign to save the Union in a way that doesn't involve being photographed with Conservatives has managed to garner just 6 friends and 47 likes on its Facebook page. I almost felt sorry for it. Even Gary Glitter's got more people who believe him than that.

Johann Lamont has learned well from Gordie, many would say she now surpasses the old master in the vanishing arts. It's much harder for Johann to hide, since she's rarely invited to international conferences in warm countries. No one in Labour's London office seems to have heard of the supposed leader of the party in Scotland, she didn't even figure on the CC list for the report into the goings on within the Falkirk constituency party, so it's hardly surprising no international conference organisers have heard of her either.

After briefly emerging to have a wee gloat over a predictable Dunfermline by election result, chicken Johann has gone back into hiding in order to avoid being asked any questions about the fulstercluck that was the role of Labour and the Unite union in the Grangemouth crisis. Labour and Unite spent the past few months attacking one another with the single minded fury of battery chickens on steroids determined to establish who ruled the roost. They forgot all about the Ineos fox intent on devouring Grangemouth's wee chicks in high visibility jaickets.

For all that they preach that Scotland should demonstrate solidarity with workers in England, Labour's pretty poor at showing solidarity with workers themselves. Grangemouth showed that Labour's sole interest is Labour. Unite's sorry role in the Grangemouth affair is nothing to be proud of either, but at least their basic point is correct. The Labour party was established by the union movement as a vehicle for workers' rights. But the Labour party has transformed the union movement into a vehicle for the Labour party.

Now the Labour party rails against the evil inquities of avaricious foxes, but when in office Labour embarked on a fox breeding programme with all the enthusiasm of their Tory predecessors, and cut down the chicken wire protecting the coops saying it was a barrier to business. They muzzled the guard dogs and sold off the chicken sheds. They created the conditions that allowed Grangemouth to be so vulnerable.

Johann doesn't want to answer any questions about this. And it's terribly unfair of us to think she should. After all, it's not like a Unite sponsored MSP and nominal leader of the Labour party in Scotland could possibly know anything about a major bitch-fest between Labour and Unite that ended up being the blue touch paper on a powder keg of petrochemicals.

Labour doesn't want us to think about its role in leaving Scottish industry a sitting duck for any passing capitalist predator, a legacy of the ex-politician on a freebie to Qatar. Instead we must allow Johann to get back to doing what she does best. Lying down in a darkened room until she can think of something to accuse Alex Salmond of. It's her only apparent purpose. She's a fat lot of use for anything else.

Scotland's Labour politicians have been known to submerge for weeks and months on end, only finally surfacing for a brief period, usually in order to accuse Alex Salmond of something. It's a skill in which they are rivalled only by Nessie, except for the accusing Alex Salmond bit, although it is fair to say there are more plausible sightings of Nessie than Gordie or Johann. It's also probably true that Nessie would be capable of giving a far more coherent account of herself, but that's by the by.

However the similarities far outweigh the differences. All are elusive cold blooded reptilians, all have a reputation that is largely mythical, and all are easy to confuse with lumps of dead wood floating at an odd angle.

Johann Lamont is an ex-politician too, she's just not admitted it yet. Perhaps in an independent Scotland a real Labour party can rise from the ashes of despair created by the current incarnation. It's unlikely that Johann or Gordon will have any role in it, then perhaps they can disappear forever.

November 2013

1 November 2013

When the truth is replaced by silence, the silence is a lie

Just as you've vented one Etna's worth of eruption because Johann Lamont has been being disingenuous with the actualité, she goes and does it again, even worse this time. She's Scotland's very own renewable resource of splenetic bile. If we could harness all the energy produced by people overcome by an urge to hurl a shoe at the telly when the wummin appears, the UK government wouldn't have to bribe the Chinese to build a nuclear reactor in Somerset.

It's not that Johann is a chancer that gets me, nor even that her political dance moves are executed with the grace and elegance of a brain damaged elephant on rusty roller blades. I can live with the fact that she wears the permanent expression of a person who's holding in a fart in case it's a wet one. I can even forgive her for having less intellectual depth than a children's TV continuity announcer and the vision of an actor in a Specsavers advert.

But what really gets my goat is the way she imagines she can rewrite the past, and expects us not to remember what she really did or said. Or more commonly, didn't say or didn't do.

Just last Sunday she denied that she'd ever said Scotland was a "something for nothing" country despite copious evidence to the contrary - up to and including videos. Now in this week's Furst Meinisters Questions, Johann has accused Alex Salmond of going off on holiday during the Grangemouth dispute, while she was valiantly saving the plant single handed.

It was only last week for feck's sake. Does she really think we don't remember what really happened? The events that unfolded allowed us to compare and contrast how the three political factions vying for the trust of the Scottish people - the Scottish Government, the UK Government, and the Labour party - dealt with a major threat to the future of the Scottish economy. And Johann did not come out of it well.

The Scottish Government had a plan A. It was to do all they could to get Unite and the representatives of the Evil One to sit down and negotiate in order to keep the plant open and save the threatened jobs. The Eck also had a plan B, in case plan A went tits-up, to find a buyer for the plant so it could be kept open and save the threatened jobs. He had been in talks with just such a potential buyer. There was even a hint there may be a plan C, in the shape of a promise that an independent Scottish government would nationalise the plant so it could be kept open and save the threatened jobs.

The UK government also had a plan A which was essentially the same as Eck's plan A, the only difference being that Tories think Jim Ratcliffe is a jolly good chappie and UK Plc needs more of his entrepreneurial spirit. The UK government had a plan B too. Admittedly it was, "Well, there's always the Job Centre," but at least it constituted some sort of statement on what might happen next. Plan C? What? By this time they were too busy discussing the Royal Christening and had lost interest. Who cares about Grangemouth, didn't Kate look gorgeous?

Johann and the Labour party had no plan at all. She didn't even get as far as Season One Episode One of Sesame Street in the lettering of plans. She had no idea how to achieve any sort of solution. Her sole contribution to resolving the crisis was to shriek that Jim Ratcliffe is an evil bastert. However just about everyone in Scotland had already formed that opinion without Johann's input. Jim Ratcliffe knew that too. The only question is why Johann imagined that he was going to back down because she was doing her beloved impression of a stairheid rammy. Like it's worked so well on Eck. But Johann doesn't answer questions, so we'll never know.

Only one of these three players is not responsible for the state of the UK energy sector, and only one does not have or did not once have the powers to regulate the sector to prevent the Grangemouth crisis from arising in the first place. Only one was not responsible for allowing the carnivores of capital to devour Scottish workers' futures, and selling off all state assets in order to sook up to the City of London. Can you guess which one children? Because Johann bloody Lamont can't.

Johann Lamont managed to make less of a positive contribution towards solving the Grangemouth crisis than the actual fucking Tories. Indictments don't come much stronger than that.

When Johann denied she said Scotland was a something for nothing country, she was referring to something that took place a whole year ago. And if you try and peer out of the furthest corner of your eye aided by the wholesale consumption of alcohol, pills, and herbal cigarettes after you've sacrificed a goat to the goddess of amnesia, you might just be able to persuade yourself that people will have forgotten that you said it, and forgotten that you'd called a press conference so they could hear you say it, and forgotten that it provoked a storm of anger and protests and derision that was all over the telly and the papers until your press guy leaned on the media to shut up with the story.

But now she wants us to forget something that just happened last week. Believing in Johann Lamont now requires short term memory loss as well as a Stalinesque facility for airbrushing last year's press conferences so they no longer contain the phrase "something for nothing". Goldfish have better memories than that.

There are only two real possibilities here. Either Johann Lamont is a liar of sociopathic proportions, who just doesn't give a shit whether people believe her or not, or she has lost all grip on reality, has long since teetered off the brink of sanity and is now in freefall imagining herself to have superhuman powers to change the fabric of reality. Of course, these are not mutually exclusive categories.

Whatever, she is unfit for public office. If she had even a nanogramme of self-awareness she would resign immediately, and offer her job to someone far more reliable, capable and trustworthy. Like Eric Joyce or Jar Jar Binks.

Under Lamont Labour has no policies. It has commissions that won't report back until after the independence referendum. It has condemnations of Alex Salmond aplenty, although many are invented and most are spurious. And it has the deep frozen silence of the vacuum of outer space. Labour gave up speaking the truth to Scotland many years ago. Now instead of a social democratic (never mind socialist) party fighting for the rights of workers we get the pathetic self-serving vacuities of Lamontism instead. Johann will go back to hiding away wherever it is she goes when she's avoiding the contradictions thrown up by her many attempts to change the recent past, and she will say nothing at all.

But as the Russian poet Yevgeny Yevtushenko said, "When the truth is replaced by silence, the silence is a lie." Every time Johann Lamont is unavailable for questions, she is lying to the people of Scotland.

3 November 2013

Union intelligence

I suppose I really ought to tackle Project Fear's latest scare story, but they scarcely raise much in the way of righteous indignation amongst Yes supporters any more. You can only give reasonable and informed responses to Unionist idiocies for so long before you start to feel that by taking them seriously you are granting them some sort of credence. Sometimes the most appropriate response really is: "Away you shut yer geggie, ya choob. The grown ups are talking."

Seemingly unaware of her boss's recent pronouncement that the indy debate was for "Scots living in Scotland", Tory Home Secretary Theresa May made a security inspection north of the Border last week, to tread her leopard print Manolo Blahniks all over us uppity Scottish people. The restriction of the debate to "Scots living in Scotland" apparently applies only to David Cameron desperately trying to make out he's not onto a loser by debating Alex Salmond.

Terry felt it was important for us to know that if we're foolish enough to opt for indy, we'll no longer enjoy the protection of GCHQ, although they'll still tap our phones, read our emails, and forward our YouTube links of trampolines getting blown away in Hurricane Bawbag to the Pentagon.

However instead of blowing away the indy campaign, Terry's arguments came across with the resounding clap of a silent fart in gale. It was like watching an airhead from Made in Chelsea trying to explain particle physics. It was more haud ma designer handbag than Hurricane Bawbag, a Tory version of Johann and Magrit's stairheid rammies.

Even the normally slavish Scottish media couldn't be arsed to give her much in the way of coverage. Perhaps they're slowly becoming aware that by reporting the contributions of Westminster Tories to the indy debate they are coming to have all the credence of Westminster Tories themselves. These are after all people who struggle to differentiate Balmoral from Balornock, yet all of a sudden are experts in Scotland's potential, or rather lack thereof, as an independent state.

But for what it's worth, Terry opined that after independence Scotland will be cast adrift and left to the mercy of evil terrorists who will insist that Johann Lamont wears a burqa. Which at least means that when she's in hiding and doesn't want anyone to recognise her she'll still be able to pop out to the shops for a deep frozen lie-pie to hurl at Alex Salmond. So it's not all bad news then.

In the accompanying press release, the Home Office warned us that Scotland and England would not enjoy the friendly relations we've enjoyed as part of the Union for "the past 210 years". The first century of the 306 year long Union was just the beta testing, so didn't really count. It's probably best to draw a silent veil over all those Jacobite wars, rebellions and invasions by General Wade. Westminster is certain they've ironed out the bugs in the game software now. Experienced users of the Union should know that the way the game is stacked against you and crashes at crucial moments isn't a bug. It's a feature.

Terry thinks small countries are especially vulnerable to terrorists, which is why the citizens of Finland are rarely to be seen on the streets of Helsinki, they're forced to sit indoors all day watching reruns of Borgen and Wallander while drinking home-brewed vodka in case a suicide bomber gets them while they're out buying sausages and potatoes. And that's with the benefit of the uncrackable cypher known as the Finnish language in which all their emails are encoded.

Scots will just have to hope and pray that no one in the Taliban learns how to speak Weegie. The Mujahaweegie would be a terrible foe, bombing transport infrastructure with piss filled bottles of Buckie and hijacking Tunnock's delivery vans. Only the Union and GCHQ can save us from public transport that reeks of urine on Saturday nights and ensure the safe delivery of teacakes.

The biggest problem we'll face, apparently, is that we'll no longer have access to UK intelligence. It doesn't appear to have occurred to Ms May that getting away from what passes for "intelligence" amongst successive UK governments is the prime motivator for many of us who seek independence. For starters there's those dodgy dossiers, the Oxbridge Communists who ran M15 during the 60s, and just about anything that comes out of Theresa's gob.

Scotland will deprive itself of the wisdom of the woman who thought up the Go Home campaign and who apparently bases UK immigration policy on Daily Mail stories. Something about immigrants giving you cancer, probably. She set up a commission of experts to advise on drug policy, but then ignored them when they gave advice she didn't like. More recently she suggested that it was condoning terrorism to object to anti-terrorism laws being used to silence legitimate whistle-blowers and the journalists who report them. How will we possibly cope without her unique brand of narrow-minded condescension?

Scotland will have little or nothing to offer proper grown up security services like M15. It's well known in London that there are only two kinds of Scottish polis. There's the cheery auld alcoholic sergeant on a bicycle who occasionally takes prescriptions to the chemist for Doctor Finlay, together with his young and naive constable who's trying to get into the knickers of the housekeeper from Monarch of the Glen and who will develop an alcohol problem after she spurns him the for dashing estate manager with the English public school accent. And then there's the morose detective with a bevvy merchant's nose who investigates junkies who murrderr one another. Since Islamic terrorists are teetotal, the Scottish police will be helpless against them because they never go down the pub.

After indy we'll be "intelligence unplugged", as Westminster has no real interest in prescriptions for antibiotics that don't cost £7 a pop or the price of a pint of heavy, and hordes of terrorist gangs, cyber criminals, and evil villains from Bond movies will descend on Scotland to use us as a base from which to attack important places - that would be London.

It's unclear why Terry thought we'd be particularly susceptible to cyber criminals, as just last month her equally clueless cabinet colleague Philip Hammond solemnly warned us that terrorists would attack our power stations and leave us without electricity. So we'll only have to worry about cyber criminals until the laptop battery gives out and then the problem will pretty much take care of itself.

When you dig a bit deeper into Theresa's scare stories, it seems that the real threat isn't to Scotland. We'll be one of those wee countries that terrorists don't bother much with because attacking us will only rate a 10 second mention on Sky News. The real threat is to Westminster, and for all their supposed intelligence there's a gaping chasm in the logic of their latest scare story.

Scotland will be hoatching with terrorist groups who intend to attack the rUK, but at the same time the new Scottish intelligence services will have little information which might be of interest to their rUK counterparts, so it's not in the rUK's interests to have a friendly and cooperative working relationship with Scotland. Instead Westminster may be forced to impose border controls all the way from Gretna to Berwick, disrupting trade and costing the rUK economy billions of pounds a year.

Hmmm. That's a really intelligent response, and by going independent we'll be depriving ourselves of such strategically joined up thinking. How will we ever manage?

They can't even think their scare stories through properly, so much for Union intelligence. So it's clear now, either they think that we are spectacularly stupid, or they are spectacularly stupid. In either case are these the people we want to have responsiblity for keeping Scotland safe? Even Theresa May ought to have enough functioning brain cells to realise the answer to that question.

5 November 2013

Breaking the Joyce barrier

Oh here we go again. It's becoming a daily ritual, ranting about Johann. I'm starting to feel like a stalker. But it's been a really bad day. I wish I could run away and hide from my problems like Johann, but full time carers don't have the same luxuries afforded to the leader of the Labour party in Scotland. In the meantime she offers a convenient target for an outpouring of pent up frustrations.

So she is actually useful for something, although I'm sure the members of Falkirk Labour party and the staff at Grangemouth wouldn't find that much of a consolation.

Anyway, on Monday we were presented with evidence that Johann lives. Ok, well maybe it's "lives" in the sense that a sea sponge lives without the benefit of a central nervous system, ears, or eyes, but the lovely Johann has come out of hiding and has admitted what the rest of the country has known for quite some time: there were attempts to manipulate the selection process for a Labour candidate in Falkirk.

Admittedly it took a front page spread in the Sunday Herald, in which Falkirk Labour party members complained that they'd been left adrift and abandoned by the party leadership, none of whom could be arsed to turn up and explain to them what's going on, before she decided it was time to "intervene".

She didn't add that the attempts at manipulation set off a chain of events that led to the greatest threat to Scottish jobs and the Scottish economy since Thatcher. Neither did she remind us that the leadership of the Labour party in Scotland then sat on its collective bahoochie replaying nostalgic old videos of conference delegates singing the Internationale. But we can take that as read. Johann has now intervened, to her own satisfaction if no one else's.

If you look up the word "intervene" in the Dictionary of Labour Party Terminology, you'll find it really means "shamed into giving a brief media interview after howls of outrage and derision over a leadership with as much direction as an inflatable banana in the Corrievreckan whirlpool", but hey, let's not quibble. Better late than never.

Scotland is on pause - oh the irony - because Johann won't do the job that she and Labour claim she was elected to do, to lead the entire Labour party north of the Border. She didn't think it was "appropriate" to discuss the situation with her fellow Unite members. She didn't think it "appropriate" to discuss the issue with the leadership of the union that sponsors her as an MSP. And she certainly didn't think it "appropriate" to speak personally to members of the Falkirk Labour party. She's only a nominal leader, a latent leader. But better latent than never.

Johann is so much of a leader that she wasn't even given a copy of the report that Labour central office carried out into the affair. It was reported on Monday that Johann had seen the report, although that's not exactly what she said. She said she "knew what was in the report". But that's not saying much, everyone knows what's in the report. It contains the contents of a Falkirk sewer and it's deeply embarrassing for the Labour leadership. Still doesn't answer the question of whether Johann is in the Labour leadership loop or not. I'm guessing not.

Decisively leaderish, on Monday Johann vowed to "have a look at" reopening the inquiry into the Falkirk serial collision. Not a definite commitment to reinvestigate the murky goings-on, just a vague statement that Johann might have a wee think about it. One of those promises that's as vague as Davie Cameron's commitment to "consider" further devolution in the event of a No vote. That's reassuring then. Though somewhat less reassuring when you realise that Johann doesn't actually have any powers to reopen an investigation or start a new one, which isn't very leaderish at all.

However in the same interview she also repeatedly stated that Labour needs to "move on" from the debacle, sweep it under the carpet and desperately pretend that it never happened. She didn't actually say that last bit, but it's a safe assumption that's where her preference vote lies.

So what's it to be, reinvestigating or "moving on"? Labour is able act swiftly and decisively. By tea time it was reported that Labour was going for moving on, rather than doing anything of any practical use to clear up its problem with declining membership rolls, and the increasing ease with which small organised groups can manipulate selection processes in sclerotic constituency parties.

They'll kick it into the long grass, let the police investigate, and pray they find nothing illegal. Hopefully we'll all forget and Johann can go back to accusing Alex Salmond of lying about something. It's a tried and trusted strategy. Worked a treat with Stephen Purcell.

"Oh that's a surprise," said a shocked Scotland over its tea as it digested the news. Before going on to ask itself just how Labour expects to persuade us that we're Better Together with the Union when the Union has been so spectacularly bad for Labour. Look what the Union has turned them into, a party that once stood for socialism and Scottish self-determination. The high road to British Parliamentary Socialism led to the cul de sac of Lamont, fiddling in Falkirk while Grangemouth burned.

The whole sorry saga was sparked off by a former officer in the Army Education Corps and sometime Labour MP who wanted to teach us a lesson in Chaos Theory. The classic version requires a butterfly flapping its wings in the Amazon to set off a destructive hurricane on the other side of the world, but Eric discovered that a fly head butting of a Tory in a Westminster bar worked just as well. It led to a storm over Grangemouth, and it seems the lasting casualty will be the Labour party. The storm ripped away their tarpaulin of lies and self-serving excuses, and even BBC Scotland wasn't able to provide much shelter.

Their only hope of recovery is the birth of a party that is really a Scottish Labour party, a party that's not always looking over its shoulder to make itself electable to Tory voters in swing seats in Middle England. A party with a proper leadership that doesn't just mouth platitudes, but demonstrates solidarity with working people by having the confidence to adopt truly progressive social democratic policies, the will to carry them out, and the powers of a parliament that can make them happen. The current party leadership will never allow that to happen, so it's up to us ordinary punters to make it happen.

It's the first lesson of socialism, the lesson that Labour have long since forgotten. If the people want change they must make that change happen themselves, because those with power will not do it for us. We can only do that by voting Yes next year. A Yes vote will drag Labour into change, despite themselves. Vote No and the Labour leadership will take it as a vote of confidence. We can expect many more Falkirks, and Grangemouths.

At least Scottish science has discovered a new principle of physics, so it hasn't been total loss. Labour under Lamont has shown it's possible to break the Joyce Barrier, the level you have to sink to before Eric Joyce is able to lecture you from the moral high ground.

As man responsible for toppling the first domino when he nutted that Tory MP put it in his blog:

"The party seems wholly unable to distinguish between competent, decent trade union organising and Unite's intimidation, incompetence and bogus politics. Either that, or it's simply too afraid. With the majority of the Scottish shadow cabinet members of and sponsored by Unite, and with a huge number of MPs in the same basket, it's looking awfully like the latter."

He added later on Newsnicht that he had no confidence that Johann was capable of taking action, a view which Alistair Darling apparently shares. But the Labour leadership is still going La-La-La-Lamont listening. It's too afraid.

But it's not the Unite union Labour should be afraid of. It's not the banks or the press. It's ordinary Labour voters, it's the people - like me - who should be natural Labour voters but are too revolted by what the party has become. Because we have it within our power to give them the biggest fright of their lives on the 18th of September next year. A fright not even Johann Lamont will be able to hide from.

6 November 2013

Ian Davidson's walnut brain tries some new thinking

Govan shipyard has narrowly avoided closure, although hundreds of jobs will still be lost from BAE's two shipyards in Glasgow. So far, so predictable, just another of the assaults on industrial communities that define the UK's economic policies. So much for the Union being the sole guarantee of a future for the Scottish shipbuilding industry. One as secure as Gartcosh or Ravenscraig, padlocked and patrolled by G4S security guards until it's sold off to a property developer.

And all this just weeks after we discovered that the Union was no guarantor of a future for Grangemouth either. So much for the "certainties" of remaining a part of the UK.

If Scotland was not currently engaged in a debate about independence, or if the referendum had already taken place and returned a No vote, Govan would close and the Proclaimers would have another chorus to add to Letter From America. It's now the poor workers of Portsmouth who will have to suffer the fate of the certainties of the Union. They don't have any prospects of an independent government that might encourage and support the yard to diversify so it's not always held to ransom by the MoD.

According to reports, the only thing that prevented the complete closure of the Govan yard was that the British Government did not want to give any ammunition to the Yes campaign. An admission that it's only the threat of independence that forces Westminster to act in Scotland's interests.

Yet they want us to vote No and give up the threat for a generation. Because afterwards they'll love us in non-specific and non-defined ways that feel more like a threat than a promise. We can have one of those relationships that doctors in clinics treating sexually transmitted diseases used to call "zesty liaisons". As if those never end in tears and suspicious rashes.

It's not even as if Scotland gets its fair share of defence contracts as it is. According to Business for Scotland, between 2007-08 and 2011-12 Scotland received £1.9 billion less than its population share of defence contracts. Westminster hasn't promised to remedy that situation, not even in exchange for a No vote.

So what was the local MP's contribution to securing the future of the Govan yard? Ian Davidson, the Labour MP who is to socialism as Jeremy Kyle is to social work, called for the MoD to insert a 'break clause' into the BAE contract, so that in the event of a Yes vote next year Westminster can pull the plug on the ailing Govan yard and cost his own constituents their jobs if they don't vote in a way he approves of. This must be that bayoneting the wounded that he spoke about recently.

It's not enough for Ian that there may be some real downsides to independence, like the very clear threat to his own career prospects. It's not enough that the significance of these downsides is exaggerated out of all proportion by Better Together. It's not even enough for him that most of the downsides are as fictitious as Johann Lamont's leadership of Labour in Scotland. Ian's on a mission to create some downsides. It's the most he's ever done to encourage the manufacturing sector.

In a bare faced attempt to justify his actions, Ian growled in an interview on BBC2's Newsnicht that there had been "new thinking" in Westminster about commissioning the new navy vessels. The new thinking being, "Here, we can use this to screw over Scotland and scare them into a No vote." Better Together for threats and blackmail.

Not that Labour get involved with Tories playing politics with people's livelihoods. Oh no. Grangemouth showed that they're perfectly able to do it all by themselves.

In Ian's Newsnicht interview Gordon Brewer didn't think to inquire whose idea this "new thinking" was, how it differed from the "old thinking", and why it had been decided it was necessary. It couldn't possibly have been Ian's bright idea now could it? Gordon was too busy interrupting the random SNP guy to bother asking.

Gordon was content to accept Ian's explanation that it was because the UK never ever ever not even once allowed "foreign" countries to build boats for the Royal Navy. Apart from South Korea. And the USA and Canada during WW2, but that doesn't count because there was a war on.

Ah but, said Ian, who was either anticipating the objection or knew that his argument was as overoptimistic as an MoD budget estimate and as inflated as his ego – readers can have nanoseconds of fun deciding which is more likely – the ships built in South Korea were just crappy tankers. Oil drums with a rudder really. Nothing high-tech or advanced about them. You could even use them as CalMac ferries. Not like the superdooper new generation of Royal Navy Type 26 Combat ships with go faster stripes.

The very idea of letting a soon to be foreign yard build the vessels. Just imagine the risk to national security. A furren yard in Glesga would have to have access to top secret building specs and blueprints and stuff. James Bond would have to sneak into the underground lair below Glasgow City Chambers after seducing Double Agent Lamont in order to save the day, but there's a limit to what even he is willing to do for Her Majesty's Secret Service. And besides, no would want to watch the movie, on account of it making viewers go blind.

Only the yard is already in possession of all that top secret information, because otherwise it would never have been able to tender for the contract in the first place, so it's not like the UK would be allowing Scotland access to sensitive information that it doesn't already possess. And the yard also knows it's a design that no other country wants to buy, so it's not like there's going to be a line of spies queueing up to buy it from an independent Scotland.

Then there's the uncomfortable fact that the Republic of Ireland is not a foreign country. Ian joins the long list of Westminster politicians and BBC reporters who are unaware of Westminster's own legislation: section 2 paragraph 1 of the Ireland Act of 1949 states that the Republic of Ireland is not to be considered a "foreign country" for the purposes of any UK legislation or law.

Defence commissioning is ultimately underpinned by law, and while the MoD can reject a shipbuilding tender from the Republic on the grounds that the Republic does not have a shipbuilding industry, they can't reject it on the basis that it's a foreign country.

So far we've had no cogent explanation from Westminster, Better Together, nor indeed the BBC, as to why the neutral Irish Republic which became independent after a bloody war against the British army is not considered foreign, but a Scotland which becomes independent peacefully, which says it wants to be a member of NATO, which will share the same head of state with the rUK, and which aspires to membership of the Commonwealth, will be considered more foreign than South Korea and as potentially hostile as North Korea. They're hoping we don't notice.

Thankfully Gordon the Beeb's incisive interviewer didn't pick up on the glaring contradictions, allowing Ian to make out he was just helpfully offering a way for the commissioning to go ahead.

But the hollowness of Ian's "new thinking" was exposed the very next day, when the announcement was made that Portsmouth was to close and the decision to keep Govan open had been made on commercial grounds. There had either been no "new thinking" after all, or Ian had been making it all up. Dinosaurs of the Labour party are not strongly associated with "new thinking", so this should not have come as any surprise.

There's not a lot of new thinking you can do when you have a brain the size of a walnut which is already fully occupied with strategies to extract as much personal gain as possible from any situation. It's the same cerebral overload that makes them confuse the light of an approaching meteorite marked "independence referendum" with limelight that they can hog. They fondly believe it shows off their most attractive features, their thick scaly hides, their grasping claws, and their eagerness to disembowel the weak and the sick.

A constant in Westminster's scare stories about independence is that not only would Scotland be a "foreign" country, it would also be a hostile one. But the only hostility we've seen so far is the hostility of Westminster MPs towards any notion that Scotland might be better off without them, and their efforts to wreak havoc on Scotland's working class communities in order to prove their point.

It's a constant as reliable as Labour playing politics with Scottish workers' jobs and the future of the Scottish economy, and it's the only certainty we can be sure of if we vote No next year. We need to vote Yes to introduce the era of the mammals, warm blooded creatures that nurture and care for their young.

9 November 2013

A field spotter's guide to the Lesser Spotted Unionist

Although Blairite McDougall (chief exec of Better Together, former special advisor to BBC Director of Strategy James Purnell and, quite coincidentally, a regular invitee to the BBC's popular news segment *Great British Right To Reply To Anything Vaguely Scottish Or I'll Call Your Boss*) claims that Scotland is hoatchin wi dedicated and fanatical supporters of the Union, ordinary punters can find it difficult to spot members of this supposedly ubiquitous species. Other than that really annoying brother-in-law that everyone's got.

Best known for its piercing and repeated mating call "I'm a proud Scot but ..." the Lesser Spotted Unionist, Latin name *Britnaticus northbrittanicus*, has failed to thrive, despite a massive campaign to develop a breeding programme which has been expensively funded by the British government and Tory oil barons who have selflessly dedicated themselves to preserving a Scottish ecosystem that they've found very profitable.

UK government policy, continued by "the greenest government ever" of Davie Cameron, has for 300 years strived to create the conditions in which the *Britnaticus northbrittanicus* could prosper, not financially but in the sense of having someone else worse off than you you could feel better than. Traditionally this was Gaelic speakers, Catholics, black people, Asian people, or anyone Continental.

Land ownership was carefully managed to ensure that most of Scotland is owned by a tiny handful, who agreed to clear out the natives in order to provide the natural conditions necessary for the successful reproduction of the species. Industrial slums were grown, sectarianism was fostered, colonialist wars were enthusiastically embarked upon, and *divide et impera brittanica* was the order of the day. Scotland was once teeming with flocks of North Britons ruling the waves and never ever ever being slaves, at least not in their imaginations.

However in the post war era, the Unionist species has gone into a precipitous decline. The demise of the Unionist coincided with the spread of the virulent Scottish nationalism virus which attacked Unionist habitats. The virus spread rapidly in Unionist heartlands, where it pointed out that it was in fact pretty rubbish that in an energy rich country there are people who cannot afford to heat their homes, it's digusting that people are forced to use food banks while the City of London continues to enrich itself, and it's an insult to democracy that Scotland is continually subjected to governments it didn't vote for who have the cheek to blag all our resources in return for a bit of pocket money.

Worrying evidence of the decline includes a marked reluctance to engage in flag waving and bunting hanging, combined with bouts of projectile vomiting whenever the BBC's Royal Correspondent appears on screen. By the time symptoms have progressed to episodes of sarcastic laughter and throwing shoes at TVs when UK politicians attempt to explain the many benefits bestowed upon North Britain by those lovely people in Westminster, the former Unionist has already mutated into a new species: *Cybernaticus caledoniensis*.

Outside their regular haunts in TV studios and between the pages of mainstream newspapers telling us how much of a majority they are, regular sightings of the Lesser Spotted Unionist prove to be difficult to confirm. Although the entirely unbiased Royal Society for the Protection of Unionists has published a number of censuses of Unionist numbers, the figures remain open to dispute as many of the Unionist breeding pairs identified in these surveys have on closer inspection been found to belong to entirely different species - most commonly *Mibbii mibbinaw*, *Wellnaw bitakidbepersuadit*, *Jistickifurstboax izerraprizefurris*, *Achtheyrawshite diznaemaiteroniewiis* or *Pissaffyapollster orahllampyeis* (subspecies *amnotellinyenuhin*).

In the interests of helping readers with an interest in the natural world to identify this vanishing creature, and so they can cross the road and avoid it when they see one coming, here's a brief guide to the subspecies of the Lesser Spotted Unionist.

B. northbritanicus labordinosaurii

The most common surviving subspecies, although only common in the sense it has no style or class, the labourdinosaurii is noted for its torn faced expression, drab plumage, propensity for feathering its own nest, and its willingness to threaten its own habitat if the habitat doesn't vote the way it wants. It's called a 'break clause': vote no or I'll break you. It's proving quite controversial in Govan, and is being widely cited in zoological journals as startling new evidence that this species may in fact be a vulture, as members of the vulture family are amongst the few birds known to shit on their own support. Called urohidrosis, the accumulation of crap on the lower members can eventually lead to sickness and death.

The subspecies traditionally thrived in industrial areas where it survived on promises of jam tomorrow. Unlike most other Unionists, the fiercely territorial *labordinosaurii* (also known as Davidson's Ringfenced Expensaccount) denies that it is a Unionist, and fondly believes that nationalism is something that only afflicts people who have the misfortune not to be British.

You can try and argue with them otherwise, but the response will invariably go along the lines of: "British nationalism doesn't count, it is of course better than any other nationalism because it's not nationalist at all. And it's not nationalist to say that. Oh look, Great British Bake Off is coming on. See, if you're independent you'll not be allowed Victoria sponge or Battenburg cake, because they're British. And not German at all."

Members of this subspecies also tend to hold that the corrupt and institutionally bankrupt British state is really an exercise in international workers' solidarity. This is in fact true, although the workers in question are only those who work as company directors in the City of London. In an effort to demonstrate this solidarity in a practical manner, the subspecies collects shiny directorships with an enthusiasm that puts magpies to shame. Davidson's Ringfenced Expensaccount holds that this shows that the system is working.

B. northbritanicus torii

More widely known by its Scots vernacular name of Yadurrtytorybasterts, a sad few bedraggled survivors are all that remains of this once dominant sub-species, which formerly produced a range of colourful varieties. The exotic attire and tartan troosers of the *Nicholas Fairbairnius* are sadly long extinct, while the *Teddy Taylorii*, a hybrid of a wee yappy dug with a Thatcherite, was forced to migrate south and was last seen on Southend Pier wearing a union jack waistcoat and a kiss-me-quick hat.

The handful of remaining examples of this subspecies huddle together for warmth in a dwindling number of leafy suburbs in the Central Belt and the Borders, however their numbers are continually diminished as adults in search of a political career flee south in search of Education Ministeries to crap all over, Defence Contractors' hospitality, and hotel bedrooms they can share with Adam Werritty.

B. northbritanicus libdemocratus

An ill-advised experiment in hybridisation with the torii has resulted in the almost total extinction of this subspecies. Successful cross-fertilisation requires parties with members of approximately equal weight and influence, but all the libdemocratus had to offer was a very wee Wullie Rennie.

Most of the better known examples, such as the Smug Ginger Rodent (variety: *Lookmammyavgoataministerialmotor*), have recently been discovered to be Tories who have adopted the plumage of *libdemocratus* in order to deceive their electoral prey. To the relief of Wee Ginger Things everywhere, the Ginger Rodent has now been reclassified as a Boris Johnston Strawberry Blond.

It's already too late for this subspecies, extinction beckons.

B. northbritanicus swivelii

The migratory *swivelii*, more commonly known as the Ukip Swivel-eyed Loon, provides a classic example of evolutionary mimicry. Despite attempting to present itself as a big scary Tory monster, the Ukip Loon is in fact a timid little Tory mutant, easily frightened off by shouts of "Nigel you're a bawbag."

More comfortable in southern English golf clubs, where it bores the bar with incessant complaints about frogs that reek of garlic, sausage-munching krauts, and whinging jocks with a deep fried mars bar on their shoulder, it is rarely seen in Scotland. However a stray Loon is occasionally found in Edinburgh pubs in the mistaken belief it's at an Aberdeen by-election where it hopes to be rewarded with some cheap headlines. It can easily be recognised by its distinctive cry of "That's anti-English racism that is."

B. northbritanicus orangensis neanderthalensis

The subspecies has gone into a drastic decline from which it has never recovered. Once the working class version of the Durrtytorybasterts, their influence was partly responsible for delivering the Conservative's infamous majority in Scotland in the 1950s, when the forces of darkness took 51% of the popular vote in a General Election.

There were a number of causes for the decline in their numbers and influence. The first was an upswelling of new religious fervour.

Scotland's four traditional religions, Protestants, Catholics, Protestant Atheists, and Catholic Atheists, found themselves in competition with a new religion sweeping Europe: Apatheism, the belief that you don't give a shit about religion. Since its central ritual in Scotland is having a long lie in of a Sunday, followed by Irn-Bru and an aspirin, it proved very popular.

The spread of the new faith was accompanied by a growing realisation that the reason churches continually banged on about personal sexual morality was because, like sex, religion is something which should only be practised by consenting adults in private, because otherwise it can lead to all sorts of unpleasantness which is really best avoided.

As the 60s turned into the 70s and 80s and turned on tuned in dropped out people lost themselves in a haze of herbal smoke and premarital sex, banging a big Lambeg while dressed in a bowler hat, a navy blue crimpolene uniform, and singing songs about killing Catholics lost much of its glamour. Even in Brigton.

But the death blow came when Orange Neanderthals up and down the land discovered that a steadfast and loyal Protestant with a Union flag fluttering from his windae box of orange lilies was still going to get made redundant when the factories, the mines and the yards got closed down, belief in Her Maj being about as useful as saying a novena to St Jude the patron saint of lost causes. So that was the Protestant Ascendency pretty much knackered, and it was knackered by the very British Establishment it pledged loyalty to. Still, irony is such a British characteristic, so that's UK OK then.

Although most closely associated with 17th century history, 18th century social attitudes, and 19th century political relevance, the Orange Sashed Neanderthal has attempted to modernise its image. The organisation now accepts gay people, who can parade in the boa their father woa, which at least makes them acceptable to Glasgow Labour cooncil.

B. northbritanicus fascistbastert

A detailed description of pondscum and fungal infections is beyond the scope of this article.

B. northbritanicus annoyingbrotherinlawensis

Because some folk are just dickheads. Although few in number, they make up for it with the sheer volume with which they make their opinions known, the loudness of their opinion being inversely proportional to the amount of hard facts and information it contains. Unfortunately their information derives ultimately from the sports pages in the Daily Record or the Sun, which makes it extremely loud indeed. Their opinion of Scotland, her people and prospects boils down to one or all of the following: "shite", "pure shite", "useless bawbags", "how can we govern ourselves when we got beat by Belarus on penalties", and "I hate that Alicsammin." Nevertheless, they're still very keen to let us know that they are proud Scots.

In the interests of balance, it should be pointed out that this subspecies has its counterpart amongst independentistas, the *Cybergnaticus caledoniensis compulsivebloggerii* - who is prone to making friends and relatives run away and hide in case they start banging on about independence again - but at least is far better informed.

In conclusion, if you are lucky enough to encounter an elusive Lesser Spotted Unionist, give them a big hug and a hearty cheer. They're performing a sterling service, converting Scots into Yes voters.

10 November 2013

Remembering peace

The United Kingdom was born in war. The War of the Spanish Succession was already raging between England and France, as they fought to exert their influence on an ailing Spain. The Union of 1707 brought Scotland into the conflict too.

The wars have continued pretty much ever since. In the 300 odd years since 1707 the United Kingdom has been involved in wars in 171 different countries. It's easier to list the years in which the UK was not fighting a war than to list the wars, conflicts, or 'police actions' themselves. They were for the most part wars of British colonialism and exploitation, wars of British political chancers and opportunists. Wars that were not in a noble cause.

Instead of the customary approach of historians and naming the wars, perhaps we should name the periods of peace instead. They're the exception to the rule of war. So here, culled from that fount of human knowledge, Wikipedia, the periods from its foundation in 1707 when the UK enjoyed peace.

1725-1740, 1754-1756, 1769-1774, 1784-1789, 1861-1863, 1874-1877, 1881-1884, 1888-1896, 1896-1899, 1904-1914, 1923-1936

And that's it. They total just 62 years out of the 306 years since the Union of 1707. I'm not entirely sure what the UK spends its £42.2 billion annual defence budget on, but if it's being spent to bring us peace it's proving to be spectacularly poor value for money.

1936 was the last year in which British armed forces were not involved in some war. 1936, when Edward VIII the Nazi sympathising monarch was briefly on the throne before he was forced to abdicate because he married a divorcee, and not because he was a Nazi sympathiser.

By way of comparison, there's a small northern European country with a population of 5 million. Denmark has had its share of self-inflicted wars, and its attempts at naked colonialist aggression. Over the centuries it's been involved in any number of spats with its neighbours. In more recent years it has participated in the First Gulf War and in the war in Afghanistan. It's not like small nations are intrinsically more inclined to pacifism than large ones.

How successful has its defence policy been at preserving peace for the Danish nation over the same period? Here are the years of peacetime for Denmark, when the country wasn't involved in any military action.

1720-1788, 1790-1800, 1814-1848, 1850-1864, 1864-1902, 1903-1918, 1920-1939, 1945-1950, 1953-1990, 1999-2002

Denmark has been peaceful for 239 out of the past 306 years, considerably more than the 62 managed by the United Kingdom.

Someone very close to me fought in two of the UK's less glorious wars as a sniper in the Royal Marines. He never speaks about what he endured and what he witnessed. He saw active service in Suez and Cyprus. He saw his friends die. He killed people. And they gave him medals that live in a drawer, gathering dust.

I asked him once why he never wore a poppy, and he said that while he'll never forget those who died, he'll also never forget that they had been sent into places where they had no business being, and had to do things no human should have the right to tell another to do. He can never forget that those who suffer most in wars are not those who fight them. He forgets about his medals, they're not important.

He stopped wearing a poppy in the early 1980s, in the aftermath of the Falklands War, when he noticed it had become obligatory for politicians and media presenters to wear one. The same politicians whose failures require young men and women to go off and die and get maimed. The same politicians who are eager to get involved in any war that's going and the press which acts as their cheerleaders.

He said he felt that poppies and remembrance were being used as a sop to justify sending more young generations off to war. He vowed to stop wearing one until the UK was no longer involved in any military action, because you can only truly honour the sacrifice of those who fought in Britain's many wars in a time of peace. It has been 30 years since he made that decision, he hasn't worn a poppy since.

The sniper from the Royal Marines is my partner. He's English, he's gay, and if you believed certain people who campaign for a No vote, he represents two stereotypes rolled into one who shouldn't be welcome here. But he is welcome, and he feels welcomed, and he intends to vote Yes next year.

Scotland isn't a place he's been sent to where he has no business being, it's his home. And he'd like to live in a country where the periods of peace outnumber and outweigh the periods of war. Then he can wear a poppy again with a quiet pride.

11 November 2013

The Clyde's oil and gas glow in the dark of the MoD

Recent reports have apparently confirmed what many of us have suspected for some time, that there is oil and gas under the Firth of Clyde in quantities which make it more than worthwhile to extract.

I remember hearing of it in the early 80s, but then everything went quiet and the prospect of a Weegie oil boom vanished along with much of Scotland's traditional industry. There was mibby some oil, but it was too wee too poor and too stupid to become independent of the ground - ground which not coincidentally was controlled by Westminster.

Obviously the Firth of Clyde is a lot smaller than the North Sea, but it was still expected that the Clyde could enjoy if not a boom, then at least a moderately biggish bang. What we got instead was a big fart blown in our general direction from the Ministry of Defence.

Even in the early 80s it was known that the MoD was not keen for oil companies to go sticking their drill bits into the Clyde, possibly in case they came up with some top secret radioactive contamination.

Despite the nuclear risks, the oil company's marketing people thought that "Clyde Oil, it glows in the dark" could be a workable slogan. After all, it worked for Ready Brek. Instead of a liability, it could have been a unique selling point. Clyde oil with added Faslane lets you fire up your central heating and light your home for free at the same time. Or you could have got an x-ray whenever you filled up your petrol tank. Would have saved the NHS millions if you don't count the radiation posioning.

But the MoD didn't want any civilians poking their noses into the murky waters of the British nuclear deterrent, its costs, its dangers, and its contamination. They'd just purchased some extremely expensive submarines and some even more expensive missiles. So the Clyde was to be left fallow, and the expensive nuclear deterrent was left defending an industrial wasteland that looked like the Russians had already nuked it.

It wasn't enough that Westminster destroyed Scottish industries, they were also hell bent on ensuring that we wouldn't be allowed access to our own waters and our own resources in order to stick a plaster on the gaping wounds.

In September 1983 the Glasgow Herald published a brief story, Ayrshire MP David Lambie had written to then Energy Minister Alick Buchanan-Smith asking him to clarify whether the Ministry of Defence was blocking oil exploration off the West coast. Buchanan-Smith was one of those posh Scottish Tories who would eventually go the same way as the Clyde's oil boom, so there is a small amount of justice in the world.

By February 1984 the paper was reporting that the MoD was indeed blocking exploration in the Clyde. David Lambie accused then Defence Secretary Michael Heseltine of blocking drilling licences.

This was the second attempt to explore for oil and gas in the area. BP had carried out some initial investigations in 1981, but was blocked by the MoD. Even after their second attempt was rebuffed, the company kept up the pressure to allow exploration to continue. Like they'd do that if the amount of oil and gas was insignificant.

Now SNP MSP Chic Brodie has reopened the issue, and it is clear that the economic potential of the Clyde was sacrificed to meet the demands of the MoD's nuclear submarines. They didn't want anyone to know just how rubbish they were, nor did they want annoying questions about the uselessness of the UK's supposedly independent nuclear deterrent, or how it might not be independent after all. A non-independent nuclear deterrent based in a non-independent country, there's a sort of logic there.

The UK wanted its nuclear subs, the people of Glasgow wanted jobs and economic opportunities. There could be no clearer illustration of how when the needs of Scotland clash with those of Westminster, Scotland loses. But that's how the Union works. We're locked into a Union where our interests are always going to be secondary. The arguments over the Govan ship yard are just the most recent example.

An oil boom in the Clyde might have brought much needed jobs and investment to a West Coast reeling under the onslaught of Thatcher's industrial amputations, although all the dosh would have ended up in the Treasury's coffers and we'd have been assured it was an insignificant amount anyway.

Shame for them really, because they missed a trick. Instead of Better Together and its pals scaring us with the dubious prospect of Shetland and Orkney deciding they didn't want to be part of an independent Scotland, they could have been threatening us with an independent Millport, and telling us we'd need a passport to go doon the watter to Rothesay. They could be telling us there was almost no oil left in the Clyde, barely enough to cover the cost of a radioactive Loch Fyne haddock.

Instead what we have is more evidence of the arrogance and disdain which Scotland is subjected to by our masters in Westminster, evidence that Yes campaigners will ensure is made known widely before next year's vote. And we've been left with unexploited oil and gas reserves that we could develop for ourselves when we finally get rid of the chancers.

The UK is founded upon the short-term gain of London and the City on the back of the long-term consequences to everywhere else in the United Kingdom. Now that strategy is coming back to bite them on the bum. It couldn't happen to more deserving people.

In the editorial in the Glasgow Herald in February 1984 we were warned: "Pessimists will say that the oil boom is over and we will not have another." Those same pessimists are still with us, still saying the same thing 30 years later. Let's make sure that we don't waste the next 30 years.

12 November 2013

Proud Scots but

Alistair Carmichael is making a keynote speech, which is Union-speak for "having a wee moan". He's allegedly upset that the Yes campaign have allegedly alleged that No voters are less Scottish than Yes voters.

The "Yes campaign" in question consisted of a carnaptious cooncillor from the SNP who had described Koalamichael as a "supposed Scot". This was a sardonic reference to the cuddly cabinet meenister's valiant defence of jobs in Govan, which consisted of assuring the shipyard workers that if they vote Yes next year they'll lose their jobs, lose their homes, their children will be sent to sweep chimneys, and worst of all they'll still have Ian Davidson as their MP.

I'll say here and now that the cooncillor was wrong. There's nothing supposed about the Koalamichael's Caledonianosity. He is as Scottish as any other person born or brought up in Scotland, living in Scotland, or possessing a Scottish accent - and that last caveat is only required because of Tony Blair, absolutely no one wants to admit to him. But none of this applies to Ian Davidson, he's not Scottish. He's not British either, his nationality is Twattish. It's a small island in the Ocean of Self-interest.

What's interesting about this, if indeed there is ever anything of interest in what comes out of a Lib Dem's gob, is that the supposed slight "supposed Scottish", doesn't work in reverse. Whatever you think of the Fife cooncillor's remark, it's understandable - perhaps not in the moral sense, but the linguistic sense. "Supposed Scot" is a phrase which has meaning. It is comprehensible, like "two faced Scottish Secretary", "hypocritical MP", or "lying Lib Dem".

The opposite, "supposed British", doesn't make any sense when used with reference to independence supporters. The reaction of yer average indy supporter to being called "supposed British" by a Unionist would be "Eh?" It's not at all clear what the phrase might mean. The utterings of apologists for Westminster are often nonsensical and frequently outrageous, but at least they consist of insults you can feel insulted by.

"Supposed British" is one of those zen koans devoid of lexical content that you find in the holy speeches of St Johann the Rarely Visible. Johann's mangled syntax is the SLab equivalent of "What is the sound of one hand clapping, grasshopper", before it slaps you across the mug.

The lack of sense of the phrase "supposed British" can only be because it doesn't make sense without the "supposed" bit prefixed to it either. Britishness is for most Scots a vague and nebulous concept, which is why the Westminster parties are so determined to make out that they are the only body able to give the word any definite import - like they're the Oxford English Dictionary or the Dictionary of Scots all of a sudden, and we instinctively turn to Johann Lamont, Ian Davidson or Magrit Curran for guidance on the finer points of linguistic usage.

The not at all supposed Scot Koalamichael is living proof that Scottish people are not immune to rank hypocrisy, wilful ignorance, or a truly astounding lack of self-awareness. He illustrated this by his warning that the Yes campaign are on dangerous ground by mixing "patriotism with politics", saying without an apparent shred of irony: "I tell you this: once you start mixing up politics and patriotism you can quickly get into dangerous territory."

No shit Alistair. All those exercises in flag waving, royal events, and Great British telly programmes are entirely coincidental. It's not mixing politics with patriotism to repeatedly warn us that we'll all become foreigners, because it's well known amongst Unionist circles that being foreign is a bad thing. And it's not mixing politics with patriotism to declare like Jim Murphy that he's a proud Scot but he's also proud to be British with the "best armed forces in the world". No patriotic grandstanding there then, oh no.

This raises an altogether deeper and more interesting question. To the No campaign, British patriotism is like British nationalism. Neither exists in their universe, and no amount of rationally pointing out to them that supporting the British state is a form of nationalism is going to penetrate their skulls. If they were truly non-nationalists and viscerally opposed to nationalism in all its incarnations they'd be arguing for the abolition of Westminster and its replacement by one world government.

Trying to demonstrate to a British nationalist that they are indeed a nationalist, and so hasn't got a moral leg to stand on when they decry a Scottish desire for independence, is a bit like trying to demonstrate to a homophobe that they are indeed homophobic. It will not compute with them. In fact, they are liable to respond angrily, because some people believe that being called a homophobe is actually worse than being homophobic, just as the likes of George Galloway will fiercely reject any suggestion that he's a British nationalist as he tours the length of the land exhorting us to "Just say naw" to indy. We'll just say naw to George instead.

Certain people and organisations habitually define homophobia in such a way as to exclude themselves from it, allowing them free rein to argue that gay people shouldn't be allowed to marry or have kids or have equal legal rights. Typically they redefine homophobia so it only means "physically assaulting a gay person out of malice or spite". It's a strategy for dealing with cognitive dissonance, allowing them to continue to discriminate without seeing themselves as discriminatory. The redefinition permits them to accuse the people they discriminate against as being the wrongdoers, and portray themselves as the victims.

This is in fact the exact tactic adopted by a number of Christian churches, not only do they believe they have the right to define the meaning of the word "marriage" for everyone, Christian or not, they also believe they have the right to define the meaning of the word "homophobia". They discriminate against gay people because they believe a god of love tells them to do so, so it cannot possibly be homophobic for campaign against legal equality for LGBT folk. It's gay people who are the bad guys, causing all that upset and fuss. And if you scratch a bit further, it's because deep down they believe that only straight people are normal, gay people are abnormal. Only those who are themselves "normal" are entitled to define "normal" meaning.

The ability of humans to hold mutually contradictory ideas simultaneously is called cognitive dissonance, and the strategy of redefining meaning to suit oneself is a classic means of achieving it. Koalamichael's pronouncements against "mixing patriotism with politics" are another example of the exact same cognitive dissonance, only this time applied to a different struggle for civil liberties, the Scottish independence debate.

The UK government and the Westminster parties want Scotland to continue as a country which isn't properly a country, and a nation which isn't properly a nation, without confronting the cognitive dissonance that this entails. They want to justify Scotland remaining a nation which doesn't enjoy the full range of rights possessed by any normal nation. Unionists achieve this by being "proud Scots but", and portraying themselves as victims of evil Scottish rupturists. Pointing out the disadvantages of Scotland remaining in the UK is a far worse crime than actually perpetrating those disadvantages upon Scotland.

Only Scottish independence is nationalist, and only mixing Scottish patriotism with the political desire for independence is dangerous. Westminster is normal, an independent Scotland is abnormal. Unionists argue that Scotland couldn't possibly cope with the challenges that face any normal country, the subtext being that Scotland is not a normal country. Naturally only normal people like Johann Lamont or Alistair Carmichael can define these concepts normally, but that's much harder sell for them.

This is certainly hypocritical of Unionists, but they're not actually lying - at least not in this aspect of their arguments - because lying entails a conscious telling of a non-truth which is understood not to be true by the person making the statement. Unionist politicians don't have that much self-awareness. They're proud Scots ... but.

Don't expect any of this to change before September 2014. As the American socialist author Upton Sinclair said: "It is difficult to get a man to understand something, when his salary depends upon his not understanding it."

15 November 2013
Just say naw to George Galloway

There's some very tortured logic lurking beneath George Galloway's stentorian oratory. George is what you get when Ian Davidson swallows a thesaurus and takes some classes in rhetoric. He's currently on a tour of Scotland, exhorting us to "just say naw" to independence. George believes he can get us to do this, in part, by flinging a bit of sectarian mud. In May this year he said:

"My own experience of growing up as a Roman Catholic in Scotland has led me to fear independence in Scotland. The possibility of Scotland being a kind of Stormont is a real one [...] Of course, most Scottish people are not swivel-eyed, loyalist sectarians but there are a large number of them. A large six-figure number, and if I were living in Scotland as a Roman Catholic I would be worried about that."

I'd never describe myself as "growing up a Roman Catholic", far less as "Catholic". Just ask my maw, to her eternal shame I was always the world's worst Catholic. Religion just didn't compute, despite enormous efforts on the part of my parents. I was dragged to Mass every Sunday until I was 15, even though I decided at the age of 10 that I was an atheist, and was sent to Catholic schools where time in RE periods was spent arguing with the priest. It was only a phase, they insisted, I'd grow out of it. And they were right. It was a phase. I'm still an atheist, but I no longer argue with priests.

Since, unlike George, I actually live in Scotland and don't view the country from afar through the wrong end of a 1970s telescope bought on Westminster expenses, I reckon this gives my views on sectarianism considerably more credibility than his. But if you want to have your views given wide coverage, it helps to be a mouthy Westminster MP who grasps at the limelight with the single mindedness of a pussy cat intent on grasping Rula Lenska's dangling ball of wool.

In the East End of Glasgow in the 1970s whether you were a "Catholic" or not had very little to do with your own personal beliefs about matters spiritual. I could have shaved my head, donned my mother's best yellow curtains, and marched up and down Shettleston Road chanting Hare Krishna, but folk would still have said: "Aye, there goes thon weirdo Catholic boay." Mind you, they said that anyway, but that's by the by.

My own experience of growing up in a Catholic family in the West of Scotland led me to the opposite conclusion from George. I learned very young that sectarianism had little or nothing to do with religion. Atheism ever so slightly rules you out from being a Roman Catholic. Not being a Catholic was one of the things I was quite determined about, but it's not like this would cut any ice with the average Orangeman, nor indeed the average Catholic parent in the 1970s. On one fundamental doctrine the Orange Order and the Catholic Church are in full agreement: Once a Catholic, always a Catholic.

So if sectarianism isn't about a person's religious beliefs or lack of them, then what is it about? There's a clue in a somewhat glaringly obvious fact which George appears not to have noticed about swivel-eyed loyalist sectarian types.

You can recognise such people, not primarily by their swivel-eyes, which could merely be a symptom of a thyroid condition, but rather by the fact that the loyalist loons are the ones waving Union flags and going on about being British and how much they love the Queen. Some of them wear bowler hats and carry furled up umbrellas. So far I'm not seeing much that would convince me I was at an SNP rally.

The swivel-eyed loyalist loons George warns us about are the ones who love being British so much that they make a point of causing traffic chaos in order to let the rest of us know about it. There's also a fair bit of singing songs about 17th century wars between the British state and Irish nationalists, often accompanied by the copious consumption of tonic wine produced by Catholic monks. That would be an ecumenical matter.

None of these, with the possible exception of the Buckie, are, distinctive symbols of Scotland, independent or otherwise. But perhaps George knows different.

The Union flag is not a cuddly all-inclusive symbol. Even now, decades later, my primary association of the Union flag is with Orange Walks. It's a symbol which historically represented the social exclusion of a large part of the Scottish population. It's a symbol which says: "We're better together without people like you."

George appears to recognise this too, at least on some level. In one of his recent lectures, George claimed that his flag is not the Saltire, and it's not the Union flag, his flag is red. It's one of these fine sounding pieces of rhetoric which on closer examination is bereft of any substantive meaning, the socialist version of "oh look there's a cute wee kitten called Karl Marx". A bit like a speech by Johann Lamont, come to think of it, apart from the fine sounding pieces of rhetoric, or any socialist references, or indeed sentences with nouns and verbs in them.

But eloquently expressed garbage is still garbage. His desire to continue having the red flag as his flag apparently depends upon Scotland retaining the Union flag. I'm not sure how that works, and I don't think George does either.

George has also failed to notice that loyalist sectarian loons are precisely those people who are least likely to be in favour of an independent Scotland, apart from Westminster politicians. So if Scottish independence is likely to provoke an outbreak of loyalist violence, that can only be because the loyalist loons identify Catholics with, or blame them for, an independent Scotland. And that in turn would mean that loyalist loons see an independent Scottish state as representing Catholics, but not them.

So why should Catholics in Scotland feel threatened by a state which loyalist loons feel threatened by because of its supposed Catholic sympathies? Does not compute. It's like RE classes all over again.

Trying to follow his chain of logic gives you a heidache that pounds like a Lambeg drum. Because no matter what way you look at it, the only folk in this equation who ought to be fearful of Scottish independence are the swivel eyed loyalist loons. And we already know that the Orange Order is an enthusiastic supporter of Project Fear, even though neither Project Fear nor George Galloway prefer to acknowledge the fact in public.

Sectarianism in Scotland is not about religion at all. And neither is it about defining who is or is not Scottish, despite what George Galloway says about the attitudes of certain SNP figures back in the 70s.

Historically, sectarianism was about defining who was British and who was not. Britishness, not Scottishness, was the most important consideration. It was never that the Irish in Scotland could not be Scottish. It was that the Irish in Scotland could not be Scottish because they were not British, and being Scottish depended upon being British first. But this is 2013, and we know better now. Everyone born, brought up, or living in Scotland is Scottish and a part of Scotland, it's the British bit that's optional.

Sectarianism is a disease of British nationalism, Loyalist bigotry and its Irish Catholic counterpart are symptoms of that disease. And the Auld Firm hoo-ha surrounding 22 overpaid baw kickers ruining a perfectly good lawn is yet another product of it. That's British nationalism for you, it even manages to screw up the fitba.

Independence will not infect Scotland with the disease of sectarianism. Independence is the cure. And given that his last attempt at election to public office in Scotland saw him gain a mere 3.3% of the vote, it may very well prove to be a cure for George Galloway as well.

17 November 2013

The dam cracks

Former Lord Provost of Glasgow Alex Mosson has come out in favour of independence. It's a bit like the end of the third movie in the first Star Wars trilogy, when Darth Vader comes over all good guy and saves his boy from the evil Empire. By that time the series was already getting a bit creaky, although the actual evil Empire is currently deep into the third of the increasingly dire prequels, but without the expensive special effects budget or Natalie Portman. All we've got left is the tortured and unconvincing dialogue and Johann Lamont. Although to be fair, Wullie Rennie does make a convincing comedy alien.

I'm no fan of Alex. Scotland is a small country, even though we're governed by a parliament stuck long ago in a galaxy far away. We don't have six degrees of spearation, it's more like two. I'm related to Alex Mosson, albeit distantly. We've never met, the Mossons not being a close knit clan, and far less cuddly than Ewoks.

Grandee and Alex Mosson are not two concepts I'd normally expect to find in one sentence. I heard all about how far short of grand he fell long before he was ever elected as a cooncillor, and before the Daily Record did its exposé on his criminal past and his former alcohol problem. An exposé which if I recall failed to mention how he climbed the greasy pole of Glasgow Labour politics in the first place. It also missed out some of the things my grandmother told me through severely pursed lips, although she rarely had a good word to say about anyone. Apparently it's genetic.

I won't be repeating my grandmother's gossip here, on account of not wanting to get sued, but Alex Mosson was one of the reasons I turned against the Labour party. He was the embodiment of Labour's machine politics. He witnessed how those politics turned a party founded by trade unionists and socialists as a vehicle for social reform into a voracious mutant with a sense of entitlement as devastating as that of an absent Highland laird during the Clearances. It sent hope into exile and treated its flock like sheep.

This would be the same Labour party in Scotland whose hierarchy is dead set against independence, not because they have any great affection for the United Kingdom, but because they know that it would spell the end to their style of politics. The endless ping pong between two identical sides who rack up points to be exchanged for peerages and directorships. We're stuck in a 1970s video game that's only of interest or benefit to those who are playing it. And even the players don't love the game, they only love the rewards it gives them.

Alex Mosson isn't playing the game any more, he's retired, as is that other Labour grandee who recently came out in favour of a Yes vote, Charles Gray, former chief of Strathclyde Regional Council. Both of them have recognised that Scotland needs a new game.

Strathclyde Region was part of an abortive 1970s experiment in killing nationalism stone dead by giving us a system of local government that was incompatible with devolution, brought to you by those fine minds that gave us the 1979 40% rule and 1997's twin vote on devolution and tax raising powers. It was abolished in 1996 when it was clear it had been as successful at dispelling nationalism as Ian Davidson has been successful in defending the jobs of Govan shipyard workers.

Alex Mosson used to work in the shipyards. It would be interesting to know what he thinks of his party colleague's, ahem, intervention, in the controversy over RN orders and the future of the Govan yard. I suspect that his declaration this weekend that he's voting Yes is not unconnected to Davidson's machinations.

Now like the rest of us Charles and Alex are viewing the ever decreasing spiral of Labour from a more distant perspective, they can see that the Westminster game's a bogey. It's not beneficial to Scotland, and it corrupts any political party that participates in it. The British Parliamentary road to socialism died a long time ago. Now it happily takes part in an anti-independence campaign alongside Cameron, Osborne - and even Nigel Farage - while accepting donations from conservative businessmen like Ian Taylor of Vitol.

Charles Gray and Alex Mosson are not alone. You can be certain that there are many more senior figures within the Labour party who harbour the notion that Scottish independence gives the Labour party its only chance to redeem itself. You only need look at Ian Davidson and Anas Sarwar to see that redemption requires something pretty drastic. The dam has just started to crack open. So much for Labour for Indy being an SNP front organisation. Labour for Indy is the real Labour party, it's Lamont, Sarwar and the rest of that sorry bunch who are the entryists.

Unionist critics will doubtless leap on Alex's past as a reason to discredit his conversion to Yes. What they need to remember is that he only got where he is because the Labour party in Glasgow voted for him. He is a creature of politics under the Union. Criticise him for his past, and you criticise the Westminster system of politics which has served him very nicely. That's a system that he, but not the Unionist critics, sees as being in need of change. Who's the hypocrite here? For those who are hard of thinking, like Ian Davidson, here's a wee clue: it's not Alex Mosson this time.

When even Alex Mosson, yer definitive Labour dinosaur, sees that the writing is on the wall for the Union, the end is in sight. I was genuinely and pleasantly surprised to find myself, for the first time in my life, in total agreement with my dad's cousin. I didn't see that one coming. So I'll give Alex the last word, the words that all Labour supporters who are unsure about independence need to hear:

"This is not a time for party politics. The decision we'll be making next September is too important for that. People need to realise that this is not about the SNP, Scottish Labour or any other political party.

"This referendum is all about us, the people of Scotland, and our right to self-determination. Once we achieve independence I'm sure people will start to regain their interest and engagement in politics, and that will be a good thing for democracy."

19 November 2013

The shape of a future past

The latest scare story from Project Fear comes in the form of a report from the IFS which apparently tells us that if Scotland becomes independent, we'll be screwed (although possibly not royally), penurious, bankrupt, beggared, and impoverished. We will in fact be so skint that it even made the BBC news at 6, so that viewers in England, Wales and Northern Ireland could also appreciate just how poor we're going to be. Since Scotland rarely makes it onto the UK national news, because if it doesn't happen in London then it's not national at all, that must mean we'll be extremely poor indeed. Are you scared yet?

How any of this differs from last month's report from the IFS telling us much the same thing is not entirely clear. That would be the report that said an indy Scotland would have to double taxes, as it would be magically unable to raise revenues any other way due to a curse put on it at birth by the wicked Fairy Godmother Osbornia. But it didn't mention that if tax raising was the only method of dealing with the UK's massive deficit, the rUK would have to raise taxes even more.

It's a bit like one dug crapping on top of another dug's turd, the reports all merge into one big amorphous toley. You don't ask which backside it came from and you don't poke it too closely to discover whether there is anything solid in there. But Project Fear collects it all anyway and flings it with the excitable glee of a troop of baboons, who not coincidentally are equally renowned for their blue arses.

Like most people I'm not an economist, instead I'm one of those curmudgeonly auld gits who believes that if a nation is only deserving of independence if it can be proven that a couple on the average wage would be £2.56 better off each week as a result, then the entire exercise is probably a waste of time.

The point of independence is that it gives Scotland the ability to do things its own way, to build a fairer and more just society, and to find our own solutions to our own problems with full control over our own resources. This desire has arisen because the present system of Westminster government only ever covers itself in glory of the jingoistic variety. Tackling income inequality, or ensuring that the country has an economic base outside the casino of the City of London are not high on its list of priorities.

However what the economists of the IFS are seemingly unable to factor into their models is that doing things differently is what the show is all about. We want independence because we don't want to do things like Westminster, yet we're presented with an economic forecast that assumes that for 50 years into an independent Scotland, we'll still be operating with the tax policies and spending priorities of the UK, circa 2012.

A long time ago I had a book called The Shape of Futures Past, it was an entertaining trawl through past predictions. Not those of the Nostradamus cyptic woo variety, although *Doth hiss foul venom the Ogre of Clota, poisoning his nest for to propitiate Tamesis*, is clearly a foreboding of Ian Davidson. This was a book about serious attempts from previous centuries and decades to predict the future. What they all had in common was that they were hilariously off the mark. None of them predicted the huge revolution in social attitudes in the post WW2 era.

Instead they concentrated on technological progress, and even then most often got it wrong. In the 1920s they predicted traffic jams of biplanes, monorails everywhere, and the City of London would be under a vast glass dome to insulate it from the harsh denuded wilderness beyond. Which come to think of it isn't so hilariously inaccurate after all.

Reading about the latest dire predictions from Project Fear, I couldn't help thinking they were really describing a wee wifie in a 1950s pinny waiting at home in her nuclear powered kitchen with futuristic 1950s appliances, making the dinner for hubby. He was at that moment flying home from the office on his plutonium fueled personal jet-pack, without his trilby getting blown off or his suit getting creased thanks to the miracle of manmade fibres, and when he got home he'd tell the little woman how the family budget was being spent.

However if you can be bothered to trawl through the IFS report, it actually says something rather different from the unremittingly negative spin put upon it by Better Together. The report tells us that:

if we continue to manage our affairs the way Westminster does,

if we adopt the exact same government priorities as Westminster,

if we collect taxes the way Westminster collects them (or rather doesn't collect them if you're a large company),

if we spend those taxes on the same things Westminster spends them on,

if we do nothing and vote No,

then we really will find ourselves under a never-ending barrage of jobbies from blue arsed baboons.

21 November 2013

Inside the goldfish bowl looking out

It was reported this week that according to study by Croatian academic Dr Jaroslav Tir of the University of Colorado's Department of Political Science, an independent Scotland could be one of the most pacific nations in history.

It's not that sort of pacific, Calmac ferries will not call at Tahiti en route to Rothesay. We'll not be blessed with tropical sunshine,

Gaugin paintings of Polynesian maidens, and hordes of Australians on weekend breaks. The kind of pacific that's in store for us is even better - Scotland will be a country which is blessed by the prospect of peace, which will enjoy freedom from war, and experience exceptional democratic stability.

This good news, which Dr Tir delivered during a recent conference at Glasgow University, was completely drowned out by Project Fear's insistence that iScotland will be unable to protect itself against rampant hordes of Russian cybercriminals, god-botherers with bombs, and Faroese trawlerboats. We're defenceless against North Korea drilling a hole through the centre of the Earth and dropping a missile though it so it can nuke Hampden in revenge for the flag incident. We'll be a little lost country, shivering alone in a big bad forest full of foreigners with dastardly ways.

Project Fear never stops to ask itself who we need to defend ourselves against, and why. In the James Bond universe of the No campaign, villains need no motive. They'll act just like Westminster will after a No vote, apparently, and will punish us out of sheer spite.

In essence, Project Fear's campaign boils down to "Vote No or we'll kick your arse, and while we're kicking your arse, these other baddies will kick your arse too - for no reason other than we're all basterts." It's understandable that they're finding it difficult to put a positive gloss on this. But if the basterts are going to kick our arses anyway, I'd rather take my chances with a Yes.

Despite the increasingly discredited and discreditable threats of Project Fear, Dr Tir's work tells us that our chances of living a nice quiet life are rather better with a Yes vote. He has analysed the process of independence in many countries, and the factors that influence how peaceful the new state becomes.

What he discovered is that there is a correlation between the peacefulness of the country's independence process and the likelihood of that country becoming involved in wars. The more peaceful the independence process, the less likely it is that the new state will be belligerent and prone to getting into artillery exchanges with its neighbours. A nation that becomes independent peacefully develops into a peaceful state.

The Scottish independence process is exceptionally peaceful. The worst that happens is that someone gets called a name, and even then the outrage is most often manufactured. It would appear that political violence in an independent Scotland will most likely consist of some politicians occasionally taking the huff over a supposed slight by some other politicians.

The rest of us can live with that quite easily, unless you're one of those peculiar people who loses sleep over Alistair Carmichael saying he's been called a nasty name. However unpleasant being called a name is for the sensitive Carmichael, it's a whole lot less life threatening than invading Iraq.

The experience of living inside a goldfish bowl is very different from viewing it from the outside. For all the supposed bitterness and vitriol of the Scottish debate, the rest of the world holds us up as a model of how a nation can attain independence.

Those opposed to Catalan independence contrast the sober and issue based debate of Scotland's pro-indy campaigners with the supposed "unreasoning passions and emotions" of Catalonia's independentistas. Meanwhile the independentistas cite the Edinburgh Agreement and the legality of Scotland's referendum as proof that the Scottish No campaign recognises the democratic legitimacy of a claim to national self-determination, even while being opposed to Scotland exercising its claim. Both sides point to Scotland and say, "See, they're acting like grown ups and that's how it's supposed to be done."

But we're inside the goldfish bowl, so all Scots independentistas see is Westminster gobbling all the fishfood and Ian Davidson doing a jobbie in the watter. Whereas Project Fear sees independentistas as a voracious carp which is about to swallow their political careers whole. Which admittedly isn't entirely incorrect.

But despite this, none of the fish in our bowlful of Loch Ness watter are killing each other. Our monsters are mythical. We've avoided cannibalism, headbutting, devouring our young. We've had no physical violence, not so much as a fin has been nibbled. Our piranhas are only metaphorical. As a nation, we need to give ourselves a bit more credit for this because it doesn't happen very often. Our non-violent independence campaign is in itself proof of the democratic maturity of Scotland.

The other major issue determining how peaceful and stable a country is going to be is them next door. Countries which can't agree with the neighbours over where the garden hedge is situated are countries which are likely to spend decades fighting over the petunias.

Here again, Scotland is exceptionally fortunate. If you've ever looked at a historical atlas, you'll be struck by the ever changing kaleidescope of borders across Europe. From around the year 1000, Poland has waxed and waned, at times stretching across much of Eastern Europe, at other times wiped from the map. After WW2 it ended up pretty much where it started 1000 years earlier. It's not just Poland. Across Europe borders came and went, populations ebbed and flowed. The end result was a whole lot of states which had claims on all or part of another country's territory, and took a chainsaw to the hedge and trampled all over the neighbour's vegetable plot.

Scotland's sole land border has been one of the most stable and enduring in Europe. For the best part of the past 1000 years it's been in more or less the same position, give or take a Berwick. Although Scots have emigrated in their hundreds of thousands, there are no solid blocks of Scottish people in some other land, calling to be "reunited" with the hameland. Scotland has no territorial claims, and no other state has any territorial claims upon Scotland.

What all this means is that Scotland is an exceptionally favoured country. It is a racing certainty that as an independent nation we will have few enemies, we will stay out of wars, our defence force will not sally from its barracks and overthrow the legitimate government, and the worst manifestation of political violence we'll witness will be the weekly hurling of insults at Furst Meenister's Questions.

The alternative we're offered is the almost continual war of the United Kingdom, "punching above our weight" in military conflicts which have nothing to do with us, and seeing future generations of young Scots going off to die in foreign fields. And we still get Johann Lamont's weekly sneerathon.

22 November 2013

Dr Ye Whit?

As any true fan of the series knows, Dr Who is not a science fiction programme for kids. It's a social realist documentary combined with a religious experience. But now, woe, woe and thrice woe, we must sacrifice John Barrowman to the Sisterhood of Karn (which, to be fair, could be a win-win), Scotland's chances of independence have been sucked into the Rift in the Space Time Continuum that lurks beneath Cardiff. It's keeping me awake at night. Curse you Project Fear!

The most fearful of all futures awaits us. Esconced in a secret underground hideout - which bears a startling resemblance to a quarry in Wales - the evil genius Master Eck, ruler of the Cybernatrons, will be able to manage a feat that even the combined forces of the Daleks, the Cybermen and the Weeping Angels were unable to achieve: creating a dominion where even the Doctor cannot tread.

Although the Doctor can cross space and time, can voyage to galaxies beyond the reach of the most powerful telescope, slips easily between one dimension and another, and can travel from the Big Bang to the end of the Universe, Project Fear insists that he won't be able to cross the border into Scotland if we become independent. It will knacker the spacetime regulatory thingy in the Tardis, and the Gallifreyan RAC won't go to an indy Scotland on account of the extra paperwork.

So said Ruth Davidson, High Queen of the Lizard People, as she addressed a nation cowering in terror behind the sofa, watching from between their fingers. Scottish Tories have been trapped in a time vortex for decades now, so you'd think she'd be a credible witness.

Wise Earthlings should heed her counsel, she used to be a presenter on the Gallifreyan version of Reporting Scotland - featuring Dalek exterrrminashuns, cute Schrodinger's kittens, and fitba. Because no matter where you go in time or space you can never escape interminable reporting about 22 millionaires ruining a perfectly good lawn. It's one of those immutable laws of physics, like the one that says you can give one billion Johann Lamonts one billion typewriters but even after one billion years they still won't have managed to construct a sentence that makes any sense.

Thankfully this latest scare story is definitely not bigger on the inside than it is on the outside, and you don't need a sonic screwdriver to deconstruct it. It's just a load of Ood pish even less plausible than an episode of Made in Chelsea starring Johann Lamont and Wullie Rennie. Which isn't very intergalactic superheroey time traveller at all, but that's what comes of confusing Ruth Davidson with the Tardis's Data Core.

The argument appears to go that because we'll not be a part of the UK, we'll no longer get BBC programmes. We'll get rubbish Scottish programmes instead of the BBC's rubbish interspersed with the occasional wee gem. While I'm prepared to concede that the great majority of telly output is indeed pish, and will remain so after Scottish independence, it's unclear why Ruth believes that Scottish telly will be incapable of producing the occasional wee gem of its own. She's a proud Scot but, not proud enough to think there's anyone Scottish capable of producing a hauf watchable telly show. Like, oh I dunno, Steven Moffat who produces Dr Who.

In any case, it is already established in the Canon of Doctor Who, in an episode penned by the very same Mr Moffat, that Scotland will become an independent nation. In the episode *The Beast Below* Amy Pond is trapped on a spaceship carrying the population of the UK to humanity's new home on the other side the Milky Way. Earth had been ruined by idiotic governments with nuclear weapons. (We're not pointing any fingers because that would just be rude.) With typical UK efficiency the space ship's engines had died the death of a thousand austerity cuts. In part because they'd used the same design as the latest submarines based at Faslane.

Amy was asked by another passenger what she was doing there when she had a Scottish accent. Amy asked why shouldn't she be there, and where were all the Scottish people anyway. "Oh," replied the passenger, "they've got their own ship." One with engines that worked.

The programme is almost as old as I am, the first Doctor I can remember was Patrick Troughton. The best was Tom Baker, and I will strangle anyone who says otherwise with a multicoloured scarf.

This devotee of Dr Who, while cheerfully admitting to being a saddo git who really needs to get out more, has never missed an episode since. Even - and I'm not proud of this - the ones with Sylvester McCoy. My weekly religious experience has taken place every Saturday evening the programme was on, uninterrupted except by dogs jumping on the sofa and partners who unreasonably insist on speaking when you are communing with the Muse of Gallifrey.

Worshipping at the shrine of the Tardis took place without fail, despite the fact we spent a decade and a half living in Spain, courtesy of a satellite dish perched on our roof and a generic satellite decoder giving access to the entire gamut of free to air UK broadcasting - all without a licence fee or a satellite telly subscription.

Scotland is a lot closer to England than Spain, Scottish residents would not require the 2 metre dish we had, which allowed us to contact passing Sontaran Battlecruisers as well as watching the BBC, alongside an impressive range of Nigerian soap operas and shopping channels selling sonic kitchen appliances. A Sky satellite dish (already installed in many homes) and a 30 quid generic satellite decoder, or a slightly more expensive Freesat decoder, and the job is done. No need to take out a Sky subscription or to find a way of resolving temporal paradoxes. And as an added bonus it inverts the polarity of the fear beams from Planet Westminsteron.

So here are the possible scenarios:

We get a reformed BBC, Scotland and rUK both contributing. BBC Scotland gets proper autonomy and a national channel. We pay the same licence fee. And we still get Dr Who.

We get an independent Scottish Broadcasting Corporation which co-operates with the BBC on programme making and shares programmes. We pay the same licence fee. And we still get Dr Who.

We get an independent SBC that the BBC will not co-operate with, instead the SBC buys popular programmes from the BBC on the international TV market. Meanwhile it can sell its own popular TV shows on the international market too. We pay the same licence fee. And we still get Dr Who.

Or there will be no SBC because the new Scottish government won't be able to organise one, for the usual reasons of weeness, poverty and stupidity. We install a satellite dish, get a cheap decoder, pay no licence fee. And we still get Dr Who.

So even in the absolute worst case scenario depicted by Project Fear, and even assuming that the BBC boycotted the new Scottish Broadcasting Corporation and refused to sell it any programming, we'd still be able to watch Dr Who and the entire range of UK free to air broadcasting. No subscription fees, no licence fee required. The total one off cost comes to considerably less than a single annual UK licence fee.

This makes Project Fear's latest scare story all the more bizarre, because even if their outrageous lie did come to pass, we'd still get all the telly we wanted, and it would cost us less than we have to pay just now.

Even Doctor Who's famously huge intellect would struggle to wrap itself around the logic of that one.

25 November 2013
Somebody else's problem

Here we go again, another day, another scare, each one dumber than the last. It's safe to say that Project Fear is now bricking itself. The anti-independence campaign which began with the intent of progressing as calmly and gracefully as a swan gliding across the glassy smooth waters of the garden pond of Scotland's media is now more like the famous Norwegian Blue parrot sketch.

The latest impossibility to occur in the increasingly improbable list of implausibilities from Project Fear is that even if we do vote Yes, we can't become independent until Westminster is jolly well good and ready. The Guardian has reported some anonymous Westminster insiders, otherwise known as the Project Fear Press Office, who warn that the Scottish Government's timetable for independence negotiations is a non-starter. It cannae be done, because there's going to be a UK general election in 2015. We can't possibly expect one UK government to be bound by decisions of a UK previous government because it breaches one of those unwritten rules of the British constitution that they've made up to suit themselves.

It's interesting that Project Fear is now acknowledging that a Yes vote is a real possibility. Couldn't be anything to do with tomorrow's publication of the long awaited White Paper which will set out a roadmap to a better Scotland, could it. Hope they tell us, always trumps fear. More on that soon, no doubt.

It's equally interesting that they also acknowledge that Westminster is incapable of medium, never mind long, term planning. It certainly explains a lot about the UK, every four or five years everything gets ripped up and we have to start all over again. What was that about volatility and uncertainty for business? Oh right, that only applies to oil and independence referendums ...

It also explains the dearth of answers from Project Fear so far on what we can expect in the event of a No vote.

If we vote no will we remain in the EU? Dunno. Nigel Farage might be very influential amongst sections of the Tory party if UKIP do well in next year's European elections. Will an independent Scotland be in the EU? We don't know, because Westminster refuses to ask the EU for a ruling. Which may not be unrelated to the fact that the ruling would most likely be along the lines of "We can work something out, like we did with German reunification." Currency union? Well they're rubbishing it but steadfastly refuse to rule it out. Let's call that one a mibbie. Extra powers for Holyrood? Depends on what you mean by "extra", "powers", "for", and "Holyrood", and on who it is you're asking. Which given the track record of the Westminster parties on this issue means "bugger all". Keeping the Barnet Formula? Looking less and less likely by the day. Keeping the UK's AAA credit rating? Oh, right ...

Still the news that a UK government doesn't have to abide by international agreements entered into by its predecessors does seem to clash with another of those unwritten rules that make up the British constitution. That's the one that says an incoming government is bound by the treaties, contracts and obligations entered into by its predecessor. Otherwise they'd have had to cancel the London Olympics in 2010 when the Labour government which was awarded the games by the IOC was replaced by Coalition. I don't recall many calls for tearing up all the Olympic negotiations and starting all over again at the time. Funny that.

This latest scare story must fall into the "making things up as you go along" sections of Britain's glorious unwritten constitution. You can appreciate why our political masters find it such a useful tool of governance.

The latest problem to confront Scottish self-determination has all the hallmarks of one of those problems that can be solved by self help manuals with titles like *Feel the Fear and Do It Anyway*, which promises to help the reader "move from a place of pain, paralysis and depression to one of power, energy and enthusiasm." Which not coincidentally is also a good description of the Yes campaign.

Project Fear's newest problem is dealt with in the popular psychology manual *Somebody Else's Problem*, a single sheet of paper bearing the words: "It's somebody else's problem."

The late great Douglas Adams described a security device based on somebody else's problem in the Hitchhikers Guide to the Galaxy. The Somebody Else's Problem Field worked just like the cloaking or invisibility devices in more traditional sci-fi, the difference being that the "cloaked" object remained very much in view. It was just that everyone ignored it as it appeared to be a trivial little piece of fluff of no importance or substance, and it was somebody else's problem. There's a similar device in the Scottish Parliament, where it's known as Wullie Rennie.

In this case the Field Generator is only functioning partially. We can see it's somebody else's problem, but we can also see that it's Westminster's problem. Holyrood will be responsible for who represents Scotland during these negotiations, Westminster will be responsible for the Westminster side. Are they really admitting that they're incapable of forming a negotiating team? If that's true why exactly would we want to stay in a Union with such a spectacularly incompetent government?

However the selfsame "insiders" who tipped off the ever willing Severin No Fear Story Too Wee Carrell also revealed that in the event of a Yes vote in Scotland, it would be Westminster which had the problem, and had better resolve it pretty sharpish. As the article said:

A political crisis over the fate of institutions like the Bank of England, the UK's national debt and its defences at the same time as a political battle over a referendum on Britain's EU membership would be likely to cause a damaging backlash from the financial markets, investors and international lenders.

A Westminster Government upsetting the financial markets just to punish Scotland? That's too implausible a scare story even for Project Fear.

27 November 2013

Paying attention

Still trying to read through the 600 odd pages of the White Paper on independence. I'm a fast reader, but am still only halfway through, and still have not had time to mull it over and digest the bits I've read so far.

That must be why I'm just a punter and not a punching above their weight Unionist politician like Alistair Darling, who seemingly not only had read the document, he'd digested it and was crapping it all out in wee pieces on telly interviews throughout Tuesday. Since he was doing this on the Beeb within two nanoseconds of the White Paper's publication, he's either the world's fastest reader or he'd swallowed a ton of laxatives and some Better Together briefing notes.

Anyway, it was a bit of a strain, what with one eye on the white paper and one ear on Alistair's bowel movements, but it was something about childcare and how we couldn't possibly pay for it, although simultaneously he wanted to know why the Scottish government wasn't paying for it right now. It was enough to gather that he had about as much knowledge of the contents of the White Paper as the average badger has of Westminster's plans for future devolution. Which is actually somewhat more than Alistair does, come to think of it.

Still at least he must feel reassured that despite being 670 pages long, and detailing the possibilities for an independent Scotland in the economy, culture, health, equality, security and development, goes into the nitty gritty of Scotland's agricultural potential, and nowhere once does it mention the words badger cull.

Of course I'm not the immense expert in the contents of the White Paper that Alistair is, what with his Olympic medal for speed reading and brain the size of a soundbite, but I seem to recall somewhere in the mass of pages an explanation that the proposed child care costs would be met by increased tax revenues generated by the greater participation of parents in the workforce - but that under current arrangements the extra revenues disappear into George Osborne's maws, to be spent on something beneficial to Scotland like a London sewer upgrade. Even I managed to pick up on that, and unlike Alistair I'm not paid to pay attention.

It all summed up what, for me, is the real reason for Scottish independence. We'd have a government made up of people who are paying attention, and if they don't pay attention we can vote them out. It shouldn't be a lot to ask for in a democracy, but if Alistair is anything to go by we'll only get it with a Yes vote. The Union gives us a political class which is paid not to pay attention, and no matter what we do can never be got rid of. They can hardly complain that we no longer pay attention to their warnings that we'll be doomed if we ditch them.

At least the BBC was paying attention to Scotland's independence debate in its own inimitable way. We got the wise and insightful words of its national commentators on the UK news, helpfully telling us benighted Scots who've been having this debate off and on for decades what it's *really* about because we're too provincial to work it out for ourselves.

Nick Robinson seemed quite let down by the lack of any razzamatazz or pandas in kilts giving a Buzby Berkley style aquatic performance in Bellshill swimming pool. He's been to the birth of quite a few new nations, he said (or maybe he didn't because I wasn't really paying attention), and this just didn't feel like one on account of a distinct lack of marching bands, Weegie fireworks that look like penises, and exhibitions of raffia based ethnic crafts.

Of course he was spectacularly missing the point. Scottish independence is not about a new nation. Scotland is not a new nation. We're a very old nation. We've got the national identity thing well sorted already thanks. Identity? Got it by the bucketload ta. In fact the very opening words in the preamble to the White Paper are "Scotland is an ancient nation." Nick's not really been paying attention either.

The White Paper shows us how we can start to find solutions to our problems and take advantage of our opportunities in ways that are not dictated to us by people who aren't really paying attention. That makes it far more exciting and substantial than the Union flag bedecked parades that pass for Westminster's attempts to imbue us with British pride.

But why should he have been paying attention anyway? He's the BBC's Westminster correspondent. Scotland is irrelevant at Westminster and always has been. Neither the Tories nor Labour require Scottish votes in order to form a majority government. They have no need to pay attention.

Scottish independence is about how Scotland governs itself and deals with the challenges and opportunities that face any small northern European nation. Independence is the radical notion that if Scotland was governed by people who were obliged to focus their attention on Scotland, they just might discover a more palatable way of doing things than the increasingly bitter range of options tossed at us by Westminster.

28 November 2013

What Mariano Rajoy didn't say

In "breaking news" during a dull ding dong of a debate on Newsnicht on Wednesday evening, we were breathlessly told that Spanish Prime Minister (Prime Minister right, so he must be someone really important) Mariano Rajoy had made an important intervention in the debate about whether Scotland should keep paying for railway lines between London and Birmingham, weapons of mass destruction, and Ian Davidson's expenses.

We really require a drum roll at this juncture, or possibly a mariachi band - yes I know that's a Mexican thing but are you telling me BBC Scotland would know the difference? - in a major new development Mariano Rajoy said ... what he's been saying for the past 18 months or so. *Nada nuevo.* Jackie Bird could have done a salsa to it, while Gordon Brewer practised imperious looks in preparation for his tango with Johann Lamont, but it would still have meant "nuhin new".

What Rajoy said was that new countries would be outside the EU. He's been saying this for quite a while now, he regularly trots it out as a threat against Catalan independentistas. It was of course covered in the Spanish media, although it came way below stories about Rajoy's unwillingness to explain how he's been managing his party's finances after a series of corruption scandals enveloped the Partido Popular. La Moncloa, the seat of Spain's government, is not in a happy place. Not much new there either.

What would have been more interesting, and you know, would have made this news as opposed to a bit of mutual backscratching between anti-independentistas, would have been if Mariano had said "Spain would veto an independent Scotland's entry into the EU and cancel flights between Prestwick and Malaga." Which if nothing else would at least make him popular with people who hate Ryanair. But he didn't say that.

Rajoy's the Spanish PM, he and his cabinet of obsessive *centralistas madrileños* decide Spain's foreign policy. If he wanted to send a clear signal that Scotland would have a tough time getting into the EU, he could have said so. But he didn't say that either.

Here's what he did say, in both the original Spanish and my English translation, as quoted in El Pais newspaper.

"Desconozco lo que dice el libro blanco que se ha presentado ahora, pero lo único que me gustaría es que se presentasen con realismo las consecuencias de esa secesión. Yo respeto todas las decisiones de los británicos, pero tengo muy claro que una región que obtuviera la independencia quedaría fuera de la UE. Es bueno que lo sepan los escoceses."

"I don't know what it says in the White Paper which has been presented today, but all I would like is that the consequences of that secession are presented with realism. I respect all the decisions of the British, but I have made it very clear that a region which obtained independence would be outside of the EU. It's good that the Scots may know that."

The El País article which the quote came from is entitled *Rajoy usa Escocia para lanzar un aviso a Cataluña* 'Rajoy uses Scotland to launch a warning to Catalonia'. Rajoy's comment was not aimed at

Edinburgh, but at Barcelona. He was reminding them that Madrid has furren pals tae gie it hauners.

What he was doing was sending a wee quid pro quo to Davie Cameron, because Westminster will share the quid with Spain but not Scotland, so Davie would say something helpful in Mariano's *Proyecto Miedo* against the Catalans. Like threatening to slap an extra tax on charter flights to Sitges or reopening El Bulli for Bullington Club reunion dinners.

The Spanish reports which the breathless Scottish media told us constituted a new twist in the debate quite explicitly said that Rajoy was merely restating a position that Madrid has held since it first heard the phrase *independencia catalana*. El País even introduced Rajoy's words with *recordó*, which means 'he reminded/recalled' as in what you do when you're reminding people of things you've already said before. But that didn't stop the Scotsman crowing that "Alex Salmond's vision of EU membership after independence was dealt a significant blow tonight."

The whole thing about it not being new and not being directed at Scotland must have got lost in translation. There's a BetterTogether filter on all news reports from Spain, nothing which doesn't support the scare story du jour gets through. Besides, "Here's something someone said nearly two years ago" lacks the sense of urgency which is a vital component of any warning of impending doom.

Despite the bluster, Madrid is not going to issue a statement saying that Spain will veto Scottish membership of the EU. It's a bit like the argument over whether an independent Scotland would retain the pound. You get a lot of "Oooh missus! How very dare you!" from Westminster, but they don't actually rule it out because Westminster knows that it's in the interests of the rUK to agree to a currency union after a Yes vote. Spain knows it's in Spanish interests to agree to Scottish membership of the EU after a Yes vote.

There are many reasons Spain knows it's in Spanish interests to welcome Scotland into the EU. None of which can be voiced before a Yes vote, for reasons of both international and domestic politics. Rajoy is hardly likely to admit to them before the referendum.

Scotland would be a net contributor to EU funds, which a Madrid with an eye on EU budgets will certainly have considered. Spain is a net recipient of EU funding, and all those agricultural subsidies and investment in infrastructure for poorer regions depend on a healthy EU balance sheet. That's not been doing too well of late, and the bottom line is that people short of dosh don't deprive themselves of potential creditors.

We also provide access to fishing grounds that provide employment to the culturally and economically important Galician fishing industry, Mariano's home region. If you've ever seen a fish counter in a Spanish supermarket you'll know what a very big deal seafood is. Then there's a whole trawlerful of other reasons, like our energy resources, the importance of political stability during a time of economic crisis in the eurozone, and enough Realpolitik to satisfy Angela Merkel at her sternest.

Perhaps most importantly, Scotland will not be the permanent obstacle to EU agreement posed by the rUK. The political geography of the EU is changed, the rUK is no longer a state on the periphery, it will be surrounded by EU members. That increases the incentive for the rUK to be more collaborative in European initiatives.

And finally there's the not unimportant consideration that the average Spanish person, doubtless including Mariano Rajoy, does not bear Scotland any ill-will. Quite the reverse actually, there is a surprising amount of affection for Scotland in Spain. Even the most fervent opponent of Catalan independence or nationhood will cheerfully point to Scotland as an example of "a nation".

But the important point in terms of Spanish domestic politics - which is all that interests Rajoy - is that Spain does not need to veto Scottish membership of the EU in order to send a signal to the Catalans. Neither does it need to do so in order to block Catalan accession to the EU.

Madrid's case for refusing to recognise an independent Catalonia rests upon grounds which are not applicable to Scotland. The constant and repeated line from la Moncloa is that Scotland has a constitutional right to hold an independence referendum, Catalonia does not. Scottish independence will be negotiated and agreed with Westminster, and will be recognised by Westminster. Members of the Spanish government have said repeatedly that under such circumstances Spain could have no grounds for objection.

In the event of Scottish independence Madrid will recognise Scotland while at the same time stating that its reasons for recognising Scotland are precisely the same reasons why it cannot recognise an independent Catalonia. They will also protest, without the slightest shred of shame, that they're not being hypocritical.

La Moncloa already has the only legalist reason it requires to block Catalan independence and international recognition, it doesn't need to damage its relationship with an independent Scotland in order to prove a rhetorical point it's not actually making. That's Realpolitik in a modern Europe.

Even Rajoy's statement that an independent Scotland would automatically be outside the EU does not imply that Spain would ensure that Scotland's negotiations to join the EU would be protracted. But it's in the current interests of Madrid to imply that they would be. There have been no independence referendums yet, so both la Moncloa and Westminster want to make out that Scottish or Catalan accession to the EU is more horrendously complex than assembling flat pack furniture with only three screws, the wrong sized Allen key, and a plastic spoon.

The point of EU negotiations should be easy to understand, even for leader writers in the Scotsman. Apart from the obvious goal of EU membership, what are EU membership negotiations for? They are to ensure that applicant countries are in accord with EU standards on a whole raft of issues, from democratic government, human rights, press freedom, the economy, the environment, and a whole lot more besides. The negotiations are extremely lengthy and complex because it takes time for a country to ensure compliance on environmental protection standards for newts, and regulations on the minimum number of newspapers willing to publish made up stories about EU banana regulations. This is what takes years to sort out.

Scotland's already done all that though, having to do it all over again would be like having to surrender your driving licence in order to use public transport. Scotland already possesses a valid EU driving licence, we don't suddenly forget how to drive because we're taking the independence bus.

What Scotland needs therefore, is not to have to take its EU tests all over again, with all the frantic swotting and overdosing on RedBull that would entail, what we need is for our licence to be validated. That's a political decision, and one which will only be revealed after a Yes vote has taken place, because in the current political landscape it's in the interests of both the Moncloa and Westminster to pretend they might do otherwise.

Confronted with the reality of a Yes vote, both will do what is in their national interests under changed circumstances. And that means Westminster will agree to a sterling union and Moncloa will agree to Scotland in the European Union.

December 2013

1 December 2013

Sun loungers and Eurosmears

I've been trying to wrap my wee brain around some of the assertions of the Better Together campaign in response to the White Paper, especially those concerning Europe. Their lack of logic and the way in which the Unionist parties insult the intelligence of voters are infuriating, but it is even worse than that. Project Fear doesn't just insult our intelligence, it panders to racist stereotypes. There can be no clearer illustration of the moral bankruptcy of the case for the Union.

Project Fear insists that the independence campaign is motivated by anti-English sentiment. It is is a classic example of accusing your opponents of your own sins. That the Scots hate the English is an ancient trope, one of a bundle of negative stereotypes about Scotland which were traditionally current south of the Border, sitting happily alongside alcoholism, deep fried mars bars, vegephobia, and a propensity to stab people called See You Jimmy.

The subtext of this smear is that Scotland has no real issues with the way in which the United Kingdom is run, that the only truly distinctive feature of Scottish political culture is anglophobia, and that the semi-civilised savages on the northern edge of Europe require the good services of Westminster to protect us from ourselves. It's a smear which tells us that we really are like the stereotypes some hold of us.

The ludicrous nature of this claim is easily exposed by the high level of participation by English people resident in Scotland on the Yes side of the argument. And I don't just mean people of Scottish heritage who were born in England. English Yes voters also include many, like my own English partner, who do not have a drop of Scottish blood. Except for that time when I dropped a glass and cut myself at dinner and bled all over his chicken tikka. He didn't eat it though, so I don't think it counts. Despite the chicken tikka incident, he fully intends to vote for an independent Scotland next year.

Project Fear's assertion of anti-English racism is in itself racist, but that doesn't stop regular airings of the claim even in a Scottish media which ought to know better. This is after all a media which is supposed to serve Scottish families like mine, which contain Scottish Yes voters who prove their love for English people every time we let them watch their crappy telly show instead of something more interesting. Our families also include English people who witness the extent of this supposed anti-English racism in their daily lives. The weird thing is that they bizarrely fail to see any.

When a media narrative contradicts the information from your own eyes and ears, you doubt the media narrative, not what you know from personal experience. Or perhaps my ex-polis former Royal Marine of a partner is so terrified of my latent anti-English racism that he's too feart to tell me? Oh. My. God. All these years he's been cowering in terror. If only I'd known, I could have got the TV remote control off him when he insisted on watching Top Gear.

Project Fear's eurosmears also trade on racist stereotypes, this time concerning the behaviour of Continentals. In fact it's really quite like Top Gear. Voting No is like voting for Jeremy Clarkson to decide your foreign policy.

One of my favourites eurosmears is that we'll be compelled to sign up to the Schengen Agreement, which provides for passport free travel between participating member states. The UK of course, refused to join, and has one of its much prized opt outs protecting the UK from the hordes of Europeans who would otherwise descend on us, creating devastated cityscapes full of nothing but shops selling interesting sausages and sour cream. The horror.

That's those things that after independence Scotland won't get, allegedly. The opt out that is, even Project Fear acknowledges we'll still be able to get wiejska, kolbasz and sour cream. Or at least they haven't actually claimed otherwise yet, it's probably just a matter of time. Anyway, after independence we'll have no choice but to sign up to Schengen and put border controls at Berwick. "They" will make us.

This was the opinion of, amongst others, the UK Government's David Lidington, the Conservative MP for Aylesbury who is also Minister of State at the Foreign Office with responsibility for Europe.

More recently, the scare was repeated by Professor Robert Wright of Strathclyde University, in a report for the Fraser of Allander Institute - the independent think tank run by former Labour leader Wendy Alexander's hubby, which just happens to produce reports that are helpful to the Better Together campaign, reports which are then gleefully splashed all over the Scottish media.

So were were told that in the opinion of some really clever academics, who can use big words and do hards sums that: "It is difficult to think of a set of circumstances that would allow Scotland to opt out and not be part of the Schengen Area as this is now the norm in the EU."

It's not actually that difficult at all, and you don't need to be a professor of economics in order to think of one. Here's a set of circumstances that will allow Scotland to opt out of the Schengen Area: geography. It's the same reason that led the Irish Republic to opt out.

They must have access to atlases in university economics departments. Scotland has no borders with any Schengen member. The nearest Schengen state is separated from Scotland by 500 miles of England and the English Channel. Perhaps the EU loves us so much that they want to take the Proclaimers song literally, and we'll have to walk 500 miles just to knock on their door.

The real question ought to be, which EU member state has an interest in insisting that Scotland sign up to Schengen? The EU itself has made no statement on the subject, neither have any other EU member states. They're not going to before there's a Yes vote. But the answer is none.

The EU knows, just as the Scottish Government and the UK Government know, that demanding that Scotland join Schengen while rUK and Ireland remain outside will damage the economies of Scotland, the rUK and Ireland, and will not create any significant economic advantages for any other EU state. Most Scottish exports to the EU go via the rUK, any advantage to other EU states to Scotland being within Schengen is negated by the reality that the rUK won't join. There is absolutely no point to Scotland signing up to the Schengen until such time as the rUK decides to sign up too.

In fact the damage that border controls along the Scottish border would cause to the Scottish economy and the economy of the rUK would likewise have a damaging effect on all their EU trading partners. This damage would more than outweigh any supposed benefits that other EU states would gain by insisting Scotland signs up to Schengen.

So why does a scare story with no rational basis continue to be repeated? It's because it rests upon racist stereotypes of Germans which Project Fear hopes will give it traction. It's Project Fear's version of German holidaymakers getting up at the crack of dawn in order to blag all the sun loungers with towels. That's the law of sun loungers, and according to the stereotype Germans are genetically incapable of doing anything other than applying rules literally and without consideration of circumstances. They're so incapable that they'll even take steps which damage their own interests, like getting out of your pit at 6am when you're on holiday even though the whole point of a holiday is to have a long lie. The Schengen Agreement has been blagged by a German towel, so naturally there's no space for Scotland on an independent sun lounger.

What Project Fear doesn't want us to consider is that foreign nations might act exactly as we would expect an independent Scotland to act: like grown ups considering their own rational interest. That means they will weigh up the pros and cons and collaborate when it suits them to do so. There is no downside to other EU countries agreeing to Scotland remaining a part of the Common Travel Area in the British Isles and Ireland, there is a downside to them insisting we join Schengen. After Scotland has voted Yes, collaboration not confrontation will be as much in the interests of other European countries as it is in ours.

On Sunday the Guardian published a poll taken in a number of European countries which showed that - by a very large margin

- their inhabitants are not disposed to do the UK any favours, and that they are thoroughly disenchanted with the recalcitrant role the UK plays in European affairs. Yet Project Fear asks us to believe that these countries will willingly damage their own national interests to punish Scotland as a favour to Westminster, all so that Westminster can wreak a bit more havoc on the common European project than it has done to date. It's not going to happen.

4 December 2013

No, an homage to catatonia

Brian Wilson, former radical socialist turned nuclear energy enthusiast, has decided to launch a new attack on the SNP and Scottish independence for being the root cause of all that is evil. It's not like he does anything else, so no one was that surprised.

In an article for the Hootsmon entitled *No homage to Catalonia*, Brian took issue with the SNP for not showing enough solidarity with Catalonia. Not like the Labour movement which was a proud ally of the Republican cause during Spain's civil war.

It's a sign of just how far the Scottish Labour party has fallen, here was Brian arguing the case for the heirs of Franco. That's some seriously depressing irony, and just too tragic to make a smartarsed remark about. Brian thinks Mariano Rajoy was quite right to gang up with Davie Cameron and thon Belgian guy, the one with the bowtie in lieu of a personality, to tell Scots and Catalans that they'll be out on their ears if they vote to govern themselves.

He starts off poorly, with some bad history. While Scotland and England were uniting peacefully, he tells us, assorted monarchs were knocking lumps out of each other to get their paws on a piece of Catalonia. Scotland on the other hand enjoyed peace, thanks to the glorious Union, as long as you don't count those Jacobite Wars which were going on at the same time.

Brian's point, however poorly illustrated, was to make out that in Europe you positively trip over ancient grievances, and it's only the fragile structure of the current configuration of states that prevents us from coming over all atavistic. Existing states good nationalism, potential states bad nationalism. And it helps to remind us that the Scottish independence campaign is likewise about "ancient grievances", and not some current grievances about the way the UK is run which it shows no willingness to address.

The spectre of war stalks Brian's imagination. If Scotland votes for independence, we'll open the doors to independence demands from everyone from Catalonia to some German Nazi survivalist in a log cabin in the Alps. The world will be plunged into chaos, and it will all be the fault of Scottish people for deciding we're not too wee too poor or too stupid after all. We'll be the standard bearers for the sort of post apocalyptic world that Mel Gibson was famous for before he did that other movie. But with Johann Lamont instead of Tina Turner, which is a lot scarier.

The possibility that other modern European nations might be just like the Scots, and be perfectly capable of sorting out their own constitutional arrangements without resorting to violence or the benefit of external assistance seems to have escaped him. But as Brian well knows, Project Fear's largest donation comes from a non-Scottish Conservative businessman who lives in England, so it's easy to see why he might have missed that point.

He goes on to ask a most curious question. "When [the SNP] talk of 'a seat at the top table', they must surely have some idea of how large they think that fabled piece of furniture should become?"

OK, I was being polite. When I said curious question, I really meant "gobsmackingly asinine question". It's a question which is so stupid it transcends stupidity, enters the realms of profundity and then comes right back to stupid again. It's stupid cubed.

For starters there's the wee issue that Brian doesn't seem to have grasped the "self" part of "self-determination". It's hardly for Scotland or the SNP to decide which other ethnic, cultural, or linguistic group is or is not a nation worthy of independence. It's unionists who do that sort of thing. Mariano Rajoy and his government do it every time they inform the Catalans that they aren't allowed to hold a referendum. Brian and his pals do it every time they invent some spurious reason why Scotland cannot possibly be a successful independent state.

Just how big does Brian think that any international organisation the UK belongs to is going to become? Perhaps the UN has an upper limit on the maximum number of states that are allowed to exist simultaneously. You'd think they would have let us know. Or perhaps new countries go into a sort of international green room, wine and nibbles will be provided until it's their turn to go on stage. Or it could be that if there are too many countries some of the older ones pop out of existence. I'm sure I saw an episode of Dr Who about something like that. But we won't get Dr Who in an independent Scotland so we'll never have to worry about it anyway.

It's more likely that Brian is trying too hard to think up another question that is impossible for the SNP, or indeed anyone else, to give an answer to. This will allow him to proclaim smugly that the SNP don't have any answers. Let's just call off this whole independence thing then.

But this unknowable can be laid firmly at the door of the SNP in Brian's world, and it is in fact the basis of his entire argument. That nice Mr Rajoy is just being sensible and statesmanlike in working with Davie and wossisname, it will come to me eventually, to prevent people doing radical and dangerous things like voting to have governments they can exercise some degree of control over.

And yet again there's nothing from Brian about any positive reason for Scotland to remain subject to governments we didn't vote for. No vision of hope, no prospect of anything better together. Vote no, it's an homage to catatonia.

8 December 2013

The difference between solidarity and stupid

Ever seen Monty Python's Life of Brian? It's a movie classic. In terms of the sheer density of surrealist ridiculousness contained in every scene it's rivalled only by any video ever released by the Better Together campaign. The only real difference is that Life of Brian is funny on purpose.

The Labour wing of the increasingly fractuous Better Together Except For Thae Basterts I'll Not Be Seen On The Same Platform

With campaign has apparently also spotted the similarity between the doughty struggle to save the Union and the comedy genius of Monty Python. It can be the only explanation for why Wee Dougie Alexander wants Scotland to play the role of the Judean People's Front Crack Suicide Squad at the end of the film. He explains this in what he called Labour's case for the Union, calling for solidarity, social justice and struggle across the UK.

The Scottish Labour People's Front Crack Suicide Squad are the ones who turned up at the end of the movie, when Brian was being crucified, yelled "Attack!" and then stabbed themselves. This is pretty much what Labour wants Scots to do in order to demonstrate our solidarity with people in England, Wales, and Northern Ireland, who are also being crucified by Tory governments. At least it's what Labour calls solidarity.

It has been demonstrated that the outcome of Westminster General Elections is not greatly affected by how Scotland votes. Even if Scotland doesn't return a single Tory MP, we cannot protect communities in the rest of the UK from Tory governments. England outweighs the rest of the UK in terms of population by a very considerable margin, the Scottish vote can only make a difference to a Parliamentary majority if the parties achieve very similar numbers of seats in England. That doesn't happen very often, and when it does happen it tends to produce governments with wafer thin majorities that don't last the full term.

Labour demands that we make a futile gesture anyway, it's the noble and self-sacrificing thing to do. Like locking yourself in the garden shed for 27 years in solidarity with Nelson Mandela. Mind you, if Ian Davidson promised to lock himself in his shed for 27 years it could well be a vote winner, sadly it's not going to happen.

It's not even as though Labour's vision has a very positive view of those we're supposed to be showing solidarity with. It seems Labour wants us to vote no so that Labour supporters in the rest of the UK can say, "The Tories are basterts, but I feel much better about myself knowing that people in Scotland are having a crap time of it too."

Which means that Labour regards solidarity as something akin to oil revenues, they should only flow from north to south of the Border.

True solidarity would see Labour supporters in England welcoming the fact that Scotland has an escape route from the Tory menace, despite it being an escape route they cannot take themselves. Solidarity in this instance would be them saying, "Flee as fast as your hairy wee Caledonian legs can carry you mate."

And in fact a not insignificant number of them are of this opinion, because unlike the Labour party in Scotland they know what solidarity means.

We are all human beings with the same worries and struggles. What Dundee faces, Liverpool faces. This is a truism. And it also applies to Dublin and a whole lot of other places that aren't part of the UK. But let's gloss over the subversive thought that solidarity also applies to non UK passport holders.

Imagine a group of friends trapped in a cave behind a rockfall, one is much smaller and skinnier than the rest. There's a narrow space between the fallen rocks that's just big enough for the wee yin to crawl through. There's not enough room for the bigger ones to follow and the rocks are too massive to shift. They'll have to go into the depths of the cave in the hope of finding another exit.

Does the wee yin stay in the cave trapped with the rest, or does she make her escape and go and get help?

Labour wants us all to stay in the cave, so no one ever goes for help. That's not solidarity. That's stupidity.

It's also insulting, because Labour tells us that by squeezing out through the rockfall wee skinny Scotland is abandoning her English friends, and will just bugger off to watch telly that can't receive Dr Who or Strictly instead of suffering the deprivations of Conservative rockfalls. The selfish article.

In fact an independent Scotland will be constructing a politics that isn't constrained by Westminster's love affair with American neoliberalism, one that can tackle social inequalities and provide a sustainable future for all. That's a vision of independence many of us share, one which will allow us to shout, "Haw here's a Tory free exit over here," down an open shaft. Then we can help our English, Welsh, and Northern Irish friends towards a way out of their own.

But there's another Tory related issue that Labour wants us to overlook when we consider our vote in September next year. And it's this, in order to get those much sought after majorities which will allow Labour to usher in a golden era of government with lashings of solidarity jam, Labour has to adopt policies that appeal to Tory voters.

It's the simple arithmetic of Westminster. The party which attracts the votes of swing voters in Labour-Conservative marginal seats is the party which forms the government. The only way Labour can do that is by dressing in Tory clothes. So we end up with a Labour party which is, to all practical intents and purposes, identical to the Conservatives. 13 years of Blair and Brown taught us that.

Labour wants Scotland to stay in the cave along with opponents of the Tories in the rest of the UK. It's not like they have any clear idea of how to get us all out, there's no Labour plan to guide us anywhere but deeper and deeper into the bowels of austerity. They quite like it down there.

That's the choice facing Scotland. We can squeeze out through an exit that no one else can use but which might shine enough of a light to let others find their own escape - or we can all give up hope and resign ourselves to gloom forever.

True solidarity delivers hope. That's why I'll be voting Yes.

12 December 2013

Every little helps

There's only one thing Project Fear has for sure, and that's an enormous barrel. How else to explain their ability to keep scraping the bottom of it to come up with a new scare story. It can't be easy to come up with some convincing goods when you aim to produce a new fright every other day.

It's not made any easier when your quality control is handled by policy wonks who think a ride on a fairground ghost train is a pants wetting journey into the terrifying unknown. We get a lurid warning of impending doom all lit up in neon flashing lights, which on closer inspection turns out to be a poorly made plastic dummy worked by clearly visible strings. But enough about Alistair Darling.

This week it's supermarkets. Undaunted by the fact that previous claims that we'd be paying more for the leckie, gas, and mobile phones were debunked even before the ghost train had passed the Abandon Hope All Ye Who Enter Here sign, Better Together have been in touch with some supermarkets in search of pricing quotes that can be used to terrify us into voting no. A couple of executives from Asda and Morrisons came up with some cheap mince. Every little helps eh?

We shouldn't blame the executives too much, at least not this time, their area of expertise is flogging baked beans. Some over-enthusiastic journalists took their comments and twisted them out of context in order to create an unidentified item in the bagging area, which Better Together promptly decided was actually an unexploded bomb and not some offcuts of tripe.

A list of hypotheticals and unwarranted speculations turned magically into a fact. Food is going to be more expensive if we vote for independence because fewer Scots eat vegetables and that will make them more expensive to deliver because they'll form a smaller proportion of overall sales nationwide. And it will cost a fortune to organise the security details and special cages to protect the petits pois from Scottish people who are afraid of legumes.

Surely however, by the same logic, since Scots eat more processed foods, then processed foods will form a larger volume of sales so will be cheaper to distribute. Or am I missing something? I thought this was supposed to be a scare story. Independence would give us slightly cheaper chocolate digestives versus slightly more expensive broccoli, the vegetable spawn of Beelzebub.

But back to reality. No supermarket chain has issued any statement saying that if Scotland becomes independent, they'll put up prices. In fact there are plenty of reasons why food prices in an independent Scotland could be lower than they are in the rest of the UK.

The story was comprehensively debunked, both by Business for Scotland and the BBC's business editor Robert Peston, within hours of Better Together's horsemeat lasagne hitting the supermarket shelves.

The intervention of Robert Peston was interesting. It's perhaps a sign that even the BBC, Better Together's biggest cheerleaders, are beginning to despair of their lamentable excuse for a campaign.

And today Newsnet Scotland is reporting that they have contacted Morrisons, who denied that they were predicting higher food prices in an independent Scotland at all. In fact the company admitted that it was possible that food prices could even fall.

Despite the scare story being dumped in the compost bin quicker than a mouthy MP can jump on a bandwagon, the Herald reported that Magrit Curran is justifying her MP's salary by demanding that Alex Salmond come clean on the price of beans in an independent Scotland. Magrit is insistent that the weekly shop will be cheaper if Scotland stays part of the UK, and added that it's a "devastating blow" to Yes Scotland because the White Paper did not give a detailed statement on the possible impact of independence on two for one offers on toilet duck. Maybe it's just Magrit who should BOGOF.

After Scottish independence food will of course be cheaper in the remainder of the UK, but only for people who are forced to get their weekly shopping from a food bank. We can be sure there will be increasing numbers of those if we vote no.

The number of food banks in the UK doubled over the last year. Between April and September this year, the number of people approaching the Trussell Trust for help tripled. The Trust runs over 400 food banks across the UK. A third of those who needed help were families with children. The Trussell Trust alone helped to feed 350,000 people, and this doesn't count the many thousands who approached other organisations running food banks.

Stagnating wages, increases in the cost of living, and cuts to benefits are forcing thousands of citizens of a rich developed country to resort to food banks to feed their kids, but the Trussell Trust reported that the problems of poverty in the UK are so deep that increasing numbers of those they help are rejecting offers of food that must be prepared and cooked. They just can't afford the fuel bills. Organisations running food banks put the increase in demand for their services very squarely down to the changes to benefits policies introduced by the UK government.

Labour has no clear solution to this problem. In fact they refuse to commit to reversing the changes to the benefits system introduced by the Coalition. There will still be food banks in the UK even with a Labour government in power. The only certainty from the supermarkets is that food prices will continue to rise, and the only certainty from the Westminster parties is that increasing numbers of families will still have to resort to food banks while a tiny minority grow increasingly rich.

There is no truth to Project Fear's claim about food prices in an independent Scotland. But even if there were, and food was slightly more expensive if we reject Westminster's policies, what sort of country would you prefer to live in? One where more and more of us subsist on poverty wages and sub-poverty benefits, or one where food was slightly more expensive but everyone has enough of an income to feed, heat and clothe themselves adequately?

I'd rather live with dignity, even if it means paying 2p more for a tin of beans.

15 December 2013

Lying liars and the lies that lie

This week's shameless spin from Better Together about supermarket prices didn't last long, but there's bound to be another scare along shortly.

It's still not clear whether the journalists from the Financial Times decided to approach certain supermarket executives entirely off their own bat, or because someone suggested to them that there might be a story in it for them if they did. But it's probably a safe bet that the journalists didn't just call the supermarkets at random, like they were conducting a telephone poll on whether your preferred brand of mayonnaise made you more or less likely to vote for independence.

Whatever precise chain of cause and effect took place, the execs obliged the journos with some quotes about hypothetical situations, and we were into the magic kingdom of the conditional. The government of an independent Scotland *could* raise fuel duty by 10 billion percent and outlaw the use of barcodes - this *would* make it much more expensive for supermarkets to operate in Scotland causing prices to rise. Another scare story for Project Fear to add to its shopping trolley.

The only surprise is that the Record didn't headline it "Salmond-Hell a threat to supermarkets". They really are losing their touch, as well as their readership.

It's all could and would. It's possible, but not at all probable. It cannot be denied that the government of any independent state does have the legal powers to raise fuel duty by 10 billion percent and to outlaw barcodes, and an independent Scottish government could go collectively insane and do it. That doesn't mean it's ever going to happen, it's ridiculously improbable. But it's still theoretically possible.

Of course a 10 billion percent rise in fuel duty and legislation against the barcode menace could also happen if we vote no. The Westminster Parliament could also go collectively insane, and there's many who believe it already has. The difference is that if we have an insane Scottish government we can vote it out. We're lumbered with the one in Westminster.

Spin finds its natural home between possibility and probability. The truth is that just about anything you can imagine is possible. It is possible that after Scottish independence the atoms making up Wullie Rennie could spontaneously rearrange themselves into a blancmange. It's just possible that people would notice.

There's even a theory beloved of those who are too stoned to make it to the all night shop for munchies that there is an infinite number of universes. And if that were the case then logically anything you can imagine has actually occurred in one of them. Which means that in at least one universe Wullie Rennie really has turned into a blancmange. But I still don't think there's any universe anywhere where anyone would notice.

However in this universe, the one where there's a Scottish independence campaign, it would mean that scientists are profoundly wrong about the basic properties of matter. That's vanishingly unlikely, but it's still possible. Even if it were the case, the probability of Wullie Rennie turning into an actual as opposed to a metaphorical blancmange would be one in some number several orders of magnitude greater than the number of atoms in the universe. It's theoretically possible, even though to all practical intents and purposes it's impossible.

So I can say that Scottish independence will cause Wullie Rennie to mutate into a blancmange, and people wouldn't notice. And it's possible it's not a lie.

But it's not possibility which is important. It's probability. I know that it's highly improbable that Wullie Rennie will turn into a blancmange. Trying to make out that a highly improbable possibility is actually quite likely to happen is what makes the statement a lie.

The ability to assess probability in any set of circumstances depends upon the amount and quality of the information you possess. When there's a shortage of information, you can't assess probability. That means there is no way of telling whether a possibility is probable or not. Project Fear's campaign relies above all on raising possibilities in the knowledge that most people don't have enough information to tell how probable they are.

It irritates me greatly that almost 2 years after the Spanish Foreign minister stated baldly that Spain has no intention of vetoing Scottish membership of the EU that the Scottish media continues to suggest that Spain would do just that. They continue to do it even after the Spanish Prime Minister refused three times in a row in a recent interview to say yes, Spain would veto Scotland.

This rant of a blog post was inspired by the fact that today, I was again asked by a Scottish person what I thought about "Spain's threat to veto an independent Scotland". The threat Spanish politicians have never made, the threat which the Spanish foreign minister has explicitly said Spain would not make.

Project Fear's Spanish scare story dominates the Scottish media, unfortunately few in Scotland know enough about Spanish politics to put Better Together's scare story into perspective. Scots cannot judge the probability of the scare, so Unionist politicians and the Scottish media continue to repeat it. They know they are not giving enough information to enable the public to reach a considered opinion. That's what makes them liars.

The only reason ever put forward for this possible Spanish veto is that Spain wants to discourage the Catalans from seeking independence. However if you accept the point of view of the Spanish government that constitutionally and legally Scotland and Catalonia cannot be compared, then the question of Spain vetoing Scottish membership of the EU becomes nonsensical. They have no reason to do so, vetoing Scotland does nothing to assist their case against Catalonia.

Spain vetoing Scotland would in fact damage the argument of the Spanish government against Catalan independence. If there is a yes vote in September, Scotland will achieve independence via a legal and constitutional route. Independence will be negotiated and agreed with Westminster. Westminster will pass an Act recognising Scottish independence.

The Spanish government argues (wrongly in my opinion) that Catalonia does not have a right to independence. The Spanish government claims that independence can only be recognised internationally if it is achieved legally and constitutionally, and is recognised by the state whose former territory achieves independence. Spain can then argue that its position vis a vis Catalonia is legitimate and legal.

Spain can argue that it is not merely being intransigent, as it does recognise situations in which independence can be legitimately achieved. If Spain were to veto Scotland on the grounds of our audacity to vote for independence, it destroys its own argument against Catalonia. Far from discouraging Catalan aspirations to independence, it would in fact give the Catalans evidence that Spain merely refuses to recognise the right to self-determination, and therefore is in breach of the UN Charter and who knows how many other international laws and treaties.

I enjoy discussing politics, because I'm weird that way. One of the things I liked about living in Spain was that people were quite happy to talk politics with you once they got to know you. Naturally the topic of Scottish independence came up frequently.

I used to live in a Partido Popular stronghold. In the more than 15 years I lived there, I never once encountered a single Spanish person who suggested that Spain might veto Scottish membership of the EU if we became independent - not even Partido Popular supporters. Not a single Spanish person ever raised the possibility, they only discussed the subject with me when I had raised it with them after reading about it in the UK media. The usual response was a puzzled look. It had never occurred to them that Spain might have any reason to veto Scotland.

In fact the PP supporters I knew had no problems at all with Scottish independence. They were in fact quite keen on it. They regard Scotland as the example that - in their eyes - "proves" that Catalonia can't become independent. Scotland was once a state, they say, Catalonia never was. They recognise that Scotland is a nation, and claim Scotland is a nation because it was once a state.

The constant and repeated theme is that Scotland and Catalonia are not comparable cases. This is precisely the line taken by the Partido Popular government of Rajoy.

The idea that Spain might veto Scotland does not come from Spain. It originates much closer to home, from Better Together and the Westminster political parties. They know Scottish people have little or no information about the intricacies of Iberian politics, and they rely upon that lack of knowledge to raise possibilities that are not probable at all.

They know their scares are highly improbable. That's what makes them liars. And that's what I told the person who asked me about Spain's non-existent "EU veto threat".

20 December 2013

What Project Fear is really afraid of

Poor Better Together, earlier this week Alistair Carmichael claimed that businesses and the media are too scared to speak up about the negative consequences of independence, in case indy supporters give them *such* a nasty look. This must be why there's never anything that paints independence in a poor light in the media then.

Indy supporters have vicious tongues, and mock those good people at Project Fear who are only asking questions - questions which can't be answered because the UK government won't supply the necessary information, questions for which there is no possible answer, and questions which have already been answered repeatedly. It's unfair to point that out.

Alistair wants us to refrain from mocking the inaccuracies, lies and outright idiocies when Project Fear releases its latest scare story. Westminster has a right to be stupid and self-serving, and we're treading all over the Mother of Parliament's democratic right to self-expression by laughing at it. It's the democratic right of a Unionist political party to trade in misinformation, lies and outright idiocies, and if they can't do that then what's the point in their existence? That's a question which answers itself.

The most ridiculous of his claims is that the media is intimidated by the independence debate, and is constrained against letting loose its full barrage of fear bombs because they're afraid of the yes campaign. Does Alistair actually read the papers?

Perhaps they're not negative enough for him, but if this is them "constrained" then only the gods know what they'd be telling us if they were let off the leash. When they're not belittling Scotland with supposed satirical cartoons or asking readers for funny names for a new Scottish currency, they've threatened us with everything up to and including partition, penury and the plague.

If your only source of information is the UK media you are left in no doubt that absolutely nothing good can come of independence. Even the SNP's proposals to scrap UK Government benefits changes like the Bedroom Tax were reported in Thursday's Express as "Salmond accused of being soft on the workshy".

Amongst the sea of pro-Union reportage there's occasionally a comment piece expressing support for independence, this must be the bias that upsets Alistair. It doesn't give the Union a fair crack of the whip. It's only Westminster which is supposed to crack whips, most commonly on people who claim benefits, the low paid, immigrants, and more recently supporters of Scottish independence.

Alistair and the UK Government have more or less admitted that the case for the Union is so weak that it cannot stand scrutiny, never mind criticism. What he's telling us is that the case for the Union can only be heard in absolute and reverent silence, followed immediately by mass applause and a choreographed display of placards in a sports stadium making a huge image of Her Maj and the House of Lords.

Alistair's complaint is that of a man who sees himself losing the argument, badly. Hence his new catchphrase, "Help me Rona."

And this is why Project Fear, bankrolled by Tory millionaires and backed to the hilt by the UK Government and all the resources it can muster, is now trying to portray itself as the little guy up against the big scary monster of the massed forces of the Scottish Government and ordinary punters with Internet connections and keyboards. They're going for the sympathy vote. It's a bit like the combined might of the US, Russian and Chinese armies complaining that they're out-gunned by the Sandyhills Boy Scouts with their peashooters and catapults.

If the Scottish Government really is that influential and powerful just now, when it must operate under the restrictions imposed upon it by Westminster, then with independence it presumably will have supernatural powers, like the ability to transmute base matter into gold. But independence is unlikely to turn Alistair Carmichael into a political heavyweight, even alchemy has its limitations.

Better Together's real beef is that Scottish deference to our political masters died a long time ago. British democracy is in terminal decline. A report published earlier this year by Democratic Audit found that the UK was moving ever further away from two of the key foundation stones of democracy, control over political decision-making, and how fairly the system reflects the population it represents. The decline was described as "catastrophic".

In Scotland we have no control over Westminster decision making. Due to the massive preponderance of population south of the Border, we get the government elected by voters in England. But even if we do vote out politicians whose performance has not been to our liking, their pals only bump them up to the House of Lords where they continue to make our laws and influence policy making. When the Labour party was first formed over 100 years ago, one of its key policies was the abolition of the House of Lords. Here we are in 2013, we're still waiting.

One of the most alarming findings of the report was the "unprecedented growth" in corporate power and influence over government in the UK. The report warned that unless this was addressed it "threatens to undermine some of the most basic principles of democratic decision making". But Westminster has no plans to address it, neither the Tories, the Lib Dems or Labour have any plans or policies to restore full democratic responsibility and accountability. That's the last thing they want. It would threaten comfortable career paths leading to well paid directorships and a seat in the Lords.

Since the political parties and the Westminster Parliament are unwilling to reform there is only one option left, we have to give them no choice. In most countries that would require a revolution, but Scotland has another option, a peaceful and democratic option - we can vote for independence. The independence referendum is a vote that will lead to a written Scottish constitution and can restore our political system to democractic accountability. That's what Alistair Carmichael is so afraid of.

22 December 2013

Tory plots, PP plans, and EU stitch ups

The Sunday Herald has picked up on the story of collaboration between the UK Government and the Spanish Government to gang up better together against those pesky separatists. According to the Herald, Downing Street's Scottish adviser (They have a Scottish adviser? Who knew?) flew out to Madrid last week to meet with Partido Popular representatives to discuss the Scottish independence referendum.

This has led Alex Salmond to accuse the two right wing unionist parties of "plotting hand in glove" and attempting a "stitch up", because it's highly unlikely that the Tories and the PP were meeting in order to have a relaxing wee social chat with wine and nibbles. It's not difficult to imagine what the UK Government might have to discuss with the Spanish Government about the Scottish referendum, and none of it is good for Scottish democracy.

The Tories and Better Together have dismissed Eck's claims as paranoia. Really, accusing them of plotting with a foreign power to undermine the democratic will if a legal vote doesn't go according to their liking ... isn't that the definition of a crime that people used to be hung drawn and quartered for? How could anyone even think they'd stoop so low.

But the Tories have previous for this. Newsnet Scotland covered a very similar story over a year ago, when it reported that Ruth Davidson and other senior Conservatives had met with Esteban González Pons of the Partido Popular to discuss the creation of a European alliance of right wing unionists.

In November 2012, the Spanish newspaper el Periódico reported the following:

El vicesecretario de Estudios y Programas del PP, Esteban González Pons, ha negociado la firma de un acuerdo de colaboración política con los conservadores británicos, que se pondrá negro sobre blanco en diciembre en Madrid. "Catalunya y Escocia son regiones distintas y tienen problemas distintos, pero la respuesta tiene que ser conjunta", asegura González Pons.

The Partido Popular's vice-secretary of Studies and Programmes, Estebán González Pons, has negotiated the signing of an agreement of political collaboration with the British Conservatives, which will be put in black and white in December [2012] in Madrid. "Catalonia and Scotland are distinct regions and have distinct problems, but the response has to be a joint one," stated González Pons.

The paper also reported that González Pons was due to meet with Conservatives and Labour in Edinburgh that December. The original Catalan language article has now gone behind a paywall and is only available to subscribers, but the relevant passages are translated in the Newsnet article. It's not a bad translation, because it was me who translated them.

The Partido Popular guy was pretty definite, he had met with the Tories, including Ruth Davidson, at the previous Tory party conference. There wasn't just an agreement, it was going to be signed and sealed the following month, quite possibly over wine, cheese, and nibbles. González Pons also had meetings with right wing parties in Romania, who want to discourage Romania's large Hungarian minority from seeking greater autonomy. His wee master plan for a European wide alliance to quash local democracy was proceeding apace.

The Scottish Tories responded instantly to the Newsnet article, although they'd previously treated Newsnet Scotland like a contagious leper. They vehemently denied there had been any agreement between themselves and the PP, because conspiring with a foreign government to screw your own country if a democratic vote doesn't go the way you want isn't a vote winner if the news gets out.

Despite the denial, the Tories refused to answer any questions about meetings with the Partido Popular. Labour also refused to answer any enquiries about the meeting González Pons said he'd be having in Edinburgh in December last year.

It's a safe bet there is no formal agreement written down on paper. What there most certainly is however is a series of winks and nods which allows "plausible deniability". The UK and the Spanish governments have quite coincidentally and entirely independently arrived at the opinion that that "new states" will be expelled from the EU simply by becoming independent. This not a legal opinion nor a fact, despite the claims of Mariano Rajoy. It is a political opinion.

Both London and Madrid refuse to acknowledge the reality that any part of any EU state which votes yes in an independence referendum will not become independent immediately, and therefore will still be a part of the EU. They don't want to acknowledge the possibility that a country can negotiate EU membership from within the EU prior to its formal declaration of independence. London and Madrid are ensuring that they make a joint political response to independence demands, because then each can present the declarations of the other to its own electorate as "a blow to independence".

Herman van Rompuy, the president of the EU council, is a member of the Belgian CDV, another right wing anti-independence party. He has also made similar statements to Cameron and Rajoy. Van Rompuy's intervention was denounced by Flemish nationalists as nakedly political.

Flemish MEP Mark Demesmaeker said earlier this week that van Rompuy's claim has "no legal basis" and is purely political. Demesmaeker states that EU lawyers, including a former judge in the European Court of Justice, had told his party that "such threats are baseless". Demesmaeker accused van Rompuy of following a "political-oriented agenda" that makes him tell "lies" that seem "truths".

Only wait, aren't Scotland, Flanders, and Catalonia totally and utterly different cases? How can the Spanish and UK governments have lots of friendly chats about situations that they keep telling us have nothing to do with one another. Unless we're not so totally and utterly different after all, I'm sure that the Catalans and Flemings will have taken note.

And so should we. If the UK government is internationalising Scotland's independence debate, then we must internationalise it too. Our struggle is not taking place in a vacuum. All across Europe there are growing movements seeking to restore national or regional autonomy or demanding independence. It's not just in Scotland that people feel the existing political systems do not listen to their demands or respond to their needs. Change is in the air.

Pro-sovereignty movements in different parts of Spain have recently started to recognise the need for co-ordinated action in order to achieve their goals of national sovereignty. The Galician newspaper Sermos Galiza reported that representatives of the ERC of Catalonia, EH Bildu from the Basque Country, and the BNG of Galicia met in Bilbao last week and agreed to work together to find effective means of collaboration between their three nations in order to achieve the right to independence referendums and to argue for a new social model within the heart of the European debate.

The debate in Scotland has centred on whether or not the European Union will allow us membership, and if so how long with the application take and under what conditions. But there is a wider argument, what sort of European Union do we want to achieve. That's the debate that the Catalans, Basques and Galicians are beginning to have.

It's certainly not the same Europe that Cameron and Rajoy want. Cameron may very well end up taking the UK out of the EU entirely, in order to better chase the Conservative wet dream of abolishing the benefits safety net, and putting what remains of public services into the hands of ATOS and Serco. Rajoy wants an EU that speaks for the ruling elites, and which defends the status quo.

Neither of them want an EU that is more accountable. Cameron and Rajoy see the EU as a means of freezing Europe's current geopolitical landscape, not as a framework within which issues of independence or national minorities can be settled peacefully and democratically.

The only way we can change this is by voting yes in September next year and ensuring that Scotland has its own voice at EU level. In the meantime Scottish organisations and political parties should strengthen their ties to other movements within the EU seeking self-determination for their own unrecognised nations. Europe belongs to us too, it's not the property of Cameron, Rajoy and van Rompuy, let's take it back from them.

28 December 2013

Forest fire in Narnia, a major blow to Scottish independence

Some in the Unionist press have a compulsive urge to present absolutely any international news as a major blow to Scottish independence. They're a bit like those people on Obsessive Compulsive House Cleaners, who visit a therapist weekly to talk about how a traumatic childhood encounter with a Scottie dog sparked off all their problems. There haven't been any forest fires in Narnia recently, in case you were worried about any imaginary forest friends, but if there were some Unionist news outlet somewhere would explain why it's terribly bad news for Alex Salmond.

And so it is with the Commentator, which reported this week on an interview which Artur Mas, president of the Catalan government, gave to the Italian newspaper La Reppublica. It's terribly bad news for those separatists, allegedly.

Mind you, in the article they did describe Holyrood as "Scotland's devolved regional government", like Strathclyde but with trams and a castle, where they presumably meet to discuss important devolved regional things like bus timetables and road signage and decide how to spend the pocket money London kindly sends. So we can't say we've not been warned we're dealing with the Daily Mail end of the Unionist scare story spectrum and a reporter whose knowledge of Scottish and Catalan politics is probably exceeded by his or her knowledge of arson attacks in Narnia.

Naturally Mas's interview was given extensive coverage in the Catalan and Spanish language media. La Vanguardia published an article in Spanish, while there was an article in Catalan from the digital newspaper Vilaweb.

La Vanguardia didn't focus primarily on the EU issue, its main thrust was that the interview contained a statement from Mas that early elections to the Catalan Parliament could be an alternative if, as seems likely, Madrid blocks other means of holding a referendum.

Meanwhile Vilaweb says that Mas used the interview to state his certainty that there would be a yes vote in the referendum, and that it would be held on 9 November.

Asked about the possible position of Europe, Mas said that he understood that Scotland and Catalonia present a problem for the current member states, but he was sure that a way of resolving the institutional issues could be found without consequences for European citizens.

So far, there's absolutely nothing here which could in any way be characterised as a "blow" to Scottish independence. But let's plough on. Oh this must be it, in the Spanish version given by La Vanguardia.

"Las presiones son fuertes. Los Estados soberanos no quieren problemas si los pueden evitar. Habrá el precedente de Escocia, que votará antes que nosotros. Después vendrá Catalunya. También he considerado que en un momento inicial, entre el referéndum y la proclamación de la independencia, podríamos quedarnos fuera de Europa. No del euro, de la Unión", comenta.

"Sería una lástima, porque nosotros queremos seguir en la UE. Sería necesario encontrar un régimen transitorio para evitar la expulsión de la UE. De todos modos, solicitaremos un reingreso. Nosotros queremos estar en el euro, en la Unión, en (el área de libre circulación sin fronteras) Schengen y en la OTAN", añade.

Translation

"The pressures [from Madrid] are strong. The sovereign states don't want problems if they can avoid them. There will be the precedent of Scotland, which will vote before us. Afterwards will come Catalonia. I have also considered that at the initial moment, between the referendum and the proclamation of independence, that we could be left outside of Europe. Not outside the euro, outside of the Union," he comments.

"It would be a pity, because we want to remain in the EU. It would be necessary to find a transitional regime in order to avoid expulsion from the EU. In any case, we will apply to re-enter. We want to be in the euro, in the Union, in (the area of free movement without borders) Schengen, and in NATO," he adds.

translation ends

I must confess I'm still struggling to see the major blow to Scottish independence here. It can't be that the topic of Scottish independence is one that European states find problematic and really don't wish to discuss just now. We know that already because one of those states is the UK.

It must be what Mas said about leaving the EU.

The key part here, which means this is very far from being a blow to Scottish independence, is the phrase immediately before the suitably scary looking "that we could be left outside of Europe". That's "between the referendum and the proclamation of independence". Mas is talking about what might occur in the aftermath of a yes vote in a referendum whose legitimacy is denied by Madrid, and that Catalonia might find itself excluded from the EU *by Madrid* after Catalonia has voted for independence.

However Mas is also saying that Catalonia would not make a formal declaration of independence until Barcelona, Madrid, and Brussels had negotiated a settlement, but that in the meantime some sort of transitional arrangement is going to be required. It's under this arrangement that Catalonia may find itself temporarily outside the EU in the sense that Catalonia would have no representation as an EU member. However Mas clearly expects the use of the euro as the currency and the free movement of goods and people to continue throughout this transitional period.

This is all up for discussion because Madrid refuses to recognise Catalonia's right to a referendum. It all depends upon how intransigent la Moncloa is going to be after the Catalans have voted, by one means or another, in favour of independence. It could well be that after a yes vote, the Spanish government will have a period of sulking followed by elections where the victor recognises that the Catalan gemme's a bogey. Catalans realise that it might take a couple of years, but la Moncloa will give in eventually. This is the worst case scenario, however the message from Mas is the whatever the difficulties and obstacles placed in Catalonia's way, one day it will be independent and a member of the EU.

In Scotland, we're in a different ball game. Scotland's referendum is legally recognised and constitutional. No one expects Scotland to be excluded from the EU the day after a yes vote in the referendum. The framework for what happens after a yes vote in Scotland is already in place. Even with a massive majority in favour of independence, on 19 September 2014 Scotland will still be a part of the United Kingdom and still a part of the EU. Scotland will not become independent until 24 March 2016, by which time negotiations will have taken place between Holyrood, Westminster and Brussels.

Mas is also keenly aware of that fact, which is what he meant by the precedent of Scotland. Catalonia is proposing to hold its vote on 9 November 2014, if there has been a yes vote in Scotland, negotiations between Holyrood and Brussels will already be taking place. Catalonia will have a model to point to.

So this news is nothing at all like a blow to Scottish independence. Instead it's an instance of Scottish independence giving a boost to Catalan independence, but that's something the Unionist media in Scotland would prefer we don't hear about. Perhaps that will also change on 19 September 2014.

January 2014

2 January 2014

The ignorocracy in action

It's a new year, and it's the same auld pish from the UK media. The Guardian, the parish newsletter of the British liberal establishment, continues to fish new lumps of rank and smelly wax from the pig's ear of its coverage of the Scottish independence debate.

The New Year edition saw the Guardian turn into the Daily Mail in a burst of racist fairy dust. Those Project Fear Christmas miracles just keep on and on, like a panto starring the smaller and more annoying Krankie - otherwise known as the Scottish Conservatives. As the paper looked forward to the new year, its sole discussion of the biggest political event in the UK due in 2014 was a piece by Simon Jenkins calling on the Conservatives at Westminster to embrace Scottish independence

Jenkins was repeating the same argument as Simon Heffer's racist diatribe in the Daily Mail in September, replete with assertions that Scots depend upon the largesse of London. Like his Daily Mail namesake, Guardian Simon's reason for conversion to the yes cause was that getting shot of us would benefit the Conservatives in England. It's the mirror image of Labour's pseudosolidarity argument, the future of Scotland being debated purely in terms of its effect on politics south of the border.

Jenkin's is the Guardian's token Tory. However the Guardian, being of an Islington Labour party persuasion, won't allow itself to indulge in naked racism of the Daily Mail variety because people tut about that sort of thing at dinner parties. But since Scottish people are members of the great British family of nations it's only a bit of harmless fun and the Guardian can have its ethnic stereotyping cake and eat it.

The article was helpfully illustrated with a photie of a red haired man with a blue painted face who is yelling something while standing half naked in a loch, because that's what Scottish people do when they discuss independence. It's just a bit of a laugh, it's not to be taken seriously. Which speaks volumes about the Guardian's and the UK media's attitude to Scotland.

This is like illustrating an article about the constitutional and political future of England with a pic of skinheads doing a morris dance, but if a Scottish publication did that it wouldn't be a harmless little bit of fun at all. It would be evidence that there's a dark cancer of anti-English racism lurking at the heart of the Scottish psyche and would provoke a special episode of Newsnicht Scotland.

Whereas Mail Simon's article was a seething mess of racist stereotypes and insults, Guardian Simon's article wasn't overtly racist, but only if you don't count condescending ignorance as racism. The thrust of Guardian Simon's piece was that Scottish independence isn't a privilege, as many in the Metropolitan bubble appear to believe that independence is a gift which only Westminster can grant, instead of a right that the people of Scotland will take if they choose to.

He starts off by telling us that the constitutional future of Scotland provokes yawns in the majority south of the border, although he doesn't seem to realise that this itself is one of the major reasons for independence. Scotland is currently governed by an ignorocracy, a political class which knows next to nothing about Scotland and which cares even less, which is elected by a country where most people know little about Scotland and care even less. It's hard to put a positive spin on this state of affairs, which is one reason for the total dearth of positive reasons for the Union.

Guardian Simon doesn't try to put a positive gloss on it. If he was a Tory strategist, he says, he'd "make light" of the Scottish vote, he'd portray Alex Salmond as a "one-tune populist, drunk on welfare transfers and windfarm subsidies" - all of which is pretty much what

Tory strategists are doing anyway. Possibly Guardian Simon didn't notice because he was yawning at the time.

The only difference is that Guardian Simon wants us to vote yes in order to give the Tories an electoral advantage in England. So we should be dismissed like an elderly servant who has outlived her usefulness as we're just a drain on the household finances. Where Scotland is concerned the Metropolitan commentariat only look at the expenditure side of the accountancy ledgers, the income side belongs to Westminster in its entirety. If we want to ruin our country by ourselves, as opposed to having Westminster ruin it for us, Simon thinks we should jolly well just get on with it. It's no skin off Westminster's nose.

It's the dominant view from the banks of the Thames. The Union is a one way affair. Scotland is just a hanger on. We bring nothing to the party except demands for subsidies. Guardian Simon views Scottish independence as the constitutional version of Iain Duncan Smith's welfare reforms, he wants to teach us to stand on our own two feet by cutting our legs off.

The solution Simon proposes is that the Tories should offer Scotland "devo max" like Catalonia or the Basque Country, which only shows that he is as ignorant of Catalonia and the Basque Country as he is of Scotland. In some ways Catalonia and the Basque Country do have more powers than the Scottish Parliament, but in many others they have less. They do not have "devo max", and they certainly don't have the right to self-determination as Mariano Rajoy and the Spanish government keep reminding them.

There's going to be much more of Simon's variety of confusion and misinformation in the coming months, and it will be a concerted barrage where even the Daily Mail and the Guardian are singing from the same Great British Proms concert song sheet. It's the ignorocracy in action.

6 January 2014

Why Cameron isn't ready for a close up

Yet again David Cameron has ruled out appearing in a debate with Alex Salmond about Scotland's future, after he was asked about it by

Andrew Marr on thon politics programme that no one gets out of bed early enough on a Sunday to watch. Cameron is desperate to avoid the independence debate becoming a debate on whether or not we want the Tories to continue to govern us. It's too late, it's already a debate about the Tories and has been since the days of Thatcher.

But Cameron is insisting that the debate is one for Scottish people to have between themselves, so he won't be getting involved at all. Fresh from a meeting with his PR strategists, he uttered the noble sentiment:

"This is not a debate between me and [Alex Salmond]. It's not a debate between the prime minister of the United Kingdom and the first minister of Scotland ... The debate should be between people in Scotland who want to stay and people in Scotland who want to go."

And all this is exactly how things should be. Except that they're not, and Cameron is the one responsible for them not being that way.

Cameron won't be getting involved in the debate at all, except when he makes a keynote New Year speech pleading with Scotland to remain in the UK, or sends cabinet ministers north of the Border to warn us that cyberterrorists will take over our Facebook profiles and post really embarrassing pics, or plans Union flag waving fiestas in the centre of Glasgow a few weeks before the indy vote, or instructs assorted UK government departments to produce reports showing that independence means all baby kittens in Scotland would be drowned, or offers helpful soundbites to Unionist press outlets, or sends representatives to meet with the Partido Popular to discuss common strategies for screwing independence movements ... but apart from that, he won't be getting involved.

David Cameron is the Prime Minister of Scotland. He heads the government which determines the Scottish budget, which decides our benefits and taxation policies, which represents Scotland internationally, which has the power to take us into war, the power to decide what laws Holyrood can make. He heads the government which is directing the campaign to save the Union. Despite this, he's somehow not involved, like Don Corleone isn't involved with the mob.

But there's another message Cameron wants Scotland to hear. Scotland's not really that important. Hardly worth bothering about.

This is consistent with the Unionist tactic of diminishing and trivialising the independence debate. They don't want people to start questioning the issues seriously or engaging with the idea of independence. So the very last thing that Better Together needs is for its real leader, as opposed to the figurehead, to be slaughtered live on national telly in a high profile debate. Voters might see.

Besides, voters in England might also be watching, and that won't look good at all, especially not if it comes just after UKIP scares the bejeezus out of Tory backbenchers in May's European elections. The only election Cameron is interested in is the Westminster election in 2015, being humiliated in a debate about Scottish independence won't help his chances.

But ye'd think that if this is, as Cameron says, Scotland's debate to be conducted by Scottish people in Scotland, then that can only mean that people in Scotland decide what the terms of the debate are, and decide who or what is relevant to it. According to a recent poll a substantial majority of voters in Scotland want Cameron to debate with Salmond, even if for no other reason than there's really not enough comedy in this independence campaign and we'd all enjoy a good laugh watching seven shades of shite being beaten out of him.

So if Scottish people say that Cameron must put himself up for debate or shut up and cease his backstage meddling, then that's what should happen. He's determined to do neither.

Davie boy says that because he has no vote in the referendum it's not right for him to debate Alex Salmond. He doesn't have a vote in the referendum, this is true, but he's got a vote in the House of Commons, he's got a vote in Cabinet meetings, and moreover in these places he's got the most influential vote. He uses that vote to decide what happens in Scotland. Cameron's vote in Scotland outweighs yours and mine combined, it outweighs the combined vote of the entire population.

Our Tory Prime Minister has the only vote that counts in the normal run of Scottish politics, yet it's not a vote that he uses with the interests of Scotland uppermost in mind. He's got no intention of telling us what he plans to do with his vote, no desire to explain to us why we think we should let him keep his job as Prime Minister of

Scotland. When it's us who vote, not him, he doesn't want to know. Equal partners in the Union? Aye, right.

We all know why Cameron won't debate with Salmond. There's the obvious reason, he'd get his arse handed to him on a plate. He'd be seen for what he is as far as Scotland is concerned - a lost tourist who's confused by the strange ways of the natives, as out of his depth as the programme makers who thought Tom Daley's Splash would make great telly. He would come to the debate with the rare disadvantage of making Alistair Carmichael appear well-prepared. And he'd be up against a man who, whatever your opinion of Salmond, is regarded as one of the UK's best political operators, on his home turf on a topic he's spent his life preparing for. It would be a blood sport the entire family could watch with guilt free pleasure, we'd be self-sufficient in schadenfreude for decades to come.

Avoiding a debate which is going to leave him looking like roadkill is not cowardice, despite what many say. Cameron doesn't want the role of the guy in the red shirt in Star Trek who gets devoured by the alien tartan monster on planet Scotland. He's a star, not a bit player. It's not cowardice, it's the arrogance of a burned out film star from the silent era.

He's not a coward, he's just confused between the Scottish independence debate and the plot line of Sunset Boulevard starring himself as Norma Desmond. Its main protagonist also spends her time fantasising about glory days long gone, and lures the unwary into an unhealthy dependency, so it's an easy mistake to make.

He won't consider a close up with Scotland, because we're not big stars like him. The question we need to ask ourselves on 18 September this year is whether we want to stay with the loopy auld bat, and end up face down in a swimming pool.

7 January 2014

The consequences of No

Nicola Sturgeon made a speech on Monday asking Better Together and the naw ye cannae campaign to spell out the consequences of a no vote in the referendum. We already know what the consequences of a no vote are, asking Better Together to spell it out is like asking Hannibal Lector to publish his cannibalism recipes in the lifestyle section of the Herald.

What we do know is that George Osborne promises another round of austerity cuts after 2015, and he wants the poor, the disabled, the unemployed and the vulnerable to bear £12 billions' worth of the £25 billion he wants to axe from public spending. The unemployed are in no position to offer retiring politicians lucrative directorships so there's little point pandering to their interests. Anyway, it's only fair, the poor and powerless caused the financial crisis by selfishly not having any money to buy things and stimulate growth in the economy. Besides, they don't make as much of a fuss as investment bankers faced with a 0.08% tax on their bonuses.

Since the Tories have promised that the benefit cuts will not affect pensioners, that means the unemployed, the sick and disabled, and carers, will cop it in the neck amidst Daily Mail headlines about welfare scroungers. Welfare is a Tory weasel word which aims to replace benefits in popular speech. Welfare reeks of alms giving, rich people tossing a few coins at the 'deserving' poor in order to assuage their consciences. Yet benefits is the better term, because a properly run and funded benefits system benefits society as a whole as well as the individuals receiving support. I want country with a benefits system, not a welfare system.

Meanwhile Labour also promises to cut public spending by the same amount. They also make liberal use of the welfare word, which is the only liberal thing about Labour these days. Labour is quite definite that Tory welfare cuts are bad cuts, but they're keeping very quiet about what they'd cut instead. Meanwhile Johann Lamont tries to pretend she never described Scotland as a "something for nothing" culture. This does not inspire confidence that Labour is committed to the principles of universality in the benefits system, nor indeed that we should have a benefits system at all. They seem quite happy with Tory ideas about welfare and the deserving versus the non-deserving.

I have a direct interest here. I do not receive welfare, I receive benefits and society benefits from the deal. I'm a full time carer who had to give up employment in order to look after my partner, who has been diagnosed with vascular dementia. You don't choose to become a carer, you do it out of love and commitment. It's the hardest job I've ever had in my life, physically and emotionally.

I don't want to use this blog to discuss my partner's care needs, but life is tough as it is, George Osborne's plans will make things even tougher. I have zero confidence in Labour, where the only difference from the Tories and their Lib Dem hangers on is that they promise to make cuts with a sad face instead of with the manaical glee of Danny Alexander. This is the future the Union offers fulls time carers, no matter how Better Together might dress it up with a promise of devolutionary jam.

In return for a full time job like caring for a person with dementia, a job requiring you to be in attendance or on call 24 hours a day, seven days a week, carers get the princely sum of £59.75 a week Carer's Allowance. Fulltime carers often work 168 hours a week in stressful and distressing conditions, and receive just short of 36p per hour for doing so. There is no time off, no set breaks, no holiday pay, no holidays, just seven days a week, 24 hours a day, working as carers or on permanent call, catching up with sleep when you can. It's not an easy job, emotionally or physically. But we mustn't grumble, at least it pays better than another Union benefit, the zero hours contract.

The local authority where we live can no longer fund much respite care due to the cuts that have already come in. Formerly those like me who get no break from caring were able to receive up to eight weeks of respite care annually, now the local authority can only fund two. Following the next rounds of cuts, it's quite likely they'll not be able to fund any at all.

I'm not complaining about having to care for my partner. It's what you do for those you love. I would do it even without the £59.75 per week I became entitled to after I was forced to stop working. All carers would, we're not doing this for the money, for career prospects, or for public recognition. We do it for unfashionable reasons that do not figure in UK Government policy making - love and loyalty.

A recent study from Carers UK found that, at an average unit cost of £18 per hour (the average cost of purchasing care services), the cost to the state of buying in care, unpaid carers save the Treasury £119 billion annually, more than the entire NHS budget across the UK.

The UK government is very much the benefits recipient here. But making the weak, the poor and the powerless foot the bill for the mistakes and misdeeds of the elite is the politically prudent choice for a Westminster politician. This will not change no matter who is in power at Westminster. No further proof is needed that our political system is terminally ill and beyond hope of redemption.

The Union recognises no benefits from us, and there are no benefits from the Union, only welfare. I dread the consequences of a no vote. No matter what promises Better Together eventually trots out on what Scotland will get after a no vote, the destruction of the benefits system remains the harsh reality.

There will be challenges and difficult decisions to make in an independent Scotland too, but those choices will be made by a government we can hold to account. There are no guarantees that an independent Scottish state will do more to lighten the burden of carers, but I don't believe anyone who says Scotland couldn't afford it.

I'm fed up with the lies and the scaremongering, of being patronised by idiots. Scotland is a rich country, if we are facing unprecedented austerity it can only be because Scotland has been badly mismanaged by Westminster. If we are too poor to afford public services when we are such a resource rich nation, whose bloody fault is that then?

If the Union has been such a grand success, why are we too poor to make it by ourselves, especially since we are positively lowpin with natural and human resources that people will pay money for - oil, gas, renewable energy, whisky, coal, leading universities - and apparently we have shale oil and gas coming out our ears too, but we're such a resource rich nation that we can afford not to exploit it. This is not a choice you can make in a resource poor country.

The reason we face unprecedented austerity is because of political choices made by a political class over which we exert no effective control. So it's time for new management, a management that can be kept on a short leash and held to account, and which has to operate under constitutional rules that are written down in black and white instead of made up to suit themselves as they go along.

With independence there is the hope that things could change for the better, that we might have a government that believes in a universal benefits system, and recognises the benefits to society that such a system delivers because it ensures all citizens have the capacity to live decent and dignified lives. I hope and believe that can be achieved with independence. I'd like to hope it could be achieved in the UK, but I don't believe it can.

There is no hope anything might change for the better with a no vote. A no vote promises only austerity, welfare cuts and a privatised dignity services provider staffed by workers on zero hours contracts. Those are the consequences of a no vote. They're not pretty, no wonder Better Together is keeping quiet.

8 January 2014

Henry McLeish and wishing for the impossible

Former Labour first minister Henry McLeish is one of the very few associated with the anti-independence campaign who has consistently called upon Better Together to present a positive reason for saying no. But Henry's pleas have equally consistently fallen on deaf ears as any attempt to establish a common position between the Westminster parties on further devolution would immediately fall apart due to their overriding need to jockey for position ahead of the only vote that counts for a Westminster politician - 2015's General Election.

In frustration at the lack of progress in positivity from the official no campaign, Henry Has made a brave stab at suggesting what a positive prospectus for the Union might look like. It's Henry's tragedy, and will be a tragedy for Scotland if we vote no, that under Westminster's brand of politics each of the five key points in Henry's attempt to write a White Paper on No all by himself is as out of place as a raised toilet seat in a convent, and just as likely to provoke recriminations, accusations, and excommunication.

Firstly he seeks a consensus "built around a positive case for Scotland's role within a modern and transformed Union: there was a consensus in 1997 when Scotland voted for a parliament, but today the nation is divided, with both campaigns making this worse. We need a cohesive, nation-building campaign."

The fly in the ointment is that any consensus on Scotland's role within the Union also depends upon a consensus in the rest of the UK, otherwise it's just Scotland demanding more devolution again, and not getting it.

But the problem is not the lack of consensus in Scotland, it's the consensus within the UK. However the consensus within the UK, which of course means the consensus of Westminster political parties, is that extra powers for Scotland will only be granted grudgingly, reluctantly, and hedged about with more caveats than a promise from Labour to think about considering to abolish the Bedroom Tax.

There already is a consensus within Scotland. By a large majority Scots want more powers for the Scottish parliament, we just differ on which of the powers currently reserved to Westminster we want transfered to Holyrood. Independence supporters want all powers transferred to Holyrood, supporters of various shades of devolution want some powers transferred. There is however already a consensus within Scotland that this nation's parliament requires greater powers, otherwise we wouldn't be having this entirely peaceful and democratic independence debate in the first place.

It's sad that Henry and other Unionist politicians don't give the people of Scotland more credit for that last point. We are not a nation at war with itself. The all too common way in which countries debate independence is with bullets and bombs or with threats of imprisonment, yet here we are in Scotland debating independence and the worst that's happened is that a few over sensitive sowels have ended up with torn faces after someone said something they found objectionable. And all this usually happens online, where people make a sport of saying objectionable things. The peaceful nature of this independence debate is a huge testament to the democratic maturity of ordinary people in Scotland - and we deserve to pat ourselves on the back for that whatever the outcome of September's vote. We're far more grown up than our politicians are.

But the really tricky bit is "a modern and transformed Union", since there's absolutely no sign of the Westminster parties getting themselves together on that one any time soon. This is all the more unfortunate since all Henry's other proposals depend upon a concrete plan for this imaginary modern and transformed Union. But if there was a cross party plan for a modern and transformed Union that will settle all questions the future of devolution and the West Lothian Question and the Barnett Formula and the oil revenues, we'd have heard something about it by now.

Westminster's track record on reform is not impressive. We've still got the House of Lords, despite abolition being a Labour policy when the party first stood for election over 100 years ago. We've still got the first past the post system which distorts political representation and allows governments with large majorities despite their taking only a minority of the vote despite decades of calls for change. Scotland only got devolution after we'd been calling for it for more than a century, and it had to be dragged out of Westminster kicking and screaming.

Better Together has less than 9 months in which to arrange a cross party consensus on fundamental constitutional reform within the UK. It's safe to say a modern and transformed Union is not going to be on the horizon any time between now and September.

Henry's second key demand is for the three main Westminster parties to jointly propose a written constitution which abandons the idea of Parliamentary sovereignty. It's at this point you realise that you're reading a belated Christmas wish list to Santa and not a political plan with any sort of plausibility. The Doctrine of Parliamentary Sovereignty has a totemic place within the Westminster system. It's the bollocks on the Westminster dog, and they're not going to give them up voluntarily.

That just leaves a wee trip to the vet where the unruly mutt can be forced to submit to the prodecure under anaesthetic. The only way this can be achieved - at least for Scotland - is by ticking the yes box on the independence ballot paper for an independent Scotland where there's a written constitution guaranteeing that the people and not parliament are sovereign. This takes Henry back to square one.

Key points 3, 4 and 5 are likewise wishful thinking. 3 is for Labour to spell out the consequences of a no vote, but they've got no intention of doing that before the referendum since it would mean revealing their

2015 election manifesto a year early and letting us know exactly what's going to happen to the Bedroom Tax, and tell us what austerity cuts they'd make. The Westminster election cycle is the only one allowed in the reserved powers lane.

With 4 he's again calling on Labour to come up with a plan, any plan, for a modern and transformed United Kingdom, and he's stressing the need for conviction and enthusiasm about extending the powers of the Scottish parliament and reforming the UK. Can you imagine Johann Lamont giving a passionate, articulate and compelling speech about the need for Westminster to transfer substantial fiscal powers to Scotland, calling for devolution of the BBC and control of oil revenues? No, neither can I. And neither can Henry McLeish, because as he says in his fifth and final point:

"Fifth, above all else, there has to be a credible, not grudging, embrace of new and radical powers for the Scottish Parliament and a new relationship with the Union."

He goes on to plead for a non-grudging Labour campaign to save the Union untainted by Tories, but isn't there supposed to be one of those already? There was thon super-high-profile one launched in a blaze of publicity some while back that we've heard nothing about ever since. The one led by Gordon Brown, the ex-politician that's still an MP for Kirkaldy. But you can't ask Gordon Brown not to be grudging. Grudging is all he does.

Henry McLeish is not a stupid man. He knows that he's asking for the impossible, he knows that there is absolutely no prospect of anything from his wish list coming to pass. His suggestion that the anti-independence campaign adopt his recommendations is either a supreme example of the triumph of hope over experience, or it's an attempt to warn them that their complacency will be their undoing - and only something drastic will save the day. But Henry McLeish writes as though he realises that it's already too late.

There has already been a steady drip of former high profile Labour politicians coming out in favour of independence, there will be others. I have it on good authority that at least three or four Labour councillors in one local authority are privately in favour of independence. There are certainly many more across Scotland, they're just waiting for someone like Henry McLeish to stop wishing for the impossible.

9 January 2014
The Bonnie White Feather Club

Just a couple of days ago, former First Minister Jack McConnell said that the referendum campaign should be suspended during the Commonwealth games. Jack doesn't want the yes campaign to benefit from any upswelling in Scottish patriotism the games might generate. But he's been entirely silent about the UK Government's intention to host a series of events designed to highlight British patriotism. Hypocrisy much?

Early in August 2014, the UK Government plans to hold a commemoration of the start of World War I. Despite the fact that London is the invariable scene of UK national commemorations, David Cameron and the Tories have decided that Glasgow is to be the focal point of the planned commemorative service, which will feature military parades and enough Union flag bunting to string up all the war mongerers who in their eagerness to teach the Kaiser a lesson caused the deaths of millions.

I can't recall a previous occasion when such a high profile UK national event was held in Scotland. But we've been assured that the decision to hold a mass demonstration of British patriotism in Glasgow is entirely unconnected to the fact that the Scottish independence referendum will take place just four weeks later. No really, the UK Government has said it's pure coincidence, and they wouldn't lie about something like that, would they? Jist hing oan a wee minute while A dae up the buttons at the back ae ma heid.

The UK has never before held an official commemoration of the *start* of any war, but the decision to hold one in Glasgow for WW1 has absolutely nothing to do with the independence referendum, and only bitter and twisted secessionists could possibly think otherwise.

The hundreds of thousands of lions who were led to brutal and early deaths by the donkeys of Westminster were told they were fighting for the right of small nations to decide their own futures. But it was a lie, in reality they suffered and died so that the powerful could maintain their stranglehold on public life, so that the rich could stay rich and the poor remain poor.

Westminster may have been able to rely upon the naivety of the public during WW1, but this is 2014 and we've had 100 years to digest the duplicity and habitual lies of the Mother of Parliaments. Of course these events are nakedly political and a blatant attempt at emotional manipulation. Despite the official hype they will indeed be a celebration of Britishness, one held at a politically highly charged time when the question of Britishness will be foremost in the minds of hundreds of thousands of Scots.

The Glasgow event will form a central part of the "emotional case for the Union" which Cameron and Better Together say they're going to make between now and 18 September and as such is a cynical and opportunistic attempt to lay claim to the sacrifice of millions of dead service people and civilians, and co-opt it for the modern political ends of Westminster. Whatever the noble dead of WW1 sacrificed their lives for, it wasn't so that Westminster politicians could continue to abuse the trust and faith of their descendants.

During WW1 white feathers were handed out to those who were regarded as cowards by the official propaganda - those who protested against the war, who refused to succumb to the jingoism used to batter the reluctant into compliance. Westminster's opportunism gives us the chance to reclaim the white feather as a symbol for the rights of small nations to decide their futures peacefully and without interference from those who glorify war for their own personal and political ends.

The symbol supposedly originates in the belief amongst afficionados of cockfighting that a cockerel with a white feather in its tail would be a poor fighter. In August 1914, Vice Admiral Charles Fitzgerald founded the Order of the White Feather which aimed to shame men into enlisting for the slaughter in the trenches by persuading women to present them with a white feather if they were not wearing a uniform. He obviously viewed ordinary working class men as some species of creature to be used in a blood sport.

In 1904, 10 years before the War to End All Wars, Fitzgerald wrote an article calling for war with Germany in order to destroy the German navy and ensure the continuation of British naval supremacy. He didn't seem to be overly concerned about the millions of deaths which would result, after all he wanted to maintain British naval supremacy so that Britannia could continue to rule the waves and despoil and exploit Africa, India and a quarter of the globe. That's the real reason the UK declared war on Germany in 1914.

Fitzgerald's deployment of the white feather was as cynical and self-serving as Westminster's decision to hold a commemoration of the start of Fitzgerald's longed-for war just as Scotland stands at the threshold of a historic referendum on the country's future.

The only appropriate way to mark the 100th anniversary of the outbreak of a world war which led to the deaths of 16 million and the maiming or wounding of 27 million more is with shame and disgrace. It was a crime perpetrated by governments and the ruling elites upon the ordinary people who suffered and died for the arrogance of those who believed they had the right to rule. Westminster politicians ought to have no part to play - they are the heirs to the warmongers of 1914, but they will be central to the commemorative events. They continue to send young men and women to fight, die and kill in their pointless and self-serving wars. It's like commemorating the outbreak of the bubonic plague with an exhibition of pedigree rats and a flea circus spectacular.

So I'm having my own wee protest about the futility of war and to express the hope that we can live in an independent country dedicated to peace, and which eschews nuclear weapons and disavows militarism. I'm starting the Bonnie White Feather Club. There are no membership lists or fees, no office holders, and no annual general meetings.

All you need to do is to wear a white feather during the month long commemoration of the centenary of start of World War I this August. The bonnie white feather represents peace, freedom from the manipulations of a Westminster which glorifies war, and the right of the small nation of Scotland to choose its own destiny. It represents the wish that never again will our youth perish in foreign lands for the glory and vanity of politicians.

I'll wear my white feather with pride.

12 January 2014

Cameron, Putin and Scotland - who is scaring who

So has he or hasn't he? According to the Sunday Herald, David Cameron has asked Russian president Vladimir Putin for help in combating Scottish independence, as Scotland is less tuneful than Pussy Riot and poses a threat the ex-Soviet voting bloc in the Eurovision Song Contest.

The Herald reports that the state owned Russian news agency Itar-Tass recently published a story claiming that the UK was "extremely interested" in gaining the support of the Kremlin in order to prevent Scottish independence. Russia currently holds the presidency of the G8 group of major economies, and Cameron hopes that Putin will support a joint statement from the G8 that Scottish independence risks the entire future of the universe - or at least threatens the future careers of Westminster politicians, which in their eyes is much the same thing.

According to the Russian news agency, Scottish independence and the situation in Afghanistan are two important topics on which the Tories want to enlist the support of foreign governments, because foreign governments will listen to Tories even if Scottish people won't. A spokesperson for Downing Street was quoted as saying that Scotland and the withdrawal of troops from Afghanistan are the "two main issues whose resolution requires international formats, albeit of different modalities". One requires fear-bombs, the other actual bombs.

However the Herald's report was immediately denied by Downing Street, the Scotsman published a spoiler piece quoting a Downing St spokes-tory who said, "There has been no approach to the Russian Government for help in the independence referendum and there won't be one."

Gosh, who to believe? It is always wise to pay close attention to exactly what is being denied when Westminster denies something. The spokesperson quoted in the Scotsman denied Westminster had asked Putin for help, but didn't deny discussing Scottish independence with him, and didn't deny suggesting to him that a statement from him on the evils of Scottish independence would be helpful to Westminster.

It sounds like the denials from the Conservatives that they've been colluding with the Spanish government to put forward the line that the EU would throw an independent Scotland out on its ear. They've not been colluding, they've reached no agreements despite the fact that leading members of the Partido Popular have openly spoken about their agreement, they've just independently and quite coincidentally arrived at the same lie and only meet regularly to congratulate one another on their good fortune.

However Downing St's denials that they've asked Russia for help were apparently contradicted within the same report in the Scotsman. The paper tells us that an anonymous source close to Cameron said that the report in the Herald "reflects more the fact that the impact of Scottish independence will not just be felt in the UK but will have ramifications abroad".

In other words, Westminster has raised the topic at an international level, but they're not colluding with foreign governments, oh no. They've not asked the Russians for help, instead they've helpfully pointed out to the Russians how - in the opinion of Westminster - there may be similarities between Scotland's peaceful and democratic independence campaign and the assorted internal wars and strife raging in various parts of the multiethnic Russia. Because a Scottish independence campaigner starting a Facebook group is exactly the same as a Daghestani suicide bomber blowing up Volgograd train station.

So if the Russian government does make some pronouncement which Westminster and Better Together can use to generate some electoral fear, it will be because Putin thought it up all by himself, and nothing to do with him doing Cameron a favour in return for some favour from the UK - like Britain not objecting to Putin's homophobic legislation, or his war in the Caucasus, or the multiple human rights abuses and rampant corruption that characterise his rule.

These people think we are idiots.

Cameron is quite happy to discuss Scottish independence with Mariano Rajoy and Vladimir Putin, and wants to raise the topic at the meeting of the G8, but he won't talk about it with anyone Scottish. It's a matter for Scottish people to debate within Scotland, he said, except for backroom dealings between the Tories and the Partido Popular and any other obnoxious regimes that Westminster thinks it can enlist in its save the Union campaign.

It is bad enough that Cameron is colluding with the revolting Partido Popular in Spain, but at least Spain is a functioning democracy. Russia is a pseudodemocracy ruled by an authoritarian kleptocracy - a condition the UK slides closer to with every privatisation and every banking or political corruption scandal that gets brushed under the carpet. Scotland will note that Cameron is willing to deal with such people, but not with us. Next week expect an announcement from Kim Jong-un that Scottish independence will be considered a threat to the sovereignty of North Korea.

We have a government in Westminster headed by a man who is willing to enter into dodgy deals with objectionable authoritarian governments in order to screw the Scottish independence campaign, but won't stand before the people of Scotland to explain to us why we think we should let him keep his job as the Prime Minister of Scotland.

What Cameron, Rajoy and Putin are afraid of is that the 21st century will be the era of the small nations of Europe. The EU consists of 27 states, but contains many more nations. Despite shedding the non-Russian Union republics of the Soviet Union, Russia still contains over 140 ethnic groups and languages. And across the continent stateless nations are finding their voice and speaking out for change. On Saturday over 130,000 Basques took to the streets of Bilbao to demonstrate in favour of Basque sovereignty and the right of the Basque Country to decide its own future.

Scotland is leading the way in this peaceful revolution. We're the first of the small nations of Europe to say - enough, we will not resign ourselves to the fate that our political masters have in mind for us. We're making history, and not just Scottish history.

The Catalans, Basques, Galicians and many others look to Scotland as an example of how a small nation can decide its own destiny without violence and without conflict. Westminster punches above its weight with nuclear weapons and armed might, Scotland does it with ideas of democracy and fairness. We don't need Westminster so we can punch above our weight, our influence is enormous.

14 January 2014
The debt we owe to the Union

It doesn't really matter how often a pro-independence organisation, website, or individual publicly refutes one the many lies perpetrated by the Better Together campaign, the lie continues to be asserted - all too often unchallenged by the supine British media. Just within the past few days, Alistair Carmichael repeated the spurious claim that Scotland benefits financially from the Union when in fact the reverse is true, and Alistair Darling repeated the multi-refuted Unionist fantasy that Alex Salmond need only snap his fingers and every indy supporter with a keyboard and an internet connection will stop taking the piss out of Better Together and its minions.

Speaking entirely personally, because I am not a member of any political party, I would love Alex Salmond to make a public statement asking people to be nice to Alistair Darling. I'd take it as carte-blanche to rip seven shades of shite out of Ali, and I wouldn't be alone. Not out of badness, well not entirely, but because it would prove that Alex Salmond is not McAstaroth directing his minor demons (my demon name is Weegingerdugaroth and my special power is frying mince). We could demonstrate once and for all that this is not Alex Salmond's independence referendum by blythely ignoring him and continuing to mock. Mind you it still wouldn't stop Darling from blaming Eck for the extra abuse heaped upon him, nor stop the media from repeating the lie.

But onto the Big Lie, the one that deserves the capital letters. It's the oil. It's too volatile, and we're lucky to have Westminster to look after it for us and give us economic stability.

The first part of this statement is true, strictly speaking. Oil is volatile. All commodities are volatile, but oil is especially volatile - in the sense that it evaporates away over time, leaving you with nothing but a rank sticky toxic mess and a stain that's impossible to shift. Which is also a fair description of Scotland's Unionist parties since the oil revenues started to flow into the UK Treasury. But the rest of the claim is utter bollocks which has been refuted more often than it's been pointed out that Bruce Forsyth wears a wig. Didn't they do well. Well, no, they didn't.

Norway passed a wee historical milestone this week. Every Norwegian became a millionaire. The Norwegian state oil fund is now worth 5.11 trillion krone, or 1 million krone per head of population - around £100,000 for every man woman and child in the country. Of course that cash isn't theirs to spend individually, it's a fund for the country's future so that generations of Norwegians to come can continue to enjoy high quality public services and benefit from first class infrastructure.

And while the Norwegians were quietly patting themselves on the backs of their expensive knitwear, what was the main topic of discussion regarding the future of the UK economy? Austerity in wongaland, indebtedness and cuts.

In the independence debate, the latest salvo is that the UK government will continue to guarantee the UK's debts. Which in many ways is is merely a statement of the obvious dressed up as news. But they did also say words to the effect that the UK government would continue to guarantee existing UK debt, including that part which would be inherited by a future independent Scotland.

This is really rather important. It is in fact a tacit admission that Westminster will accept a currency union with an independent Scotland, and an admission that Westminster cannot force an independent Holyrood to accept a single penny of the UK's £1.4 trillion debt. Scotland will of course accept a share of the debt, which will be owed to the UK, but only in return for a proportional share of UK assets. It helps to smooth the path of future negotiations on independence, and as such is a major advance for the yes campaign. Not that the media would report it like that.

But the point remains, they were discussing debt, not the vast assets of Norway. If an independent Scotland had started an oil fund when

Norway started its fund, we would currently be discussing Scottish assets, not Scottish debt. If Westminster had established a UK oil fund then Scotland would now be discussing what share of it was ours. Instead it's all about debt.

Norwegians are millionaires, but as part of the UK Scotland doesn't have an oil fund, we have public debt. Our public services are bleeding to death, and our straining transport and communications infrastructure cries out for investment. If we remain in the UK we are screwed economically and face unparalleled cuts in public spending - not so much cuts, as amputations and decapitations.

Monday's Newsnight on BBC2, the one for grown ups in London not the 20 minutes at the end tacked on to assuage Scotland, spent much of the programme discussing the extent to which the services of the UK state will be axed or privatised. We live in a UK where all the main parties agree on the need for cuts. They just differ on the presentation.

Scotland's oil bonanza was pissed away on Tory tax cuts, benefits to the millions thrown onto the scrap heap of unemployment as Thatcher used people's lives as a tool to break the unions and destroy heavy industry, casino banking, privatisations, nuclear weapons, and the odd foreign war or three.

Yet we're supposed to believe that Westminster is a competent manager of Scotland's economy. Better Together operates in a peculiar little bubble of parochialism where it imagines that not only are Scots unaware of the news from furren pairts, we're also unaware of the news from the rest of the UK. The big oil lie exposes itself as a lie every time we read another headline about austerity. They want to spend what remains of the oil revenues on more wars, nukes, privatisations, casino bankers and tax cuts for the well off.

And that's what really gets my goat about Alistair Darling. It's not that he defends a system that benefits the few not the many. It's not even that he exercises power without responsibility - because mere electoral rejection can't kill off a Westminster political careerist. It's that he expects to be beyond criticism, and beyond mockery. He's so eager to avoid being mocked he's turned Better Together into a joke without a punchline.

A Scotsman, an Englishman, and a Welshman got into debt. It's the way you tell them, Alistair.

16 January 2015

Slapping Alistair Carmichael with a wet fish

Alistair Carmichael is at it again. This time he says Spain is going to veto Scottish membership of the EU unless we grant them access to fishing waters where the Spanish fishing fleet doesn't currently have full access. But the icing on the cod was Alistair's claim that Scottish fisheries get a better deal from the UK than they would from an independent Scotland. Alastair said:

"Spain has long wanted access to North Sea fishing rights for its fleet as part of the Common Fisheries Policy because there are provisions within the CFP, which favour the UK fleet in the North Sea. I cannot think Spain would be very keen to offer Scottish fishermen the deal that they get as being part of the United Kingdom."

So in other words, according to our representative in the UK Cabinet, Spain will veto Scottish membership of the EU, thereby losing access to the entirety of Scottish fishing grounds, unless we grant them increased access to an area they don't currently have access to. Hmmm. That'll make the Partido Popular really popular amongst customers at the fish counter in Hypercor.

The peculiar assumption underlying Koalamichael's fishy threat is that Scottish fishing grounds aren't Scottish at all. They're European, or they're British, or they're Spanish. They're anything but Scottish. Claiming that Spain will veto Scottish membership of the EU unless they are given a part of Scotland's fishing grounds is a bit like saying that Italy would veto Scottish membership of the EU unless the branch of Domino's Pizza in Paisley high street was declared Italian soil.

Naturally Spain is intensely interested in maintaining the access its fishing fleet has to Scottish waters. And that's precisely why they won't veto Scotland, because vetoing Scotland means that Spain loses access to much of the North Atlantic as well as the North Sea. And that is politically unthinkable for a Spanish government, especially a Partido Popular one.

However as a negotiator, Alistair Carmichael is clearly more suited to the depths of the toddler pool in Bellshill Baths than the icy waters of the North Atlantic. In this instance, it's Scotland which holds the cards, not Spain - because if Spain does not cooperate with Scottish membership of the EU an independent Scotland could veto Spanish entry into Scottish waters, which would have political consequences in Spain that Mariano Rajoy could not survive. He needs our fish more than we do.

Throughout Iberia, seafood makes up an important part of the diet. Despite their many other differences, Basques, Catalans, Castilians, Andalusians, and Galicians are all united in their love of fish and shellfish. The Spanish fishing industry is huge, and as rapacious as the Iberian appetite for its product. Between 2000 and 2010, the Spanish fishing industry benefited to the tune of €5.8 billion (approximately £4.83 billion) in subsidies from the EU and Spain - far more than the industry of any other EU state.

The fishing industry is particularly important in Galicia, where Spanish PM Mariano Rajoy comes from. Well over 50% of the entire Spanish catch is landed in Galicia. The fisheries sector employs 4.6% of the active population in Galicia, a much higher percentage than in any other European country. It is estimated that 12% of all jobs in Galicia directly depend upon the fishing industry. In coastal areas, this figure reaches 40% to 50% and the economy of many towns and villages is entirely dependent upon the fishing fleet.

As well as being the home of Mariano Rajoy, who represents the Galician city of Pontevedra in the Spanish Parliament, Galicia is one of the main power bases for the Partido Popular who benefit greatly from their links to the owners of the Galician fishing fleet, many of whom are important donors to the party. Angering this powerful lobby is not a step that any Spanish Government is going to take lightly.

A Galician friend informed me that 65% of the Galician catch comes from the waters of the North Atlantic off the coasts of Scotland and Ireland. I've not yet been able to find a referenced source for this figure, but it is certainly a large and significant percentage of the total catch. According to Greenpeace Spain, the Galician fleet in the North Atlantic - excluding those trawlers who fish off the coasts of Iceland, Greenland and Newfoundland - consists of 46 deep water trawlers and 194 longliners.

If Spain were to veto Scottish membership of the EU, it would instantly lose all access to a large part of its fish catch. The effect on the Galician economy would be devastating and the powerful Galician fishing lobby would withdraw its traditional support for the Partido Popular. Meanwhile shoppers across Spain would be deprived of their *bacalao* and *merluza,* and the politicians they'll blame for that would be the ones who decided to veto Scottish EU membership in the hope of getting a bigger slice of our fish cake.

Alistair's claim that Spain would veto Scottish membership of the EU unless we allow them even greater access to our fishing grounds does not hold water, and neither does his claim that Scotland's fishing industry benefits from Westminster rule.

Westminster has mismanaged the Scottish fishing industry and used its interests as a bargaining chip to be traded away for benefits to the farming industry in the south. Tory PM Ted Heath infamously traded away Scottish fishing rights in return for agricultural subsidies for large southern English farmers in 1973, and Westminster has pursued similar policies ever since.

According to figures from the Scottish Government, Scotland receives just 41% of the UK's European Fisheries Fund allocation despite accounting for 87% of the total value of UK fish landings - 37% of the total EU Total Allowable Catch (TAC). Scotland receives just 1.1% of European fisheries funding although the Scottish fleet lands 7% of the total EU catch of wild fish and 12% of European aquaculture production.

The only way that Scotland can protect its fishing industry is through independence. Alistair Carmichael is clearly not up to the task - he's a man who doesn't recognise a bargaining chip when it comes in the form of a wet cod slapping him across the face.

24 January 2014

Witch hunts, and who's afraid of who

The Daily Mail has embarked on a witch hunt of "evil cybernats". It's the same old story from a publication which panders to the basest instincts of the uneducated and the willfully misinformed, it's only the target which has changed.

Back in the early 1980s, during the Aids hysteria, an acquaintance was outed by a newspaper. It was one of the usual suspects given to demonising innocent and powerless members of the public, either the Daily Mail or the Express, I can't remember which now. His 'crime' was to organise private parties for gay men, and his punishment was to have his personal details and photo plastered all over a gutter rag, describing him as a sleazy pervert.

He wasn't out as gay to his work or his family, this was the early 80s after all. The newspaper report caused him to lose his job and estranged him from many of his relatives. He struggled to keep up with his mortgage payments and almost lost his home.

My friend was not involved in anything that would raise an eyebrow these days - nor even back then if you were a normal human being instead of a tabloid rag. He did not organise sex parties, just quiet and very douce gatherings where gay men could meet up and chat in an era when there were few public spaces available and many gay people were suffering dreadful social isolation. Most of us, myself included in those days, were not out as gay to our families, straight friends or work colleagues. We had few opportunities to meet other gay folk.

Even though the events were strictly sex-free zones, my friend rigorously enforced an age bar and refused to allow anyone under the age of 21 - then the legal age of consent - to attend. But the law in those days permitted gay sex only in private, and 'private' was legally defined as no more than two persons being present on the premises. Any gathering of more than two gay men, for whatever purpose, was a target for tabloid purience.

When the tabloids see you as a vile and disgusting sex-beast, any gathering becomes a 'perverted sex orgy' even when the most orgiastic thing that happens is cooing over how delicious the home baked cakes are, and if you were lucky swapping contact details for later and more intimate meetings.

My friend had the misfortune to live in a day when gay people were one of the tabloids' favourite bogeymen. According to the Sun and the Mail, we were all part of an international conspiracy to destroy the family and spread disease. Their current demonisation of the mythical cybernat conspiracy is very much in the same diseased and deformed mould.

That wasn't something any of us expected to change back when gay people were seen by the tabloids as the number one threat to public health and morality. You had to learn to ignore the insults, the slander, the threats and the oppression, but it took a toll and eventually something snapped inside me.

One day I woke up and thought "fuck this for a gemme o sodgies" and resolved to tell my family and friends the truth. It wasn't easy back in the 1980s in a working class part of Glasgow and a deeply Catholic family, but it was the best decision I ever made. And I wasn't the only gay man or lesbian making that decision. The closet doors were popping open across the land. We weren't going to stand for it any more. 30 years later the gay rights campaign has won all the legal arguments, and legal discrimination is a thing of the past.

Yet here were are 30 years on and the tabloids have found a new target. Now it's independence supporters who are part of an imaginary conspiracy to destroy all that is Great and British. In 1980 I never imagined that one day it would not be permissible to insult and threaten me for being gay, but perfectly acceptable to insult and threaten me for being Scottish. That's what happens when a minority get "uppity", and currently from the perspective of the London media bubble, Scots are very uppity indeed.

The lesson I learned was that you can only be silenced when you collude with those who seek to oppress you. Fear lives only inside your own head. The tabloids seek to create fear and by targeting a few individuals hope to dissuade others from putting their heads above the parapet. But when you are out and proud, tabloid threats have no purchase - what are they going to do? Tell my mother I have sex with men? She already knows. It's not me who is afraid, it's the tabloids who seek to demonise. They are afraid of me.

Those who have been targeted by the tabloids for daring to express opinions in favour of independence need to realise that they are not the ones with cause to fear. The fear the tabloids seek to generate within you is a weapon you can use. Instead of provoking fear it provokes righteous anger, and that anger provides the energy to continue to fight against them. And you already know that you scare them.

When you live in the light you cannot be threatened by the darkness. The way to avoid the fear provoked by the tabloids and the media is to give them no purchase against you. If you haven't already done so, tell everyone you know that you support independence, it's not a shameful secret, it's something to be proud of. Be out, be proud, live without fear. Then when some sleazy tabloid reporter doorsteps your neighbours or your colleagues and tells them you are an evil cybernat who says nasty things about Unionist politicians they will reply, "So what?"

Gay people have largely won their struggle for equality, despite forming only a small minority of the population. Independence supporters make up a far far larger proportion of the Scottish population. This is a struggle we are not going to lose unless we collude with the Daily Mail. That's not going to happen. Just like the late 1980s when closet doors burst open and gay men and lesbians refused to live in silence, the independence closet is well and truly open and Scots are going through it in droves - out into the light.

This uppity Scot has every intention of continuing to be uppity, and I'll keep doing what I can in my own small way to get it up Westminster politicians and their lackeys in the press some more. I won't be alone. Cybernat conspiracy my arse, it's the anger of righteous indignation.

28 January 2014

Feeling the lurve

It was recently revealed that Better Together are to embark on a new phase of their campaign. The fearmongering and the scare stories just aren't cutting it any more, and have only resulted in increasing support for a yes vote in opinion polls, so we are to be love-bombed by Unionist politicians and celebs who are going to tell us how much they love us. To date we've seen at least two examples of this new loving tactic, neither of which have left anyone feeling moist. Although there have been quite a few tears of laughter.

First up was John Barrowman in an excruciatingly embarrassing performance for Burn's Night. It contained enough ham to supply the Danish bacon industry for a decade, but failed to convince that Rabbie Burns would have signed up to the Unionist cause. John was attired in a tartan jaiket last seen on a 1970s TV presenter - the only thing missing was his hand up a muppet's arse, but one muppet fisting another muppet was probably deemed too meta for a prime time audience.

However in the true style of an overly friendly 1970s telly presenter, John tried to make out that Westminster's abuse was actually a loving act. He did this by mugging to the camera with a glaikit expression and a series of pish poor jokes about Alex Salmond and how fat he is. As an exercise in love-bombing it was a dismal failure - the first time anyone has attempted to employ toe-curling as a sexual practice.

John Barrowman emigrated to the USA before he hit puberty, so I'm not going to criticise his Virgin midAtlantic accent. It's quite normal for people who move to another country in early childhood to adopt the accent of their new home, or a facsimile thereof. Unfortunately however, John's concept of Scotland is also prepubescent, as he doesn't think we're a grown up country capable of grown up decisions. John takes his intellectual cue on all things Scottish from the Krankies, and believes we're in safer hands with the 1970s TV presenters.

Next up was something with a bit more intellectual substance. That's substance in the sense of that suspicious brown matter you find inside a dirty public toilet. Martin Woollacott, formerly the Guardian's foreign editor, published an article in the paper telling Scotland how much England loves us and warning us that we will miss them when we go. Martin employed the tired old divorce metaphor, which has already been done to death, and made a number of references to thon movie starring that Australian American with the dodgy politics.

Anyone following the independence debate knows that a Braveheart reference in any discussion of Scottish independence is a reliable indicator that the person making the reference knows less about Scottish politics than they do about copra harvesting in the Comoros Islands. It's a bit like discussing Leonardo Di Caprio and Kate Winslet in a technical report on ship building standards and the risks posed by icebergs. No wonder Better Together is holed below the water line.

According to Martin's fact free zone of an article, which was ignorant and patronising in equal measure, Scottish independence will have a devastating effect on England's self-esteem. The English, he tells us, are terribly afraid. I immediately telephoned some English members of my family in order to reassure them, asking if their sense of personal well-being might suffer if Scotland declared independence. However the reply was, "Eh? Are you on drugs?" I took that as a no.

The truth is that a large majority of English people are indifferent to Scottish independence. A minority want us to stay, another minority supports independence, but most don't give a shit - and why should they. They know what Martin Woollacott and a plethora of pro-Union commentators don't know - that the independence debate is about Scotland, it's not about England at all.

Of course the obvious question which Martin's article raises is that if this guy was the paper's foreign editor, and he's so ridiculously clueless about the affairs of a country so very close to his metropolitan home, just how reliable are the paper's reports about places further away? Or indeed, their reports on anything at all.

That's the big problem Better Together's love-bombing campaign will not be able to overcome. They're relying on people who know bugger all about us, and their ignorance is plain to see for a Scottish readership. Every time some clown puts his grinning mug in front of a camera and makes a fool of himself for the Union, a little bit more of Scotland's rapidly diminishing faith in the UK media dies.

Better Together has spent the last 18 months trying to frighten us with alarmist tales and scary stories. Now they're telling us how much they love us and need us. That's not love bombing. It's stalking.

Of course, I am just saying this because of the SNP microchip implanted in my brain ...

29 January 2014

We can work it out

Mark Carney, the governor of the Bank of England made a much anticipated speech in Embra on Wednesday giving his opinion on the sterling currency union the Scottish Government proposes post-independence. His opinion boiled down to "we can work it out", saying that the Bank of England would implement whatever agreement Holyrood and Westminster came to during independence negotiations following a yes vote.

For those of us who are neither economists nor central bankers, that's pretty much all we need to know. A sterling currency union between an independent Scotland and the rest of the UK is perfectly possible, and perfectly sensible. Yes, there will be issues to be sorted out, but they can be sorted out.

Carney took pains in his speech to state that he was neither pro nor anti Scottish independence, but that hasn't stopped a barrage of negative commentary in the Unionist press telling us that Carney's speech means we're all doomed and will have to buy the weekly shopping with cowry shells. It's all very predictable from a UK media which tells Scotland that winning £1.5 trillion on the oil lottery is a very bad thing.

Better Together have already rushed out a press release saying that Carney's remarks "quietly demolish Alex Salmond's claim that Scotland could keep the UK pound" when Carney had in fact said no such thing. But then Better Together are doubtless employing the same speed reading skills they used when the White Paper on independence was published last year.

The Guardian's resident ray of sunshine, Severin Carrell, warned us that an indy Scotland would have to "cede sovereignty" if it wanted a sterling currency union. Which kinda implies we have sovereignty just now under the Union, an obvious nonsense. It was a misrepresentation of Carney's words, what the Governor of the Bank of England actually said was:

"An independent Scotland would need to consider carefully how to develop arrangements with the continuing United Kingdom that are both consistent with its sovereignty and sufficient to maintain financial stability."

This is not quite the same as "an independent Scotland would be in thrall to George Osborne", which is what the Guardian was trying to imply.

However "ceding sovereignty" is not the "ooo you're not really independent then are you" which Carrell would have us believe. Independent countries cede sovereignty all the time. The UK has "ceded sovereignty" to the UN, NATO, the EU, and to just about every other international organisation or country with which it has signed a treaty. Because that's what treaties mean - two or more nations commit themselves to an agreement, and in the process surrender a part of their sovereignty by the mere fact of making a commitment to one another.

However what Carrell fails to point out is that while an independent nation can choose to cede sovereignty by entering into a treaty with another independent nation - the other nation which is party to the agreement also cedes sovereignty. It's not just Scotland which would "cede sovereignty" by entering a currency union, it's the rUK as well. It's this element of the rUK ceding sovereignty to an indy Scotland which has got the Unionist knickers in a twist, as they typically fetishise the supposed sovereignty of the Westminster Parliament. But that's their problem, not ours.

The other point Carrell fails to mention is that an independent nation which cedes sovereignty in this way has not lost that sovereignty forever. If times and circumstances change, an independent state can withdraw from a treaty commitment at a time of its own choosing.

The difference between this set of circumstances and what we have now ought to be clear. At the moment Scotland has ceded all sovereignty to Westminster and we won't get any back unless we take it from them in the independence referendum. They're certainly not about to give it to us if we ask nicely. Independence means Scotland has choices it does not have just now - that is the real point.

If at some point in the future a Scottish government decides that it wants to join the euro, create a Scottish currency, or use Norwegian kroner, it could do so. Westminster will not be in a position to refuse or to prevent us. That's what sovereignty really means.

During independence negotiations Scotland will hold some very strong cards. The UK Government has already conceded that it will remain responsible for the UK's existing national debt, currently sitting around an eye watering £1.5 trillion. Scotland may take on a portion of the UK's national debt, and become a debtor to the rUK Government, in return for a share of UK national assets, but the bottom line during negotiations is that the debt remains Westminster's problem. In theory the Scottish delegation will be able to say "stick yer debt". This would cause a serious economic crisis in the rUK which would be in no one's interests, however it does give Scotland the freedom to decide which of the UK's debts we are going to shoulder. Westminster will not be able to unilaterally decide which debts we will be lumbered with, and if they want us to take on any of their debt - well they'll have to cede part of their sovereignty to Scotland by agreeing to a currency union won't they.

The thing that always intrigues me in Unionist discussions of independence is the underlying assumption that Westminster will always get its own way. That's certainly the case just now under the Union. Unionists inhabit a mental universe where it would remain the case even after independence. That's not merely missing the point, it's completely misunderstanding the entire argument. And that's why they're going to lose.

30 January 2014

Honour and dishonour

Thatcher's former Governor General of Scotland, Ian Lang, made a wee speech in the House of Lords in which he said that Scottish independence would dishonour all those who had fought and died in the UK's assorted wars.

As far as I can discover, Ian Lang has never seen active service in the military. Instead he's made a very lucrative career for himself in Tory politics, followed by his pretendy Lordy title and a series of directorships. According to Businessweek magazine, the privately educated Lang has amassed a very profitable portfolio of part time directorships which bring him in over £240,000 annually. It's the natural career path of a Tory poshboy.

So I asked my other half what he thought about Lang's intervention. Himself is a former Royal Marine who saw active service in Suez and Cyprus, two not especially honourable episodes in Britain's imperial past - but we'll gloss over that. He killed people, his friends died, and he got some shiny medals for his pains. After leaving the Royal Marines he served for 25 years in the Metropolitan police, where he continued to protect the likes of Ian Lang.

The other half is English, not a person of Scottish parentage who happened to have been born down south, he's yer actual Englishman with the yew wot accent and everything. He fully intends to vote yes in September's referendum. His exact words on hearing Lang's comments were: "Lang can go fuck himself. He doesn't know what honour means. He won't tell me what I fought for."

I wish I hadn't asked, because the other half then went into an extended rant about how a former Thatcher cabinet minister has no business telling anyone what is or is not "honourable". It's pretty rich for an exserviceman to be called dishonourable by a man who spent his career betraying working class servicepeople and took a leading role in a government which slashed the services those servicepeople now rely on when they are infirm or disabled.

All across the UK, frail and elderly ex-servicemen are left lying for hours in their own shit because care provision has been axed. Where's the honour when you reek of stale urine Ian? Thanks to Ian Lang and his colleagues, former soldiers freeze because they're forced to choose between eating or heating. Where's the honour Ian?

If that's the honour Ian Lang speaks of, who is dishonouring who?

If anything, my partner fought for the Britain of consensus, the Britain of the NHS and the welfare state, the Britain of free education, the Britain that cares for the infirm, the disabled, the elderly, and those who've been dealt a bad hand by life. He did not fight for the Britain of ATOS, the Britain of cuts and privatisation. He certainly didn't fight for the Britain of illegal wars. But that's the Britain Lang has created, and now he has the audacity to claim that we dishonour the selfish nasty and narrow little Parliament that is a tool of the misrule of those who know no honour, only profit.

No Ian, we are not dishonouring servicemen by voting for independence. We are honouring them, because we're protecting them from your betrayals, your cant, and your lies. With independence we can create a land that really is fit for heroes. We can preserve those good parts of the postwar consensus that you have made it your life's work to destroy.

We are dishonouring you Ian, because dishonour is all you and your so called "Lords" deserve.

I do hope the Daily Mail is listening, because this particular instance of cybernattery comes from an English ex serviceman who has never used a computer in his life.

February 2014

1 February 2014

Wee things make a difference

It can't be easy being Johann Lamont. It's bad enough being promoted well beyond your talents and abilities, placed in an important public role which mainly involves communicating with the public, while possessed of poorer linguistic skills than someone who's recently suffered a brain injury. People in semi-comas can communicate more effectively than Johann, at least blink once for yes and twice for no is comprehensible, which is a lot more than can be said for most of Johann's public utterances.

Come to think of it, Alistair Darling blinks so frequently that he looks like he's sending subliminal messages in Morse Code. All the time he's spouting his increasingly implausible mince, his subconscious can't help revealing the truth. I... A ... M... A... L... I... A... R...

Most over promoted managers can hide away in their office and blame their junior staff. Johann has to do it in public and then when she screws up the entire country points and laughs. She can't even blame her junior staff, at least not in public what with Labour party tribalism trumping all and everything. Besides, if it came to a fist fight between Johann and Jackie Baillie it's not at all certain that JoLo would win. That only allows her to blame Alex Salmond. Poor wee thing.

So it was Furst Meenister's Questions, and Johann had been handed a big, if imaginary, stick to beat over Alex Salmond's head in the shape of the UK media and Better Together's misrepresentation of Mark Carney's comments about sharing the currency. There she was, armed with all the weaponry that the massed forces of the British state and its propaganda department (AKA the newspapers and the BBC) were able to give her, and it blew up in her face in a single throwaway line. When Johann goes off script, she goes off the rails.

Johann thinks that the possibilities unlocked for an independent Scotland are just wee things - like getting rid of Trident, tax and benefits policies, or whether or not we invade a random Middle Eastern country. Johann and the Labour party are focussed on the big picture, the things that are important and relevant to the people of Scotland. Things like airguns, letting Labour councillors pay themselves extra for sitting on ALEOS boards, and the amount of dog shit on the streets of Shettleston.

Although Labour has tried to slough off Johann's wee things comment, and as cold blooded reptilians they have plenty of practice at sloughing, her words were unintentionally very revealing. They show that Labour in Scotland has a wee horizon, a wee vision, and a wee spirit. The satnav on the Labour bus is firmly pointed down a privatised Tory highway where every pothole is blamed on Alex Salmond. They are genuinely, and scarily, bereft of any vision of where Scotland is going. Who cares if the passengers are unceremoniously dumped in a post-industrial wasteland at the end of the line, all that matters is that the drivers arrive at a seat in the House of Lords.

I've been walking a neighbour's dogs this week, as she has recently had an operation and is still a bit too tender to take her dogs out herself. Last night when I returned with her pets, she asked me about the referendum. She was interested in the wee things, would we be able to get rid of Trident, would we get rid of the bedroom tax. I told her it was a big yes to both.

The neighbour is not a fan of Alex Salmond or the SNP. She's not a big fan of Labour either, and gave up voting in elections many years ago. "I cannae even remember the last time I voted," she said. But she added that she's definitely going to vote in the referendum, and she's going to vote yes. It's the wee things we'll be able to do that interest her.

Like ensuring that her daughter, who is in the army, won't be sent off to get blown up by a roadside device in some foreign land in one of the UK's many illegal wars.

It's people like my neighbour who will decide the outcome of the referendum, people who do not normally vote. It's not that they don't vote because they have no interest in politics, or that they don't care about how this country is governed. They don't vote because they know that under the Westminster system they have no effective voice. Their vote doesn't matter, doesn't count, and doesn't make a difference to the likes of Johann Lamont.

But they'll come out to vote in September, and they'll vote for the wee things that aren't important to Johann Lamont's political career. It's a point worth repeating - people who are alienated from politics are not going to come out and vote to keep a system that alienates them. They're going to vote for change, they're going to vote for the wee things.

2 February 2014
The real racism in the independence campaign

The Guardian / Observer has proven to be the big disappointment of the independence campaign. If you do manage to construct a coherent shelving unit out of the Guardian's one dimensional flat packed reports, you'll get a shoddy and poorly manufactured piece of crap that won't take the weight of a lying leaflet from Better Together.

You'd expect that sort of thing from the Mail or the Telegraph, but when the referendum campaign kicked off I did, naively perhaps, harbour fond hopes that the liberal traditions of the Guardian might just allow the Scottish indy case a fair shake of the stick. But no such joy, the Guardian out-Mails the Mail in its eagerness to depict independence supporters as atavistic English haters. The UK media is united in singing from the same "ooo aren't they racist" songsheet.

The Guardian's Sunday sister, the Observer, was at it again this week. A report on Alistair Carmichael's latest fact-free whinge contained a number of accusations that the independence campaign has been disfigured by racism and intolerance. Of course it's only Yes campaigners who do that sort of thing, what British nationalism being the only non-nationalist nationalism ever.

I can't be bothered dissecting the contents of Alistair's interview. He's a waste of space and if he didn't exist no one would feel the need to invent him. Ali wants us to take him seriously, and gets upset when we don't. You don't get respect for talking out your arse, Alistair, you get mockery. The rest of us learned that lesson in nursery school.

However he raised a couple of points that should not go unchallenged. Alistair said that it was wrong to claim that the people of Scotland and the people of England have different values. And this would be true. The people of Scotland and the people of England do, by and large, have shared values. We share those values with the rest of Europe, and just about everywhere where most people aren't fundamentalist god-botherers of one sort or another. The problem however is that this is not about sharing or not sharing values with ordinary English people, it's about Scotland not sharing values with Westminster. It is convenient for Alistair and Better Together to confuse the difference.

Alistair was very annoyed that he'd been called a Quisling. He was called that because he diminishes Scotland's prospects and potential, he either knowingly lies or he repeats untruths he does not challenge, and he colludes in the stereotypes and racism which form the prism through which the Westminster elites view the Scottish independence campaign. But this is not the same as rounding up Jewish people at the behest of Nazi occupiers and sending them off to death camps, which is what yer actual Vidkun Quisling did. People were afraid of Quisling, with very good reason. Alistair is not a Quisling, he's an Uncle Tam - a figure of fun and ridicule, not fear.

However it allowed the reporter to indulge in another bout of mud slinging. Ooo aren't the Scots terribly racist. We need Westminster to keep our atavistic impulses in check for us.

When the Guardian does deign to cover Scotland with something approaching intelligence, it discusses the effect independence might have on England - or to be more exact, on the English political elite. Because in Guardianland Scottish independence isn't really about Scotland at all.

How foolish of those Scots to complain that Scotland has a different political culture to the rest of the UK. Scotland is exactly the same as England, only with scenery. Scotland is nothing more than a region of the UK with a burning hatred of all things English due to ancient historical grievances. That is, to the Metropolitan commetariat, what defines us. If Scotland is defined as nothing more than a region of the UK where people hate the English, then any Scottish independence campaign must be a racist campaign.

But the reports in the UK media of the racism that supposedly disfigures the Scottish independence campaign are themselves racist. They play to racist stereotypes of semi-civilised Scots who need Westminster to civilise us. They do this in the hope that voters will be discouraged from engaging with the independence debate, so that the power of the Westminster elite will remain unchallenged.

The real racism in this campaign lies with the Guardian, the Daily Mail, and the Uncle Tams. Racism, like homophobia or sexism, is fundamentally about power. Who has power, who exercises power, and who is to be subject to that power. The British establishment have the power, and they use it to keep Scotland shut firmly in a constitutional box where the democratic wishes of the people of Scotland can be contained and ignored, and Scotland's resources and potential can be harnessed to the demands of the Westminster elite. In order to maintain their privilege, Scotland must be trivialised and diminished. Calling supporters of independence racist and anti-English is a means to that end.

3 February 2014
Bias by omission

The recent paper from the University of the West of Scotland on bias in the Scottish broadcast media has not been given any coverage in the media which is the subject of its study. Scotland's broadcasters don't want their audience to know that they are biased, partial, and only covering one side of the story.

BBC Scotland's management have mounted an extraordinary attack on the paper and its author, but undaunted the paper's author Dr

John Robertson has come out all guns blazing and has published the snotty letter he received from the BBC, together with his devastating critique, on Newsnet Scotland.

There can now be no doubt that BBC management are deliberately downplaying the referendum and equally deliberately are favouring the No campaign. However the report from UWS only covered stories which actually get airtime. Dr Robertson pointed out in his reply that he had not studied the bias involved in story selection, and said that he believed that the Scottish media was also skewing its coverage of the independence debate by not giving airtime to many stories favourable to independence.

There was yet another example of media bias by omission today. On Monday the Financial Times, no supporter of Scottish independence, published an article detailing the financial situation of an independent Scotland, using UK government figures. The bottom line is that we'd be in the money - every man woman and child in the country would be almost £1400 a year better off.

The FT showed that the Scottish government would immediately have some £7 billion a year on top of the existing Scottish budget of £64 billion - and this is under the assumption that the government of a newly independent Scotland would continue to spend according to UK priorities. Even if we were daft enough to keep paying for Trident, and other "UK national" projects like London Crossrail, the High Speed Railway between London and Birmingham, and the London sewer upgrade, we'd still be in a much stronger financial situation than we are at the moment.

Neither do the figures account for companies operating in Scotland who currently pay taxes via head offices in England - taxes like Corporation Tax or VAT for example. After independence these companies would have to pay taxes on their Scottish operations to the Scottish government, not the UK Treasury as they do at the moment. It's very difficult to quantify just how much extra this would bring in, but it's certainly a substantial amount.

When we take all these other things into account, the financial situation for an independent Scotland looks extremely rosy indeed.

You'd think that this was important and relevant information for people who are making their minds up about how to vote in September, and that it would be plastered all over the Scottish media - especially since, as Dr Robertson pointed out in his reply to the BBC bosses, the Scottish media focus almost exclusively on the economic aspects of independence and seek to reduce the argument to one about pounds and pence.

But there's been not a word about the FT's report on Reporting Scotland - Scotland's national news programme according to the BBC. Today BBC Scotland chose to lead with a story on ecstasy. There was not one single mention anywhere in our supposedly professional media of an important story which goes right to the heart of the independence debate on the very grounds that the media have chosen to present that debate. The media in Scotland have chosen to reduce independence to economics yet when presented with clear evidence, from a Unionist source no less, that Scotland would be a far wealthier country as an independent state, they don't report it.

As Dr Robertson noted in his reply to the BBC, the Scottish media almost entirely ignores the democratic or political reasons for independence. There is little or no discussion on telly about the relative merits of a country choosing its own government, or having its government chosen for it by a much larger neighbour. It's not hard to see why the media don't want to discuss that. Equally it's not hard to see why they have suppressed Dr Robertson's report and don't want to discuss their biased presentation of the independence debate.

Under the Union, Scotland is not a fully democratic country. A free and fair media is not an optional extra in a democracy. Without access to full facts and information, citizens cannot make principled choices about how they wish to vote. The Scottish media does not allow Scotland to make principled and informed decisions, and that's just the way they like it. They only want us to talk about what they think is important, they are determined to shape the debate and direct it onto a Unionist path, they are not content with simply reporting.

The state of the Scottish media is now an issue in this independence campaign. We're not just campaigning for national independence, we are campaiging for the basic democratic rights that define any democracy - the right to access to information, and the right to have the full range of Scottish opinion represented.

If we want a media that truly reflects our nation, there's only one way we're going to get it. Vote yes in September.

5 February 2014
Things that make you go hmmmm

What leads a business person to make a public statement about a sensitive political matter in a country where he neither lives nor is a citizen? Moreover, what makes him do it when no other figures in his industry have made such a public declaration?

Indeed senior figures within the industry have restricted themselves to saying that the decision is one for the people of Scotland to make and they will continue to work in Scotland regardless of the result. Meanwhile the industry continues to make record investment in Scotland, despite the fearmongering of Unionists that the indy debate is discouraging investment.

So did Bob Dudley Chief Executive of BP wake up one morning, and entirely off his own bat decide that he was going to give an interview to the UK media in which he parrots the Better Together line about uncertainty and help-me-mummy-I'm-frightened? It's not impossible.

However in my limited experience of the business world, the real currency is back-scratching. This is not always for financial gain (and I am certainly NOT alleging or implying any financial motives or impropriety of any sort in this case), quite often it's simply a wee favour for a mate. You do them a good turn, and at some point in the future when you may need a good turn, they will be predisposed to help. It's the social grease that lubricates any business.

So I'm genuinely curious about the chain of events that led to this intervention, an intervention which was apparently far more important than any positive story about independence ever since the dawn of time, or at least since the dawn of the BBC. It must have been pure dead significant though, after all it made the main 6 O

Clock News on the BBC so even people in London could see it. It was followed up as the lead item in Reporting BetterTogether at half past, just to stress even more just how important it was. No pro-indy story has ever enjoyed such publicity on the Beeb.

I've never been one for conspiracy theories. When something goes awry it's usually a cock up not a conspiracy. Westminster is expert at cocking things up. And I have no knowledge about what transpired in the lead up to Bob Dudley's "gaunnae no vote for indy" moment.

However isn't it interesting that there are two very prominent pretendy Lords who are senior "advisers" to BP plc. I'm sure it's entirely coincidental, and I have no idea whether either of them have ever so much as mentioned the Scottish referendum in any of their contacts with Bob Dudley.

According to the House of Lords register of members interests, Chris Patten, former Tory cabinet minister, is a paid adviser to BP. That's the same Chris Patten who is also the Chairman of the BBC Trust. They have busy lives these folk.

Another high profile pretendy Lord with links to BP is George Robertson, former backing singer in the Tony Blair band and NATO lead singer who is best known for his hit records "Killing Nationalism Stone Dead", and "We Have No Culture or Language". According to the Lords register of interests he too is paid by BP plc as an adviser. His Wikipedia entry says he is a board member of TNK-BP, a Russian company jointly owned by some assorted Russian oligarchs and BP.

George and Bob go back some way together in BP. George was the white knight who rode to Bob's aid back in 2008 when Bob was President of TNK-BP. He made a statement to the media supporting Bob, who was at the time having some difficulties at the hands of the Russian authorities, as was reported by the BBC.

So if you were an American businessman, heid bummer of a company operating in Scotland and you were paying George Robertson as an adviser, and George had been so helpful to you in the past - what do you think - entirely hypothetically of course - that he would advise you to say about the independence referendum? Hmmm.

So what is it? Senior businessman in the oil business intervenes in the Scottish independence debate entirely off his own bat, or senior businessman in the oil business makes intervention in the indy debate because George Robertson or some other Unionist politician had a wee hand in helping Bob articulate his concerns, directly or indirectly? As Private Eye always says, I think we should be told. Because it makes a bit of a difference to the context of Bob Dudley's concerns, don't you think? "George Robertson's business associate makes intervention in independence debate" may not be an exciting headline, but it may be closer to reality than the BBC's presentation, in which Bob's words were received with the rapturous and unquestioning enthusiasm of the Pope getting a handwritten letter from the Virgin Mary.

I'm sure the next edition of Reporting Scotland will uncover the truth. Unless of course something more important comes up ... like overflowing litter bins in Airdrie and how it proves we can't hack it as an independent state.

6 February 2014
Defending Scotland's interests

This week Scotland has witnessed the Westminster state in all its arrogant and patronising glory. It started off so well over the weekend, with a series of good news stories for Scottish independence, but we're not allowed to dream of a future which isn't determined by Magrit Curran, the Fandabidozy Alistair Twins and the massed ranks of posh Tory public schoolboys, so the state propaganda department made sure that none of it was reported.

Instead we got a manufactured, and deeply implausible, scare story from the mooth of wee moothed George Robertson's pal in BP - killing nationalism stone dead by proxy. Then we got Alistair Koalamichael, aided and abetted by la Magrit, standing up in the Commons to make ritual denunciations of ordinary Scottish people who dare to challenge Westminster's agenda.

Alistair actually commended the Daily Mail's campaign of vilification of people who have broken no laws and committed no crimes, because the very worst thing possible is calling someone a rude name. Calling folk rude names is far worse than invading Iraq, axing housing benefit for the disabled or ill, or rewarding the bankers who brought the country to the brink of ruin. It's worse than lying, manipulating, threatening or bullying. Westminster does all those things, but they're doing it to preserve the Union, and that makes it hunky dory.

Even more remarkably, or perhaps not, Alistair denied that any vilification or hatred originated from no campaigners, saying : "I know of nobody suggesting that anybody on the pro-UK side of the debate has acted in that way."

Is he deaf and blind as well as stupid and blinkered? Or more to the point, does he think we are? Actually that's insulting to deaf blind people, who have a form of tactile sign language which allows them to communicate effectively with their hands. Alistair only feels things with his arse. The plooks on his bumcheeks spell out "I love being kicked by Tories" in braille. If the Unionist parties get their way and destroy Scotland's unprivatised NHS, the entire country will suffer from the same acne related condition. But Alistair thinks that's a good thing.

There's some vitriol fur ye Alistair, to add to your collection. The no campaign is defined by negativity, insults, abuse, and a simple minded reductionism. It's what they do. Alistair is like those antigay campaigners in the 80s and 90s who complained about dreadful homosexuals and how intolerant they are of decent homophobic bigots. And no, I'm not calling him a homophobe, I am merely pointing out that he employs the same tactics, albeit on a different target. When you are a hypocrite Alistair, you do not deserve respect.

So Nicola Sturgeon didn't receive death threats on Twitter, an elderly yes campaigner in Edinburgh wasn't attacked by a no supporter who broke his wrist, Alex Salmond has never ever ever not even once been called a dictator and didn't receive insulting and abusive messages after the death of his father, Simon Heffer's racist anti-Scottish diatribe in the Daily Mail was just a harmless wee joke, a unionist in Glasgow wasn't up in court this week on charges of sending death threats to yes campaigners, the abuse which litters the comment sections of any online newspaper - but not the BBC because it won't allow comments on Scottish stories - is entirely from yes supporters and there's no such thing as a unionist troll, pro-independence websites have not been subject to denial of service attacks, companies are not being pressurised or threatened by Westminster to make anti-independence statements ...

None of this has happened in Alistair's wee world, but apparently BP chief executive Bob Dudley was described as a British nationalist after his intervention in the indy debate, and that was terribly terribly wrong. It's a foul insult to call people nationalists as it might discourage them from participating in the debate.

If Alistair wanted to discover evidence of abuse originating from the Unionist campaign, he wouldn't have far to look. Much of it comes from his bosses. Lying to people, denying them access to full information, and threatening them is a form of abuse, yet it's Westminster's stock in trade, and Koalamichael has the enthusiastic support of Labour and the entire UK mainstream media. Alistair doesn't want to look, and he doesn't want anyone else to look either.

I'd glad Alistair has cleared everything up for us. It's reassuring to know that the Secretary of State for Scotland is doing such a sterling job of defending Scottish interests.

7 February 2014
Taking the Buchan out of buccaneering

Not content with lecturing Scotland from afar, David Cameron stood atop a podium in the Olympic velodrome in the East End of London on Friday and begged people in England, Wales, and Northern Ireland to lecture Scotland from afar as well. He wants folk in other parts of the UK to phone their Scottish friends and relatives to beg them not to vote for independence because he's unwilling to have a conversation with Scotland himself. He's quite happy to lecture and hector, but he runs back to nanny if there's any possibility that Scottish people might answer him back or ask him questions.

So instead we had the surreal experience of Cameron describing the UK as the most brilliant buccaneering country in history. I thought the world's most buccaneering country was Somalia, but never mind. It's unclear why Davie boy thinks buccaneering is a good thing, what with piracy being illegal under international law and everything, but he doesn't want Scotland to become independent because we'll take the Buchan out of his buccaneering. That just leaves him eerily erring.

Was Cameron saying we should take to fishing boats and hold North Sea ferries to ransom? It's more likely that our tin eared PM just doesn't know the difference between buccaneering - piracy, robbery, and hostage taking (which in themselves are the epitome of British Imperial values, although not ones Michael Gove wants to admit to) - and swashbuckling, which is pure dead glamorous if you're a 1930s movie star with a moustache to twiddle, as opposed to a Westminster politician talking twaddle. However when Scotland looks at Davie Cameron, we don't see Errol Flynn abseiling down a galleon's rigging, we see thon guy in the top hat tying a Scottish maiden onto a railway track and running away before anyone clocks him.

Cameron spoke in front of a backdrop draped in bicycles which looked like it was designed by Norman Tebbit, Thatcher's axeman who told unemployed Scots to get on their bikes and seek work dahn sarf. The subliminal message we were meant to receive was that this was the venue where Chris Hoy won his gold medal for Britain, because we're supposed to decide our country's future on the basis of whether some guy can pedal a bike really really fast. Instead the real lesson is that if we remain in the Union, future generations of Scots will have to get on their bikes and emigrate to find work. That's if they can afford a bike.

Davie had no answer for that, so he spoke of patriotism and attempted to make an emotional appeal to the heart. Wasn't it the Yes campaign that was supposed to be based on irrational emotions and an appeal to a rosy eyed version of the past? But that's all we get from Better Together because they have no positive case to make. They love us so much they threaten us with oblivion and poverty, they denigrate and diminish, insult and impugn. There's a difference between loving and stalking which Cameron doesn't seem to have picked up on.

He had nothing to say about the future, his speech was entirely about the past, appealing to the nostalgia of those who still believe that the UK is important and has the power to effect change in the world, as opposed to the dismal reality of a lapdog of the Pentagon which promises only more austerity and more savage cuts. Cameron doesn't care about Scotland, he only cares about his own role on the world stage. His patriotism is the patriotism of a personal ego massage. Scotland doesn't want to live in the past. We're looking to the future, and Westminster's brand of patriotism has nothing to offer.

Westminster's patriotism is the patriotism of selling off everything that's not nailed down to the highest bidder, the patriotism of tax avoiding big business, the patriotism of demonising the poor, and the patriotism of milking Scotland Wales and Northern England dry to finance the bloated ego projects like the Olympic Velodrome where Cameron delivered his sermon. Cheering for Britain doesn't come cheap.

The real issue, which Cameron conveniently overlooked, is that the Westminster Parliament doesn't cheer for the whole of the United Kingdom. It only cheers for the City of London, the banks, and feather bedding London and the South East and those on high salaries at the expense of the rest of the UK. The Tories have sold off all the institutions that once glued the United Kingdom together, it's scarcely surprising that few of us know what "Britishness" is supposed to mean nowadays. So they only have themselves to blame that Scotland has logged onto the website comparethepatriotismservicesprovider.com because we're not happy with the customer service or value for money we're getting from our current supplier. We've discovered that other options are available.

So he should applaud Scotland's decision to hold an independence referendum and see it as another instance of privatisation. He's very keen on flogging off national assets and making the state smaller. We can make Cameron's state smaller simply by putting an X next to the box marked YES, and take Westminster's bloated ego down a peg or three in the process.

That won't just be good for Scotland, it will be good for Wales, Northern Ireland, and the English regions too. No wonder the most highly rated comments on the BBC News site were those from folk in other parts of the UK urging us to vote Yes, and begging for us to take them with them. Those phone calls are going to be interesting.

9 February 2014

Better Together has an ely

Well that went well, didn't it. Despite being hailed by some random Tories, and even the Observer, as one of the most passionate and eloquent speeches Davie Cameron has ever delivered (there's low expectations for you), the reaction in Scotland to Cameron's plea for us to remain under his thumb, sorry, remain a part of bright and shiny Brand Britain, has been a mixture of anger and scorn.

Dave has reduced us to a brand. Marmite, that's a brand. The difference between Marmite and Dave is that even people who like Marmite would still be nauseated by seeing Dave over the breakfast table. The guy just doesn't get it. We're not interested in product promotion, but even if we were the basic expectation any of us have from an advert is that it tells us what the product will do for us. Dave couldn't even do that.

In history books yet to be written, Dave's wee impression of a used car salesman in the echoing emptiness of London's Olympic Velodrome will be seen as the moment when the Union was lost. What it showed was that the Westminster elite are blind to the perspective of Scotland, deaf to her voices, and do not feel the shifting of Caledonian tectonic plates.

Dave chose the venue because of the symbolism it represented, to him. All he has are symbols, there was nothing of substance in his words. He didn't understand that the value of a symbol is in the experience of the perceiver. He thought he was stirring up an image of a common British experience, but he could not see why a Tory lecturing Scotland from afar, in front of a row of bicycles, might stir up images of other Tories lecturing us to get on our bikes. The din of a distant Olympic roar deafened him to the complaint from Scotland that our taxes had helped pay for it, yet it brought no benefit to us - like so much Westminster does. He spoke of the damage to the prestige of a Parliament that most of us believe is already too arrogant by half.

Dave still thinks it's all about identity. That's the mistake he's been making since the independence campaign began. He hasn't realised that Scotland is already quite sure of its identity, it's an identity that doesn't need Westminster to define or validate it. And we're increasingly of the opinion that it's an identity that doesn't include Dave, a man who talks at us but never listens to us and won't be questioned by us. And who, most certainly, is not accountable to us.

All Dave's misjudged plea did was to confirm that opinion. How can he claim to share an identity with a country he doesn't even begin to understand? The immense irony of this debate is that despite the accusations of Better Together that independence will turn us into foreigners, we are already foreigners to Westminster. They do not even know who we are.

For the past year and a half, Better Together and the Tories have smugly congratulated themselves that all was going to plan. But as the polls show that the no vote continues to evaporate away, they're starting to get the awful feeling that something, somewhere, has gone terribly terribly wrong. While they've been talking down to us and talking us down via their total control of the mainstream media, people in Scotland have been talking amongst ourselves. We've been having a different conversation, a conversation about our future not our past.

The late great humourist Douglas Adams once published a book called the Meaning of Liff. Adams thought that there were many useful concepts for which the English language lacked words, and many words - in the form of place names - which have no modern meaning. So he decided to pair them up. Liff, the village near Dundee, was defined as "A book, the contents of which are totally belied by its cover. For instance, any book the dust jacket of which bears the words. 'This book will change your life." Spookily descriptive of just about any Better Together press release. Meanwhile the Cambridge city of Ely is "The first, tiniest inkling you get that something, somewhere, has gone terribly wrong." This week Better Together had an ely.

This realisation seems to have dawned on Tory MP and former Eton schoolboy Rory Stewart, the one that called for 100,000 Unionists to stand along Hadrian's Wall bearing torches so they can gaze northwards into Northumbria and ward off the advancing Picts. Not sure why he thinks that will help his cause, but it does give something of an indication of just how clueless English Tory MPs are about the Scottish referendum, even those who, like Rory, profess to be as Scottish as haggis pakora and Irn Bru.

On Friday night's Newsnight on BBC2, Rory went to a pub in the East End of Glesga along with the BBC's Alan Little in order to persuade a few Weegies that the Tories really get Scotland and would be diminished without us. Rory's the Ross Kemp of the posh end of the Tory party, and he was going to lovebomb where even Ruth Davidson's drones fear to fly. It was one of those "ooo let's get the popcorn" moments.

What Stewart discovered, much to his surprise, was that the independence debate isn't about identity, or even nationalism. He was genuinely perplexed. He was even more perplexed that the camera crew only managed to find a single No voter. He had the look of a general who had just discovered he'd won an overwhelming victory in the wrong war. It's not about Scotland's identity questions at all. It's about Westminster's.

Does Westminster stand for fairness, for equality? How does it express the will of the Scottish people? Does it listen? Is it accountable? Does it tell us the truth? The evidence suggests very strongly it does none of these things. That leaves the biggest concern of all, how is Westminster going to reform itself between now and September 18 to lay Scotland's concerns to rest.

Rory didn't have an answer. There isn't one. That's why Scotland is going to vote yes.

12 February 2014

Where did the love go?

To the list of things that are wrong with Better Together, we can now add premature ejaculation. There we were, lying back and thinking of Scotland and expecting a love bomb, it lasted 2 minutes and the only person who spurted was Dave. And the bastard never called. It's back to the scares and the threats.

It's the currency again. They're going to keep on at this one, because they reckon it gives them some traction. Sharing the pound is the only thing that Scotland is asking Westminster for after a yes vote, so Westminster wants to do its utmost to make out we won't get it.

Better Together operates on the unspoken assumption that many Scots traditionally had about our country, it's a relic of the cringe. This is the belief that Scotland is weak and powerless and holds no cards of its own. But that is very far from the truth. The truth is that there is far more that Westminster wants from Scotland than Scotland wants from Westminster. Better Together knows this too, which is why they're doing all they can to scare us.

Think about it logically. Let us suppose that Scotland has nothing that Westminster wants or needs. If that were the case, then the scare stories and hysteria being whipped up by Unionist politicians and their media hangers-on can only be motivated by a deep, selfless, and charitable concern for the well being of Scotland. They know us better than we know ourselves, and have only our best interests at heart. Stop laughing at the back there.

OK, having a low opinion of the altruism of Westminster is highly subjective, even if true and based upon many years of witnessing and suffering what passes for their altruism. However we need to be logical here and remove all personal feelings from the equation. This involves imagining that you are in a universe where George Osborne really does put Scotland's interests in his wee box of precious things - alongside his signed photie of Maggie Thatcher, his bank details and his gimp mask - so mind bending drugs may help.

Right, so Scotland is poor, weak, and helpless, kept afloat solely by the good graces and financial acumen of the UK Treasury, steered through the choppy waters of the big scary world by captains who love us and cherish us and let us on the boat for free. See, sometimes drugs do work.

We're a charity case with nothing to offer. But this is the condition Scotland is in after being governed by Westminster for over 300 years. The Union has left us as damaged goods, a basket case reduced to pleading for free passage. And that's despite the industry we no longer have and those we still do, like the oil and renewables and the whisky and all the rest. It happened even though we have a highly educated and skilled population who inhabit a country with an embarrassing excess of natural resources.

Someone must have mismanaged those resources terribly. Who could that have been then? Oh... And we're supposed to be Better Together with these people?

If you accept the premise of Better Together's case, it doesn't take long before you find yourself mired in logical contortions and confusion. There's more logic in a Tennessee school textbook that says we can't be descended from the apes because Ian Davidson is still around.

So let's be logical. An independent Scotland wants only one thing from Westminster - for them to stop being dickheads about a currency that's as much ours as it is theirs. The reason we hear so much about the currency is because it's the only card they have, so they want us to think that it's a high value card.

What do they want from us? Scotland has far more going for it than Westminster or Better Together want us to believe. We have some very strong cards indeed.

There's Trident, Westminster needs a new base for it and they can't just stick it in a multistorey carpark in Reading for the time being. They need us to be obliging about Faslane and Coulport until they can sort out an alternative. Or they could just abandon it and leave Scotland with the clean up and disposal costs. Which we could afford, since according to the time honoured legal principle of *quisquilliae defutatae tuae sunt, eas purgabis tu** we'd simply deduct the money from the amount of debt Westminster expects us to take on. Whatever way you look at it, we've got them by the ballistics.

And talking of that massive national debt that they want us to take a share of. That will be the national debt that Westminster has already conceded that it and it alone, will be responsible for after Scottish independence. £1.4 trillion of it. That's a lot of maxed out credit cards. Scotland could, if it wanted, walk away debt free. Sure, our international credit rating would be low for a couple of years, but since we'd be starting off with zero debt and an ocean's worth of assets we'd manage just fine. More than fine. We'll only take on debt in proportion to the assets we're due. Nae assets, nae debt. The pound is a shared asset too. Apparently it's one that Westminster values very highly, which must mean not getting our share in it must be worth oodles of debt we won't be taking on.

There's the status of the rUK as the sole successor state to the UK. There is a very strong legal case that Scotland could make in international courts that the rUK was not in fact the sole successor state. There is no guarantee that the rUK would win the argument, not all nations love Westminster the way that we're supposed to love David Cameron and Alistair Darling. Westminster requires Scotland not to object to its claim to sole successor state status.

And neither last nor least there's Scotland's substantial contribution to the UK's balance of payments. Without Scotland, the UK's deficit would double and they lose one third of their international exports. Business for Scotland has detailed the figures for those of you who can cope with figures. The bottom line is just that. If Scotland didn't use the pound the arse would fall out of it, because it would no longer be backed up by Scotland's massive contribution to the UK's balance of payments.

As if all of the above were not enough, Westminster cannot actually stop an independent Scotland from using the pound if we wanted to. What are they going to do, send hit squads to every Scottish branch of Tescos to stand by the till ensuring shoppers pay in euros, Canadian coins left over from visiting their auntie, and an unidentified token they found in their granddad's shed? Scotland can use the pound without any agreement with Westminster. Naturally that means Scotland won't have any control over the currency it uses - which is exactly what we have now. The difference is we'd also have an independent Parliament that controlled all the other economic levers. And this would be terribly bad for Scotland because ... ? Nope, I can't think of anything scary either.

But this scenario also means that Westminster has no control over when Scotland decides to stop using the pound, and switches to its own currency or adopts another existing currency. This would be bad for them because the demand in Scotland for rUK sterling would vanish overnight, and the currency would suddenly lose value.

Scotland will be free to make that decision when it suits Scotland, the Scottish Treasury will not be constrained by any agreements with the rUK Treasury. Scotland could switch to a new currency at a time of its own convenience, without having to concern itself with the effects on the pound or the economy of the rUK.

But hey, we give them the same degree of consideration they give us right? Mutual respect and good neighbourliness and all that...

The point is not to make threats. Better Together provides plenty of those all by itself and the independence cause isn't served by adding more. The point is that Scotland is not powerless against the threats from Westminster and Better Together. The threats they make prove only one thing - they need us more than we need them.

They're in no position to make demands, and they know it. The growing hysteria and mounting threats are because they're realising that more and more people in Scotland know it too. But it's not working. We're not scared.

 * *It's your fecking mess, you clean it up.*

13 February 2014

If you're going to tell a lie, tell a big one

Better Together, they're like a lonely hearts advert saying "Stalker seeks someone to love. Don't bother with a pic, I'll take one through your bedroom window while wearing a Maggie Thatcher fright mask." They've really not got the hang of this love bombing business have they.

Today we had George Osborne saying he would be "unable to recommend" a currency union between an independent Scotland and the rest of the UK. Like Scottish people care deeply about what Osborne recommends. And there was us thinking that he was going to rule it out definitely. Still, if Mark Carney's studiedly neutral speech was presented by the media as a major blow to independence hopes, it's easy to understand why our media sooked up George's words like viagra for the wilting Better Together campaign. They're treating us like idiots again.

It was another of the UK cabinet's hit and run exercises - paid for out of your tax bill. Osborne came up to Edinburgh and ran away back to London after taking a few questions from the tame media pack. He had no intention of debating the issues with anyone who might challenge his waffle. What the Chancellor of the Exchequer said was economically illiterate, intellectually risible, and morally bankrupt. Will this be pointed out by the economic experts trotted out by the BBC? Don't go holding your breath.

Never mind Project Fear, the guy in charge of the UK economy doesn't understand some of the most basic principles of finances and economics. The kind of principles that the rest of us understand every time we buy anything with a credit card. Now that's really scary. It's either that or he's lying through his teeth, which is equally unsettling. But what's scariest of all is that it's equally plausible that Osborne is ignorant or a liar - or indeed both simultaneously. My pounds sterling are on the latter.

George made the jawdropping claim that if Scotland refused to accept a part of the UK national debt because Westminster refuses to let us use the pound, we would be in default and would be castigated by the international markets. This is sheer nonsense. It is a lie of epic proportions, a big lie constructed out of wee lies and wrapped up in a multicoloured tissue of untruth.

You cannot default on a debt which doesn't have your name on it. The debt was issued by the UK government, it bears the name of the UK government, and the UK government has already stated that it alone is responsible for all existing UK debt. So how can Scotland default? The debt isn't in our name. In no legal system can you be held accountable for a debt which belongs to someone else.

There is precedent for this. When the Soviet Union broke up, all its national debt was inherited by Russia. The other former Soviet republics did not take on one rouble of the USSR's debts. They were not considered financial pariahs because of it. George's threat that Scotland would be a pariah is baseless. The only pariahs in Scotland are Tory MPs.

In fact Scotland is prepared to accept a proportional share of the UK national debt - even though we are under no legal obligation to do so - but only in return for a due share of UK assets. The proposition put forward by the Scottish Government is that if the UK Government deprives Scotland of her rightful assets, Scotland will not accept any debt relating to assets which Westminster retains in full. Nae assets, nae debt. It should be simple enough even for George to grasp.

In order to make the claim that Scotland would be defaulting on its debt, George sought to deny that sterling is a joint asset. If sterling isn't an asset then Scotland cannot justifiably claim a share in it. George dismissed Scotland's claim to joint ownership of the pound, saying it wasn't a CD collection. Which is true. Stick a tenner in your CD player and it won't play anything by the Better Together Toryboyband. A currency is not a thing, it's an abstract concept.

Continuing with the CD collection metaphor, Osborne wants us to believe that the debt the UK accrued building up its collection of the greatest hits of the Royal Artillery Marching band and its expertise in bunting bedecked musical interludes will be Scottish debt after independence, even though George is hanging on to all the CDs, the sheet music and the stage directions. We walk away from ownership of the Philip Sousa band, he told us, but oddly he doesn't want us to walk away from the costs involved in acquiring it, training it, and developing it. In George's wee world, Scotland should still be financially liable for the UK even after we've become independent. This is such an arrant nonsense that it really shouldn't need to be pointed out.

For George, ownership apparently only extends to physical objects. A man who worships filthy lucre, who comprehends worth only in monetary terms, and he's unaware of the concept of intellectual property. Sterling has a reputation in the international money markets, it's a reputation based in part upon the massive contribution Scotland has made to the Union - you know all that oil, whisky, industrial exports, and the rest. Sterling is like the goodwill and reputation built up by an existing business, which influences its value when the owners decide to sell. The UK's reputation for financial stability, the reputation George wants to protect, only exists because Scotland contributed to building it up. That reputation is as much ours as it is the rUK's.

However if we were to accept George's view that sterling is not an asset - then by definition it cannot possess any worth or value. Perhaps he views sterling like a much loved and battered teddy bear or a used rubber bondage outfit. No one else wants them, but George really loves them. Which in turn raises the question of why he's so keen to maintain sole possession of something which is worth nothing commercially.

And all this over a non-issue. Because Scotland doesn't require Westminster's agreement to use the pound, as has been pointed out by organisations like the Adam Smith Institute, no friends of Scottish indy. It's worth repeating their comments in full.

Sam Bowman, director of the Adam Smith Institute said:

"An independent Scotland would not need England's permission to continue using the pound sterling, and in fact would be better off using the pound without such permission.

"There is very little that an English government would actually be able to do to stop Scottish people from continuing to use the pound sterling if they wanted to.

"As the American economist George Selgin has pointed out, what the Prime Minster really means is that the Bank of England would not act as a guarantor for Scottish banks or the Scottish government. Lucky Scotland: the implied promise of a bailout from the European Central Bank is exactly what allowed Eurozone banks and governments to borrow cheaply and get themselves into a debt crisis.

"Scotland's position would be closer to that of countries like Panama, Ecuador and El Salvador, which use the US Dollar without American "permission", and, according to research by the Federal Reserve of Atlanta, consequentially have far more prudent and stable financial systems than if they were part of a formal currency union.

"An independent Scotland that used the pound as its base currency without the English government's permission, with banks continuing to issue notes privately and private citizens free to choose any currency they wanted, would probably have a more stable financial system and economy than England itself.

"It's up to Scots to decide whether they want independence, but the Chancellor's announcement today should be seen as a feature, not a bug."

Whatever way you look at Better Together's arguments, they mire you in confusion and contradiction. So no change there then. Just more lies, more threats, and more fear. And this shower of miserablist selfish self-servers want us to think that we're Better Together with them. They're not painting a very attractive picture of themselves are they.

14 February 2014

The Fat Man of Fear Bombs

According to the Herald, a "senior figure" in the Coalition UK government has said that even if Scotland delivers a yes vote in September's referendum, this does not necessarily mean that Scotland will become independent. Described as a "senior colleague" of David Cameron, the anonymous source said that Westminster would refuse to grant Scotland independence if we refuse to roll over and let them kick us in the nads. Westminster's idea of negotiation is for Scotland to agree to each and every demand they make of us. Demands like "We'll tell you how much debt you'll take on and what assets, if any, we let you get. And you'd better be grateful."

Yes, he really did say that. If "independence talks "do not go smoothly" from the point of view of Westminster, "the status quo would be maintained". Conversations like these between anonymous sources and journalists are conducted in a form of code. What was really meant was the following:

"The Edinburgh Agreement was just a ploy to get Alex Salmond to shut up," said the unknown ToryDem, "we never meant for anyone to take it seriously. We never took the referendum seriously. We've never taken Scotland seriously. To be honest we thought that we'd get a massive majority for the Union without breaking into a sweat and the whole Scottish question would just go away.

"Now it looks like the Scottish question won't just go away, the rest of Scotland will go with it. We haven't just broken into a sweat, we're shitting bricks.

"Some people think that the Tories would benefit from losing Scotland. But if Cameron loses Scotland he'd face a vote of confidence in the Commons, especially after it comes out just how bad the accounts are without our Caledonian top up. And we've spent the past couple of decades telling voters in England that we subsidise Scotland - they'll be expecting tax cuts if Scotland leaves.

"Cameron will lose the vote of confidence. There would be an early election, and we'd all be annihilated. Dave's screwed. George is screwed in a way he doesn't enjoy. Danny Alexander's totally screwed. Michael Gove will be screwed and foreign. We're all screwed. We didn't plan for this. So we're pressing the nuclear fearbomb button.

"We've changed our minds. Screw independence negotiations. There won't be an electoral backlash in England over it, and who gives a shit what the Scots think. We've always told you what you're going to do, and voting yes won't change anything. We're the sovereign Parliament and we won't give you independence unless you do what we tell you. The Union is the default position.

"Mind you we also said that voting no was the default position, so perhaps that's not such a great example... "

The signs are the nuclear fearbomb is a bit of a dud. It went off with the explosive force of a pettit lip. So far, amongst other belters, Scotland has been threatened with having our airports bombed, our power stations destroyed by terrorists, and the forcible annexation of Faslane, all of which are exciting and dramatic scare stories which could very well involve James Bond, fireworks, explosions, and even a secret underground lair. And they'd already be in 3 D so we wouldn't have to pay extra for the special glasses. This is how we judge a good scare story in Scotland these days.

So when Georgie boy came to Embra promising a nuclear scarebomb, we ought to have got something really spectacular. But unfortunately George has not been paying attention to the development of the BetterTogether franchise, so what we got was: "We won't let the Bank of England be your lender of last resort, even if it means hacking off my own limbs."

It's a scare of two halves, but it scores null points for dramatic impact. We'd only care about George's self-harming if we cared about George. They're your limbs George, hack away.

What it means is that an independent Scotland wouldn't have the Bank of England to bail out our financial sector, so Scotland will have to introduce strict regulation to stop Scottish banks indulging in the wilder excesses of casino capitalism and make sure they behave responsibly. Wow George, that's such a scary threat. I'll be sure to vote no now. Imagine those poor bank executives we'll be disappointing.

That would be the consequences for Scotland, and naturally we'd be debt free since we'd be deprived of our assets, like our share of the assets of the Bank of England which include over a quarter of the UK's national debt. We'd have no credit rating, but we're a peaceful democratic country in a quiet and stable part of the globe, with a highly developed economy and a shitload of natural and human resources. We would still find lenders and investors.

That's what's really got George worried. For all his talk of Scotland "reneging" or "defaulting", he knows that we'd be perfectly within our rights to refuse to accept the debt if we are deprived of our due share of the assets. And for all their bluster over Scotland's powerlessness and lack of friends in the world, Westminster knows that Scotland would insist the matter was put to international arbitration. How confident are they they'd win their case? Not very, judging by the loudness of the squealing.

Today's revelation in the Herald is part 2 of George's nuclear fearbombing campaign. He really really means it, because the stuff about the debt has the Treasury well spooked. So George came to Edinburgh and dropped Little Boy, now some anonymous briefer has dropped Fat Man via the Herald.

It will land with all the explosive impact of Eric Pickles falling into a muddy puddle in Somerset.

15 February 2014
Ed Balls signs Labour's suicide note

This week the UK Labour party in Scotland signed their suicide note. It was for the best, the party has been dead from the neck up for decades, and the body is atrophied and weak. All that is left is for it to be buried. If we plant an independent tree on the grave it can take the nourishment left in the rotten carcass, and grow into something vibrant and fresh. That's the only thing that Labour in Scotland is fit for now.

The events of the past few days have stripped away any pretence that the party leadership has the slightest concern for the best interests of people in Scotland. For the Labour hierarchy, the sole imperative is winning UK General Elections. That's all the party exists for, that's all it does. It has no real idea of what it will do when it gains power, gaining power is the means and the end. The Labour hierarchy is as imperious as the Tories when it comes to the absolute power of the Westminster Parliament.

Tony Blair, Jack Straw, John Prescott. Nuff said. All have offspring who have been selected as Labour Parliamentary candidates or who hope to be. Euan Blair, Will Straw, and David Prescott hope to repeat the ploy previously played by the Sarwar and Martin clans in Glasgow. In the English town of Corby, local Labour MP Andy Sawford also inherited his seat from his dad. Ed and David Miliband owe their preferment within Labour to their late father's party connections, as do Wee Dougie and Wendy Alexander. Labour's local government spokesman, Hilary Benn MP, is the son of Tony Benn, and Tony's granddaughter Emily is set to become a Labour councillor. Jack Dromey's selection as a Labour MP was not unrelated to the fact that his wife is Harriet Harman, he was also considerably aided by his extensive links to the trades unions. And it was recently reported that Jack and Harriet's son Joe is very interested in seeking selection as a Labour candidate. What's the betting he's got a better chance of making it than a random Labour activist from Motherwell?

The next generation of Labour politicians will be the same as the last. Labour is as dynastic as North Korea. The key to advancement in the party is family and social connections, not politics or policies - a strategy which blew up in Labour's face in Falkirk. But as the wreckage fell around the workers at Grangemouth the party leadership was nowhere to be seen. Like the Catholic hierarchy when faced with child abuse scandals, the priority of Labour's leadership was to protect its own reputation and standing.

It's clear now that when you vote Labour, you're voting for someone else's interests. You're voting so that a self-selecting political elite can continue to rule us like lairds, collecting our votes in lieu of rent. And if the party perceives anything that might stand between the leadership and their career plans, it will be evicted as ruthlessly as a crofter in the Clearances.

This week the party reached a nadir not seen since George Cunningham's shameless betrayal of democracy in 1979, when on the eve of the Home Rule referendum the Scottish born Labour MP for Islington introduced a measure ensuring that the votes of the dead counted as no. Labour's shadow chancellor Ed Balls stood shoulder to shoulder with George Osborne and Danny Alexander to threaten and bully Scotland and demand that even after independence Scotland must bend its knee and submit to Westminster's will.

Labour is as complicit as the Tories in the theft of Scottish assets. Theft is the accurate term for it. Labour, the Tories, and the Lib Dems have come together to assert that the Bank of England will not be shared with Scotland. It's a state owned institution with assests totalling £402.8 billion, but Scotland will get no part of it.

A large part of the assets owned by the Bank of England consists of debt owed to the bank by the UK Government. Much of this money was created out of thin air as a part of Quantatitive Easing, which the BoE spent on buying up UK Government bonds. The UK Government pays the interest on these bonds to the Bank of England, which in turn repays it to the UK Treasury. Scotland issued this debt along with the rest of the UK, but Westminster wants Scotland to repay it to them alone.

Labour, along with the Tories and the Lib Dems, want Scotland to take on its share of this debt but without conceding that Scotland is also an issuer of it, so that the debt repayments will continue to flow into the coffers of the UK Treasury and Scotland won't see a penny. We're just a colony which must do as it's told. So much for the world's most successful partnership of nations.

Westminster in its arrogance believes that Scotland must continue to subsidise the UK Treasury even after independence, while they deprive Scotland of assets that are rightfully ours. Above all they want to deprive Scotland of the very assets that would reduce the debt burden on a newly independent state. That's why the Scottish Government is hinting that it may refuse to accept a share of Westminster's debt, and they are perfectly justified in doing so.

The reason for all this is obvious. Scottish independence will expose just how much cash flowed from Scotland to the Thames, it's a greater figure than even official figures suggest. The UK parties have spent the last 3 decades persuading voters in the rest of the UK that Scots are subsidy junkies. When the truth comes out the electorate of England, Wales and Northern Ireland will be furious that they have been lied to for years.

Labour voters in Scotland were infuriated this week when Ed Balls sang from the same songsheet as George Osborne. The threats and bullying were identical. Vote Labour, vote team Tory.

As a full time carer who has to remain at home most of the time, I'm scarcely in any position to gauge public reaction. But the other evening my brother and sister in law called to ask me what Osborne and Balls really meant. They were convinced it was just more scaremongering, and wanted their opinion confirmed. They were angry with the Tories, the default position for the average Glaswegian, but most of their ire was directed at the Labour party they've always voted for. I'd always had them down as leaning towards a no vote, but that's changed now.

And it was the same story with two other acquaintances. Unprompted, both spoke to me about their disgust and anger that Westminster politicians were shamelessly bullying and threatening Scotland. They don't understand the details of quantatitive easing - neither do I - but they know enough to see that we're being ripped off. It's like a mugger telling you you ought to be grateful that he's taking your purse. Both were previously don't knows, both are now inclined heavily to yes.

A few wee straws in the wind, but the same story is repeating itself in homes across Scotland. We have seen that the UK parties are incapable of coming together to offer us the increased devolution most of us wanted before the referendum campaign started, but that they'll come together at the drop of a credit note in order to steal from us. They have revealed themselves to us in all their avaricious and mendacious glory as the penny drops that this referendum will not be the shoe-in for the Union that they had expected. The panic has scarcely started.

Judging from the response so far, all they've done is to alienate Scotland even further. Labour signed its death warrant this week. They signed the death warrant for the UK too.

20 February 2014

Wowie Bowie

Written after David Bowie intervened by proxy in the referendum debate.

There's god-awful cuts in welfare
and Scotland's saying nae mair
But the Tories are yelling "No"
though we've told them we want them to go
And Johann is nowhere to be seen
As she walks
through the shattered dream
of a party that's gone true blue
Labour's hooked to the Tory scheme
But Westminster's a saddening bore
For we've seen it
ten times or more
So we'll spit in the eyes of fools
As Scotland will focus on
MPs lying through their back teeth
Oh man!
Look at those cavemen go
it's the Commons freak show
Take a look at the pressman
Feeding all the Scots lies,
Oh man! But we already know
It's a one sided show
There's no truth on Marr.
It's to Osborne's threatening vow
That our country
will not kowtow
And we Scots will rule our ain hame

so we can't be sold out again
by the media's ignorant hordes and careerists and the hopes they've
whored
So we'll keep on using the pound
and are deaf to the scares of clowns
'Cause Westminster's a saddening bore
and we've stood it
ten times or more
Vote no and it comes again
And that's why we focus on
Food banks stretching down the high street
Oh man!
But what would a rich singer know
about this Tory freak show
Take a look at the pressman
Feeding all the Scots lies,
Oh man! But we already know
It's just the Westminster show
There's no truth on Marr.

21 February 2014

The fearbomb hat-trick

There's something that's been bugging me for a while. It's Irish people. Not that Irish people bug me, far from it. It's the total absence of discussion of Ireland and the Irish in the context of this debate Scotland is currently having about who is furren and who isn't.

Speaking personally, and I'm quite sure my sentiments are shared by the overwhelming majority of Scots, Irish people are no more nor less foreign than English people or Welsh people. Which is to say, not very foreign at all then. People who know what tottie scones and sodie breid are can't possibly be foreign, even if they do call them potato farls and soda bread.

So the question I keep coming back to, when I hear Unionists warn in the direst terms about the awfulness of us becoming foreigners to the rest of the UK and breaking those shared bonds we have, is what exactly is it we share in terms of culture, identity and history with the Welsh and the English, but not with the Irish as well? Because all those shared things are shared quite independently of the bonds of the Westminster Parliament, which seems to be the only bond in the equation - we're bound by their decisions and don't have much in the way of remedy. More a shackle than a bond.

The bad news for the Better Together mob is that the only single answer is "the Royal family". It's dubious whether the Windsors could be considered "culture", though they are a parasitic growth which could be grown in a petri dish, so I suppose that's culture of a sort.

However Irish people tend to have quite strong opinions about the British monarchy, especially those in the northern bits, but it's also far from foreign amongst those in the Republic. This is not something you often find amongst people in properly foreign parts. Properly foreign foreigners have no more interest in the Windsors than the average Scottish person has in the King of Thailand. Can you name the King of Thailand without Googling it? No. Neither can I.

In any event we'd still have that particular circus after independence, what with Liz already being Queen of Scots quite separately from her claim to the throne of England - or to give her her more accurate title north of the border, "Queen of Those Scots Who Give a Shit About the Monarchy". There's more than a few Scots who fully intend to press for us to go down the Irish route with respect to the Windsors just as soon as we get independence, so republican sentiments are not really something we can be told we don't share with Ireland.

This can only mean that citizens of the Irish Republic are foreigners who have cunningly disguised themselves not to seem foreign at all. So even if we do end up as foreigners to the rest of the UK if we vote for independence, we can just borrow the cloaking technology from Dublin. Sorted.

However some clown in the Telegraph was opining the other day that since the UK is a constitutional monarchy where the sovereign is bound to act on the advice of the Prime Minister, Davie could have a wee word in Liz's shell-like and advise her not to become Queen of Scots after independence. Bash. Kapowie. Blam. Take that Scottish separatists. You'll be proper foreigners without the Queen.

Peter Oborne, who apparently gets paid to write this stuff, wrote:

"Cameron has already denied Scotland the pound sterling. He is entitled to deny the Scots the House of Windsor, especially since the Scots had their own separate monarch before James the VI and I unified the crowns of England and Scotland in 1603."

He then goes on to suggest Scotland invites this mad auld Spanish bat to become Queen, the conveniently titled Duquesa de Alba, because she's a direct descendant of the Stuarts and has an unfortunate resemblance to Phil Spector in drag. At first I thought he might be making a witty play on the wummin's title and the Gaelic name for Scotland, but that would require some actual knowledge of the country Oborne is so ready to denigrate.

His staggering lack of understanding was already illustrated in his first sentence, when he said Cameron had "denied Scotland the pound", so I should have realised. Scotland can't be denied the pound, we can use it without Westminster's permission - and we can leave the debt behind too. This might not be the preferred option of the Scottish Government, which proposes to be studiously reasonable and helpful to the UK Treasury post-independence, but it sure as hell is mine.

The only reason Oborne mentioned la Duquesa is because she's stinking rich. Obscenely rich. This allows him to make a Metropolitan sneer about how she'd be able to bail Scotland out. Oborne, like the rest of the London commentariat, suffers from the quaint delusion that Scotland is the Big Issue Seller of Europe, dependent upon the charity of good people like him. And we jolly well ought to be grateful. Someone's in for an unpleasant shock after Scottish independence, and it's not going to be Scottish people.

Nevertheless, I'd like to add my wee voice to Oborne's plea to Cameron to tell Liz she can't come over all queeny in Scotland. It would save Scottish republicans the bother of having to campaign for a republic post-independence, and it would piss off Scottish monarchists no end and drive them into the yes camp. So it's a win win.

We'll have our Dublin made not-foreign cloaking devices, a Scottish republic, we'll still use the pound and have no national debt. Thank you Westminster for giving us the hat-trick. Can we have more of these fearbombs please? They're really pretty tasty.

22 February 2014

Nul points

Project Fear has got around to delivering a special fearbomb just for Scotland's gay community, or more specifically, middle aged gay men who find the Eurovision song contest hysterically funny. Exploding in a shower of sparkly dust and some cast off feather boas came the threat that Scotland won't be allowed to enter the Eurovision song contest if we become independent.

The rest of Europe will enjoy an evening of expressing historical grievances through the medium of collective camp, but there will be no spangly tartan fabulosity for Scotland set to a dire tune with meaningless lyrics, and we'll be left with the drab surroundings of a karaoke hymn night at John Mason's church. Or if we're really lucky, indoor bowling from Coatbridge.

The Daily Mail, thrilled that it had finally found a way to piss off gay people, lovers of kitsch, and Scots simultaneously, reported that an independent Scotland would be forced to leave the European Broadcasting Union and would have to reapply to join. The EBU is the international association of broadcasters which organises the Eurovision Song Contest, and entry is only open to EBU members. So it's the whole EU schtick all over again, only this time we'll be vetoed by a chorus line of Slovenian drag queens dressed as air hostesses.

According to the Mail, when they telephoned the press guy at the EBU fishing for a quote they could manufacture into a scare story, he told them that membership of the organisation is not automatic.

So there ye go. Membership is not automatic. That's us telt then. Without the blessings of the UK we'll never get to score nul points. That's just how crap we are, we can't even fail properly, we need the BBC to fail on our behalf. Scotland could never dream of producing an artiste with the expressive range and sensitive vision of a UK Eurovision entry like the Brotherhood of Man. We have no clapped out performers well past their sell by date as we've exported them all - there's another Union benefit we'd never considered - although it might be a possible new career for Ian Davidson after independence.

Mind you the thought of a bespangled Ian Davidson singing Save All Your Kisses For Me goes so far beyond the line between bad and so bad it's funny it ends up somewhere deeply disturbing. So maybe not.

However it seems that the substance of the Mail's scare lay in nothing more than the statement that membership of the EBU is not automatic. Which presumably means there are conditions which must be fulfilled for membership. The Mail did not specify what these conditions might be, it sufficed to tell us that the list was "long and complicated", but it's probably a safe bet that one of them is that there must actually be a Scottish national broadcaster to apply for membership, and a set of Scottish broadcasting regulations for it to operate under.

Unaware that telling us we don't currently have a Scottish national broadcaster or control over our own broadcast media is actually a reason for independence and not a threat as such, the Mail ploughed on in its very own descent into so bad it's funny kitsch.

In all seriousness, the paper warned that Spain might veto Scottish membership in case it gives the Catalans the subversive notion that they too have the sovereign right to demonstrate an affection for camp self mockery while singing Ring-dinge-ding. Mariano Rajoy is already looking for a clause in the Spanish constitution that forbids it.

Certain by now that Scots will vote no when we realise that we won't be able to join the Nordic block voting bloc after all, and smugly exchange douze points with Iceland every year because we're both world renowned experts in tastefully shot videos of people in knitwear singing on mountaintops in the rain, the Mail explained that we'll lose the UK's opt-out, or rather opt-in. The UK is one of the big five you see. Britain's vapid pop star wannabes are vapid pop star wannabes with a seat at the big table. The BBC, and the national broadcasters of Spain, Italy France and Germany pay the largest share of the costs of the contest, their entries automatically get through to the final so Graham Norton can witter some cheery double entendres about them.

Scotland would have to go through the qualifying rounds and get to the back of the Graham Norton banter queue. It could be like the World Cup in Argentina all over again, same piss poor choreography, only with sequins. The very horror.

However the number of Scots whose decision about how to vote in September depends heavily on our chances of Eurovision success is probably equal to the number of votes secured by the UK's dire Eurovision entry in 2003. It scored nul points too. And falling into the category of ye couldnae make it up, the song was called Cry Baby.

Project Fear, another Cry Baby that's scoring nul points.

23 February 2014
Puerile bile and contemptuous invective

We're doing things all wrong you know. After spending the past 18 months or so sneering contemptuously, ignoring all positive arguments for independence, and belittling Scotland's chances of making it as an independent state, the Observer/Guardian has decided that Scots are not having the debate we're supposed to be having. Apparently we're being childish and puerile. And this from the paper whose response to the announcement of the referendum question was to publish a cartoon saying "Do you think that Scotland should just f*** off."

In Guardian Towers the view is that there's too much bile in the independence debate. No shit Guardian. And it's mostly coming from the pages of Guardian editorials, aided and abetted by the Daily Mail, the Telegraph, and the BBC.

I'm quite happy to admit that my blog posts are often childish and puerile. I can do contempt and invective too. That's the appropriate response to being treated like an idiot, and being patronised and dismissed by clueless ignoramuses whose knowledge of Scotland and its political landscape begins and ends with a vague awareness that Scotland doesn't like the Tory party. Contempt and scorn is the only possible reply to Unionist politicians and their media outlets who deliberately lie and misinform in order to preserve their career prospects. You can't have a debate with liars.

But it seems that it's just childish bile to point this out. Calling someone a liar is unhelpful to a debate, even when they are indeed liars and so are preventing the possibility of any meaningful debate taking place. In fact, that's the entire strategy of the Tory funded Better Together campaign and its peculiar lack of any public engagement.

Westminster didn't want this debate to happen, doesn't want electors to engage with it, and is doing its utmost to cover the entire process in mud and misunderstanding in an effort to prevent Scots from participating. Only one side is represented in the media. It's the exact opposite of a debate in a representative democracy.

And the Guardian/Observer enthusiastically goes along with it. So much for their liberal credentials. We expect this sort of thing from the Mail or the Telegraph. But when the supposedly progressive Guardian does it too it adds an extra seasoning of hypocrisy to the bubbling pot of bile. It's a recipe from the George Osborne Cookbook.

Because there is no doubt about it. Does the Guardian/Observer honestly believe that Alistair Darling and George Osborne don't know that Scotland cannot legally default on UK national debt? Does it understand that our political masters know that Scotland cannot be prevented from using Sterling? Does it believe that Barroso didn't know that in making his statement on Scottish independence he was exceeding his authority, interfering in subjects that are not his to opine on, and undermining the democratic basis of the EU Treaties?

Does the Guardian/Observer not know all these facts too? Because if that's the case, what is it doing describing itself as a newspaper - there's more rigorous investigative journalism in a primary school newsletter.

And if the writer of Guardian/Observer editorials does understand the simple and self-evident truth, that Scotland cannot be prevented from using Sterling and no one can be held legally responsible for a debt in someone else's name, and that the EU is pledged to support, defend, and *accept* the legitimate constitutional processes of representative democracy in member states, then it's still not a newspaper, it's a lying propaganda sheet. And as previously pointed out, you cannot have a debate with a liar.

Unionist politicans have many many faults. But they are not actually suffering from perceptual disorders or learning difficulties. I understand how dementia affects a human being, and Alistair Darling doesn't suffer from it. That doesn't prevent him conveniently forgetting things he said just a few weeks or months ago - like his statement that a currency union would be in the best interests of both Scotland and the rest of the UK.

They know the truth. They just choose not to tell it, and the Guardian/Observer, the BBC and the rest of the Unionist media pack choose not to investigate the veracity of their statements. They simply present them uncritically as a "major blow to independence".

This is our debate Guardian/Observer. We will have it on our terms, not yours. And we've been having an informative and bile free debate here in Scotland. You're just not reporting it. Scotland welcomes you to participate if you want to participate in a real debate. But if the paper is going to continue to lie, smear, misinform and patronise, the Guardian/Observer and its leader writers can just fuck off - and you can take Alistair Darling, George Osborne, and Alistair Carmichael with you. There's some puerile invective you can add to your collection.

March 2014

3 March 2014

Back from London, but London's not backing Scotland

Well I'm back from my visit to London. Had a great time in the belly of the beast. It's a great place to visit, but I wouldn't want to live there. Unfortunately, if we vote no in the referendum we won't have much choice. We'll be a suburb of London whether we like it or not.

Meanwhile Michael White, the Guardian's chief political bod, has decided it's time to lift his wee heid out of the Westminster bubble for all of 10 minutes to pass down his words of wisdom on the speech given by Alex Salmond to the New Statesman. Michael thinks that Eck made a fine speech, but the Guardian's politics savant is still not convinced by the case for independence. Now there's a surprise.

According to some statistics which were scrawled down on a fag packet by a random drunk person in a pub, and are therefore considerably more reliable than anything that issues from the Office for Budget Responsibility, 97% of people in Scotland have never heard of Michael White. 2.95% of Scottish people are vaguely aware who Michael White is but don't give a toss about his opinion. Meanwhile 0.049998% are indeed interested in Michael's opinion, but only so they can snort derisively at it in the Guardian's comments section. Which leaves 0.000002% who believe Michael's opinion is a serious and significant contribution to the debate, that would be Blair McDougall.

Michael's description of the Scottish debate is like reading a review of a movie by someone who hasn't seen the film, hasn't read the book it's based upon, and doesn't know that the book is non-fiction and not a novel. It's not just that Michael lacks knowledge of Scotland, he struggles with the distinction between the Scottish constitutional claim and that Broons strip where Daphne got jealous of Maggie's new hat.

The Guardian puts the anal in Scottish political analysis. The Guardian's chief political analyst's argument against independence can be summed up in a single sentence, which saves the bother of reading his piece. It boils down to "wanting Scottish independence is just like supporting UKIP". He writes:

They all [UKIP and supporters of Scottish independence] invite us to believe that everything would be easier if we could only be free of international obligations - not free of the benefits, of course, but free of the costs and the constraints.

The constraints on Scotland which Mikey so lightly glosses over are considerably more onerous in the case of Westminster and Scotland than anything the EU imposes on the UK. The EU does not decide whether the UK goes to war. It does not decide what UK spending priorities should be. It does not collect all our taxes and give us some back in return, calling it a subsidy. UKIP and Scottish independence supporters are not opposed to similar obligations. But that's only the start of the differences that Mikey is blind to.

UKIP wants to take the UK - and Scotland with it - out of the EU to exist in a glorious isolation where our political elites are free to ape the worst excesses of US capitalism all wrapped up in the vinegar soaked brown paper of a Little Englander's Romanian phrase book, whereas Scotland wants independence so it can connect directly to Europe and the wider world without David Cameron or Nigel Farage as intermediaries. This is not a distinction that Michael has considered. Or is even aware of. He still thinks it's about Daphne's hat. He doesn't bother offering us any method of solving the questions and the troubling lack of accountability or any commitment to equality in the UK. He contents himself with the observation that Ed Miliband's vision of social democracy has yet to take hold. Once it does, it will be like sprinkling the debate with a thick coating of magic fairy dust. Or maybe not.

As political analysis Michael's Caledonian musings are not even anal, he just makes an arse of them. It's more than a wee bit alarming that a politics guru can't get over the simple word "nationalism" and appreciate that common or garden words mean different things in different contexts and that this is true in spades of political words. You'd think that would be the most basic tool of his trade.

The goal of a movement which seeks self determination for a country without a state is qualitatively different from the nationalism of a political party which seeks to aggrandise an existing state and isolate it from the world in a red white and blue wet dream. The goal of Scottish independence is diametrically opposed to the goal of UKIP, and many if not most supporters of Scottish independence are nationalist only in so much as they recognise the existence of Scotland as a nation.

Recognising the existence of matter doesn't make you a materialist, recognising the existence of Scotland as a nation doesn't make you a nationalist. It makes you a realist. And the only realistic way in which Scotland can find and act upon solutions to the many problems which confront this country is to have the powers that independence bring. Westminster isn't going to solve our problems for us, they're too busy milking us dry to feed the beast that is London. That much ought to be clear even to the most thrawn Guardian political correspondent.

But Michael is representative of the dominant view of Scotland in the Westminster bubble. It's a view best exemplified by the recent BBC2 documentary Mind the Gap, which supposedly explored the effect that the increasing dominance of London is having on the rest of the UK. The programme told us that London is a UK national asset. Fair enough, in that case Scotland is owed - at the very least - Camden, 3 tube lines, a chunk of Crossrail, and Chinatown - because we like Asian food and aren't afraid of immigration.

The programme offered us a paean to London's growth at the expense of the rest of the UK, and told us that not only was it inevitable, but there is no alternative. Scotland is merely the most distant of London's suburbs, far beyond the end of the Metropolitan line where it can safely be forgotten. If you cannae get somewhere with an Oyster card it's probably not worth bothering about.

Although touted as an examination of the tensions that London's economic and political dominance were causing, the programme got through its entire 1 hour running length without mentioning the biggest tension of all, the possibility that Scotland will reject Westminster's decision to treat the rest of the UK as a supplier of people, capital, skills and talent for London's benefit and that we will take 10% of the population, 30% of the landmass, 37% of the balance of trade, and over 90% of the oil with us.

In the view from the London commentariat, Scotland, her needs, her distinctiveness, her challenges and her opportunities are entirely invisible. When they do force their way onto the Westminster agenda, they are met with a mixture of contempt, scorn, and utter incomprehension. They can countenance no alternative to putting all our eggs in London's financial basket.

And that's why Michael White sees UKIP and Scottish independence as evil twins. In very different ways both threaten the dominance of the London that White has made his career in. UKIP threatens to take London out of Europe and isolate a city that depends upon networking and communication with other financial centres. Scotland threatens to take away a significant part of the wealth and resources that the city requires to operate. For Michael and his ilk, the rest of the UK exists to service London. Scotland's argument, that this wealth and these resources should be used to benefit and develop the nation of Scotland, is not an argument that is easily understood by the Metrocommentariat. They can't see the difference between Scotland and Stevenage.

Is Scotland a country, or a neglected far off suburb? We can be a country which makes its own decisions and forges its own path in free cooperation with other nations, or we can be a dingy station at the far end of a closed down London commuter line.

I know which I prefer.

7 March 2014

Outshined by a potato

John McTernan, former aide to Tony Blair and erstwhile special advisor to Jim Murphy, has been crowing in the pages of the Scotsman that the independence referendum has already been won for the Union. The nasty separatists have lost, brought down by the combined forces of the Westminster Avengers. George Osborne will grasp at any opportunity to dress up as Captain America in a skin tight leotard, and Ed Balls was hoping his Iron Man costume would let him outshine Ed Miliband. Though to be honest, you can do that with a potato.* Even Wee Danny Alexander was thrilled when he was asked to play the comedy sidekick.

And ever since then we've had a succession of concerned businesspersons with absolutely no business or personal connections to former UK cabinet ministers lining up to tell us that if we vote for independence they'll jolly well move south of the border and take their bonuses with them. And then we'll be sorry.

So it's all bash, kapow, slam. And all us rupturists or herniaists or whatever we are this week have been besieged out of existence. So I am not writing this and you are not reading it. We don't exist. They're always telling us that the indy debate needs to raise its tone, and here we are already in a Kafka novel and it's all thanks to John. That's yer actual Czech philosophy that is. And we have the Union to thank for it. If we were foolish enough to vote for independence we could go through our entire lives without having an existential crisis like Czechoslovakia. Oh wait, bad example ... sorry John ... And there's former Czech President Vaclav Klaus thinking Scottish independence isn't a bad idea, just to pour salt in the split pilsner.

John's looking forward to a return to business as usual. It's just as well, because he doesn't have many special powers and doesn't look good in a superhero costume. Tights are so revealing. But still, we ought to listen to him when he warns us fissurists that we've already lost because John fondly believes that his secret superpower is his ability to manipulate public perceptions. He's done exceedingly well at this. The results speak for themselves.

He was a spin doctor for Tony Blair, a man unrivalled in popular affections - everyone hates him. It takes a very special public relations spin doctor talent to achieve that. Mind you, the illegal wars did help a bit too. John helped spin those too.

He masterminded the Labour campaign in the Scottish elections of 2007, which managed to avoid any incidents in Subway Sandwiches even if it still ended in defeat. Defeat for the first time and the first of many more. Ouch. Then he went off to Australia to spin doctor for Julia Gillard, only for her to get turfed out of office by her own party. And then the Ozzie Labour party went on to lose to Ozzie Tories that make Boris Johnstone seem like he's in touch with reality. You know that when John has his finger on the pulse, it's about to turn into a corpse. Thank god he never took up a career in nursing.

So John truly has the most impressive spin doctoring abilities. They're on a par with putting a heavy bag over your head, and rocking gently back and forward inside a dark wardrobe while muttering "Why did you leave me Tony". And when he's trying to manipulate public opinion, sorry, writing an important article for the Scotsman, we should pay attention.

John wants us to stop all this constitutional nonsense. For the first time in decades untold thousands who had previously given up on politics with disgust [waves shy hand] - in no small measure due to the machinations of the likes of Tony Blair and his troll minions - are discussing politics, with passion, interest, and for the most part an enormous dollop of good humour. Calling him a troll minion is good humoured, because it makes me think of one of those wee plastic figures from the fun fair. Only with a grumpy face.

But it's the wrong sort of politics, and John doesn't approve when people stop taking him seriously. He says it's "the politics of the magic porridge pot". He's quite right there, there is no magic porridge pot, there's only a magic gravy train in Westminster. Labour's Scottish contingent know a lot about that.

Back in the real world, as opposed to Project Fear's pale imitation of manga, John's sole superpower is the uncanny ability to hitch his horse to the wagon with the broken wheels and Magrit Curran as satnav. When you're a Blairite and only have Jim Murphy to talk to, you don't have many choices. And if we vote no in September, neither will we.

That's why John is looking to the future with barely restrained glee.

And I too shall place my faith in John's political antennae. Because you know that whatever he's predicting, the opposite will happen. He's reliably unreliable, just like the rest of his former colleagues at Westminster. I know that. The dug knows that. The woman along the street knows it, and so do her pals at the bingo. The only person who's heid is in a spin in John's.

He's longing for things to get back to normal when Scotland has already changed forever. Things will never be the same again. John's normal is the normal of back room deals, of Labour establishment and Pacific Quay together in cosy harmony. That normal died when 13 years of majority Labour government gave us ATOS, the first incarnation of the bedroom tax, wars, privatisation, PFIs, and Stephen Purcell's cocaine fuelled implosion which went mysteriously unreported.

What he's trying to do in his crude spinning way is to send a message to the unengaged that there is no point in discussing independence since the game is a bogey. But we know how his game works, which is why we're playing a different game.

John's game is called "not giving any answers, and gloating like Gollum". It's as close as he's ever going to get to a positive case for the Union. He only thinks he's winning because he lives inside his own spin. The problem with spinning is that everything around you is a blur. It's a game played in TV studios and in newspaper columns.

Our game is called "talking to people, not at them". The rules are simple, when someone asks a question about Scotland's future, give an honest answer. Provide them with information, or show them where to find it. That's not a game Westminster can play. It means looking people in the eye.

It's a game we're winning.

* Seriously, potatoes really do shine more brightly. All you need is a potato, a wee LED light, and a couple of other household bits and pieces. Science fun for all the family, and infinitely more illuminating than John McTernan:

http://science.howstuffworks.com/innovation/everyday-innovations/how-to-make-potato-powered-light-bulb.htm

9 March 2014
Expat groundhog day

Can we not lay this one to rest? *Jayzuz*, here we bloody go again. The Sunday Times is claiming that Alex Salmond has acted illegally by denying the vote to expat Scots. Because it's behind a paywall, and wild horses would not drag me to give money to Rupert Murdoch, I had to rely on third party reports so am unclear on what grounds the Times can make its allegation. Though they're probably along the lines of "See that Alicsammin, I hate him hate him hate him. He's smelly and racist against English people. Did I mention I hate him."

Onieweys, for the umpteenth time, and for the benefit of very small children, the joined up thinking challenged, and dumb as soup Times journalists, expat Scots cannot vote in the referendum for many reasons, none of which have anything to do with Alicsammin and his eevyle desire to install himself as our alien lizard overlord.

\<pedant>

And by the way, it's expat, no hyphen, because it's short for expatriate, which comes from the French expatrier "to banish, exile". It's not derived from ex-patriot and doesn't contain the ex- meaning former. An ex-pat is a Patrick who's had the operation and is now called Marina.

\</pedant>

Neither, by the way again, do the real reasons expat Scots cannot vote in the referendum have anything to do with them deciding not to live in Scotland. It's common practice in many countries to allow expats to vote. UK citizens living in other EU states retain a vote in UK General Elections for 15 years. Spain, France, and the USA organise ballots for their citizens who live abroad. When Latvia recently held a referendum on whether to grant the Russian language equal constitutional status to the Latvian language, a ballot of Latvian citizens in the UK was organised by the Latvian embassy in London.

Amongst the large Scottish diaspora, of which I was once a part before returning to live in Scotland, there are many many thousands who did not actively choose to leave Scotland. A great many did so only reluctantly, because it was the only way to get a decent job. That is one of the reasons we are campaigning for independence, because the economic policies of the Union prevent Scotland from offering livelihoods and opportunities for all Scots, and forces our children and siblings to leave. Scots who were forced to move south or move overseas because of the neglect and deindustrialisation wreaked by successive Westminster governments are victims of the Union's ill effects on Scotland, they are not dirty stop outs who chose to leave and by leaving surrendered their voice.

Of course expat Scots have a right to a voice. But they don't have a right to a vote in the referendum, and they can't have the right to a vote. The real reason is very simple. So simple and obvious it is overlooked - even by supporters of independence.

The reason is that Scotland is not an independent country yet. Since Scotland is not an independent country, there is as yet no legal definition of a Scottish citizen. You cannot legally be a citizen of a state which does not legally exist. And if you cannot define who is or is not a citizen of Scotland, then how do you define who has the right to vote in the referendum?

The Scottish Parliament has no legal authority to hold any sort of ballot outside of Scotland. That's a power reserved to Westminster. So the only body capable of organising a ballot of expat Scots to allow them to participate in the referendum is the Westminster Parliament. However that would mean that the Westminster Parliament would have to determine some basis for deciding who would be a citizen of an independent Scotland - but that is not something that Westminster can decide. Only the Parliament and constitution of an independent Scotland can define who is a Scottish citizen. Tory MPs from Surrey don't have that right, not even if they're Michael Gove.

The only way in which the Westminster Parliament can pass the necessary legislation would be after consultation with the Scottish Parliament. But the current Scottish Parliament doesn't have the legal authority to determine who would be a Scottish citizen. Westminster could negotiate with the current Scottish Parliament in order to reach a provisional agreement on who might count as a Scottish citizen for the purposes of the referendum. But that would mean prenegotiating Scottish independence, and the Westminster Mob have already made it clear that as far as uppity Caledonians are concerned they don't do negotiations, whether of the pre or post variety.

So if you are an expat Scot in say, Woking, who is aggrieved that you cannot vote in the referendum, then write a stiff letter of complaint to your local Conservative MP, demanding that Westminster opens negotiations with the Scottish Parliament forthwith.

However Scotland might insist that Westminster adopts the fitba rule, and anyone with at least one Scottish grandparent could qualify for the national team. That would mean Davie Cameron would have a vote and he'd no longer have any excuse for not debating Eck. You can see why he might not be so keen.

11 March 2014

Gordie's own brand diversionary jam

Gordie Broon's promise of mair powers for Holyrood if we vote naw signals that the Labour party is getting serious about the constitutional debate, at least according to highly paid politics analysts on the telly. Course, independent art house movies are dead serious too, but they're still works of fiction, and often just as badly acted. Having said that, even 145 minutes of existentialist angst in Romanian with Italian subtitles is more comprehensible than a speech by Gordie endogenous growth Broon. And invariably more entertaining.

Ming Campbell has been getting serious about more powers for Holyrood too. At least if you're to believe Ming. There's lots of things I'm serious about as well, like removing those annoying hairs that grow out of your ears, and understanding the difference between a commitment to do something from a person who actually has the ability and will to make it happen and a party which changes its mind as soon as someone calls out "ministerial motor for Danny Alexander".

Neither man is in any position to make their suggestions come to pass, neither has a firm timetable for bringing them about, and both are faced with entrenched opposition from within their own party ranks. The saccharine jam substitutes of Gordiedevo and Mingindevo are not going to happen. Any new constitutional proposal is going to have to gain the support of an electorate south of the border which has been fed on a diet of deep fried subsidy junky myths. It will be bye bye Barnett and hello budget cuts.

Both Scotland's leading representatives of the zombie community spoke of the need for a new UK constitutional settlement. And that's the worrying bit. A new UK constitutional settlement means only one thing when it's uttered by people who have spent their Scottish political careers in a tribal spat with the SNP, and who want it to be introduced in the aftermath of a no vote in the referendum. It means a new Union created by an Act of the Westminster Parliament. You know, that body that claims it is the sole repository of sovereignty. A no vote gives it the chance to having another go at killing Scottish nationalism stone dead.

Irrespective of your opinion of the SNP, it is a fact of Scottish politics that Scotland's constitutional concerns are only addressed when Westminster is in a panic about the forces of Eckness. The rest of the time, Scotland's on mute while Gordon Brown played Angry Birds on his Nokia.

Gordie Broon spent 11 years playing at being chancellor of the exchequer while not busy with his full time job of plotting to get Tony Blair's job, followed by a few dismal years when he'd got Tony's job only for it to become apparent to one and all that he didn't have a scooby what to do now he'd got there. Throughout all that time, when he actually had power and influence, and not a clue what to do with it, he was even less interested in addressing Scotland's demand for greater home rule than he was in pretending he loved the Arctic Monkeys. The SNP did not have a majority in Holyrood, there wasn't going to be a referendum. Gordie could safely file it under ignore and make like the North Briton.

And that's what he did, apart from that time that Wendy Alexander told Eck to "bring it on", and Gordie had to slap her down, aided and abetted by her brother. Gordie wanted Scotland to remain filed under ignore. There was his big chance at a lasting legacy, and he didn't notice until it was far too late. Story of his life eh. Now he's stuck with the legacy of the bust he said he'd abolished.

Ming's no better. He's the man who told Tavish not to countenance going into coalition with the SNP after the 2007 elections, he's the guy who sat down with Donald Dewar to design a voting system for Holyrood that would ensure Labour and Lib Dem coalitions in perpetuity. Neutering the threat posed by the SNP is as high on his agenda as it is on Gordon Brown's. The pair have previous for choreographed attempts to do down the SNP.

Now all of a sudden it's vitally important to the pair of them that the UK finds a new constitutional settlement. Nothing to do with there being an independence referendum then and the SNP posing a bigger threat to their personal careers, their parties, and their parliament than ever before. They see no distinction between the demands of Scotland as a nation, and the demands of the SNP. That's a major reason they keep calling it Alicsammin'sreferendum. In the aftermath of a no vote, they will do their utmost to ensure that Scotland can be kept filed under ignore forever. They won't see it as anti-Scottish. To them it's just party politics, and they want to get back to playing it their own way.

You can be quite certain that any new Act of Union devised by the Westminster parties will define the United Kingdom as a single nation. It's the inclusive and British thing to do after all. And you can be even more certain that the new constitutional arrangements will ensure that Holyrood can't go scaring Westminster with independence referendums. Westminster will be the sole sovereign body. We've already seen that they don't like sharing. So no doubt there will be some provision saying something to the effect that any future changes to this new constitutional settlement must be put to a referendum of the British nation as a whole. Because that's terribly British and inclusive. And is just another way of saying - you'll not be having any more of those Scottish independence referendums.

The Guardian's editorialist thinks a new constitutional settlement is a good idea, and wrote

"The strict logic is on Sir Menzies's side, but Britain's asymmetric devolution is not unique. Structures for Catalonia and the Basque Country likewise sacrifice a tidy constitutional organogram to political realities."

I thought an organogram was what Hannibal Lector got as a surprise during his birthday party, a combination of entertainment and takeaway meal in one singing package dressed up as a sexy cop. Somehow I get the feeling that Westminster wants to be the birthday boy and dine on Holyrood's beating heart. I wouldn't put that past Michael Forsyth.

As stupid suggestions go, few can beat the Guardian's idea that constitutional arrangements in Spain are somehow a model we should copy. It's way up there with "Hey, Scottish people will start voting Conservative again if we introduce the poll tax a year early."

They can't have noticed that Catalonia is pressing hard for its own indy referendum, is going to vote yes when the vote comes, and the Basque Country won't be far behind. The pressure has only increased because of Spain's constitutional ban on independence referendums, the debate is more fraught, the risks far higher. That's not a model anyone sensible should want to adopt. Sadly, "sensible" has little to do with the electoral calculations of Westminster politicians.

Brown and Campbell did not actually come out and say that it should be illegal for Scotland to hold an independence referendum. But it is a view widely expressed in the Unionist camp, by the likes of Michael Forsyth, and yer man Aidan O'Neill QC who's now saying it's illegal not to allow Scots outside of Scotland to vote in the vote he thought was illegal to begin with. Oh and Michael Moore in January 2012, who was at the time the Secretary of State for Scotland and was expressing the view of the UK government to the House of Commons. And just about every other Unionist politician at the time.

The job of Gordie and Ming is to promise some diversionary jam. With a no vote, Scotland will get stuck back in the dusty filing cabinet. Only this time they'll lock the drawer.

13 March 2014

The Cherlie letters

Personally I've never seen much need for the monarchy. Vast wealth and landholdings, tax breaks, civil lists, free castles, and all the RAF helicopters you can commandeer seems a bit pricy for a head of state in waiting. For that sort of expenditure you expect a George Clooney lookalike with the intelligence of Einstein, the wit of Bill Hicks, and the humility of Gandhi. Instead we've got Cherlie Boay. We're being seriously shortchanged.

Windsor Junior is a veritable Disgusted of Tunbridge Wells when it comes to writing to politicians. But unlike the average punter who writes letters of complaint to their MP, Cherlie Boay and his maw have a legal right to be consulted in any matter which affects the interests of the Royles. They can, and apparently regularly do, "request" changes to be made to forthcoming legislation, which is one reason why the family remains the UK's biggest benefits scroungers.

The average claimant of Housing Benefit doesn't have the legal right to be consulted on forthcoming legislation and to make requests to change it which cannot be ignored. Otherwise Jim Royle could have sent a wee letter to Iain Duncan Smith saying "Are you fecking mad?" and he'd have been forced by Royal Protocol to agree. So much for British Fair Play.

By the way, it's important that we all cram in as many British cultural references as we can just now, as after a yes vote we'll all turn into foreigners and won't understand that Breetish sense of humour any more. Even worse, Spain's going to veto our use of Central European fart jokes and George Osborne is demanding sole custody of the deep fried mars bar stereotype. Mind you, Westminster is a joke we're better off without - bit of politics there, as Ben Elton used to say when he could say a bit of politics there without people screaming back at him "piss off you hypocritical sell out". There's another British cultural reference right there, and so it's quite appropriate that Better Together provokes a very similar audience response.

But back to the politics of princes, which are still smelling suspiciously machiavellian. The Guardian, with its liberal and progressive face on because it thinks it's not something related to the Scottish referendum, has been campaigning to get Cherlie's letters released to the public, so we can see exactly what changes he has 'requested' to legislation so that his interests are not damaged. But the Attorney General for England and Wales, Dominic Grieve, doesn't want us to know. And if he doesn't want England and Wales to know, Scotland doesn't get to know either, even though Dominic's writ does not, in theory at least, extend north of the border.

According to the Guardian, "They were letters of advocacy so blunt that Mr Grieve has argued they have to be repressed in order to avoid compromising the public perception of the prince's political neutrality."

It's more important that it continues to look like Charles is politically neutral, than to ensure that the supposedly politically neutral royal family is in fact politically neutral. Even when they know, Charles knows, and we all know, that he's anything but the sort. He is, whisper it, an upper class self regarding Tory who's spent his entire life being protected from the consequences of his lack of intelligence and imagination and believes his privilege is a right. Like that comes as a shock to anyone.

Conscious of the fact that one day he hopes to get a lordy title, and you cannae be a lordy without a king or queen to be lordy to, Dominic Grieve refused to accede to the original Freedom of Information demand for the letters, and overruled the information tribunal which had agreed to the release of the documents. He didn't go through the appeal procedures, he just vetoed the release, citing reasons which had already been considered and rejected by the information tribunal in its ruling.

Dominic just didn't want to spoil the magic of the monarchy for us. Isn't that nice. Now we can all be patronised by chinless wonders and feel warm and cosy inside. It almost makes me stop having those recurring visions of drowning Nicolas Witchell in a vat of Duchy Original treacle.

The Appeals Court has now ruled that ministers do not have the right to veto legal decisions in the way Grieve did. The UK Government has appealed against the appeal, and the matter will go to the UK Supreme Court. The ban on the release of the letters remains in force.

But like so much of what goes on in the rest of the UK, this incident does have a bearing on the Scottish independence debate. We have no written constitution, and the status and role of the royal family is defined by precedence and practice as much, if not more, than written and explicit law. Charles has as much power as he chooses to exercise and immense patronage to wield, within certain common sense British limits of course. The limits are marked by a sign saying "Caution, one is now entering things which the commoners might find out about". At least that's what it says on the side Cherlie sees. The side facing us says "Crown Property Keep Out". When we are not allowed to see what goes on behind the keep out sign, precedence and practice is what they choose to make it.

Lack of transparency doesn't just permeate the British system of government, it is the very core of its being. There is little prospect this will ever change. The privileged will continue to exercise their privilege hidden away behind glossy media events presented by obsequious reporters. The magic of the monarchy will keep weaving its spell. Only it's not a magic spell, it's just a cheap and tawdry trick and Dominic Grieve is Debbie McGhee.

Paul Daniels finally saw sense and took that stupid wig off. We can vote to end the charade too. We can vote yes for independence and a written constitution, for explicit rules regarding the conduct of future heads of state in a constitutional monarchy where the people are sovereign not the crown. We can vote for a country whose future supposedly politically neutral head of state can't try to influence government policy behind the backs of the true holders of sovereignty.

And if our future head of state is unhappy about that, then Scotland can always cite centuries old Gaelic traditions regarding kingship. Monarchists like that sort of stuff don't they, and it is after all the very foundation stone of the Royal House of Alba, apart from that other stone that keeps getting stolen. It's the Celtic institution of the tànaiste rìgh, which loosely translates from the ancient tongue as "Suck it up. Because we can easily find another chinless wonder to do your non-job. Or we can choose a republic."

14 March 2014

Unionist commentators and the tolanometer

When I was a wean, I went to a Catholic primary school that happened to be in a different parish from the church where I got dragged to mass of a Sunday. From time to time one of the priests would visit the school in order to talk to all the children from his parish. I used to dread the announcement that we had to go along to see Father Tolan. Father Tolan had a superpower. He could make time stand still when he spoke.

Father Tolan droned on in a monotonous tone. I can't actually tell you what he was talking about, except that it probably involved Jesus. His little chats never lasted longer than 10 minutes, but they seemed like they went on for hours. He had nothing to say that was of any relevance or interest to a 10 year old obsessed with apemen, dinosaurs, and languages. There was nothing for it but to count the flakes of dandruff gently settling on the shoulders of his black suit and wish it was dinner time. Over 40 years later, and Father Tolan remains my own personal boredometer.

Folk south of the border seem to have woken up to the fact that Scotland is about to hold an independence referendum, and they've taken to expressing their opinions about it in the comments sections of the newspapers. Which they have every right to do and is perfectly reasonable and fair. But for those of us who have been arguing, campaigning, debating, and discussing Scotland's future for pretty much the entirety of our politically aware lives the opinions of uninformed non-participants in Scotland's referendum score over 5 tolans. I've long since given up paying attention and am counting the flakes of dandruff that settle over their oft-cited irrelevances. If I enjoyed being lectured like a small child, I'd have been happy to trot along to see the priest.

There are a number of common themes. Those on the right harangue us about currency and how we're surrendering to Brussels, or possibly Berlin as some of them are under the delusion that they're still fighting WW2. Those on the left harangue us about currency and how we're betraying the working classes by pandering to nationalism - which is just the same as fascism you know. There's a generous sprinkling of nutcases who bring up ancient history and genetics. And there is the overwhelming consensus that it's all about the sly manipulations of a wily Alicsammin. He's always wily, just like the coyote in the roadrunner cartoons. But Alicsammin's ACME independence rocket sled has a fatal flaw they cry, and then raise some point which people who've been paying attention have long since debated, discussed, and put to bed.

Above all there is a boundless capacity to see anti-English racism in innocuous remarks which don't refer to English people, even obliquely. It's a strange thing, taking offence. If you go around expecting offence, then you'll certainly find it. When you are convinced that the person you are debating with is motivated by anti-English racism, you will see anti-English racism in every utterance they make.

Then there are the assumptions, more legion than the Romans who marched off into the Caledonian wilderness and never returned. "Scotland wants independence, but wants England to keep underwriting its debts," they sniff contemptuously. The assumption being that Scotland is subsidised by the goodwill and deep pockets of English taxpayers.

But they've got it the wrong way around. Scotland does not rely on the UK Treasury to underwrite it. Quite the reverse, Scotland was underwriting the UK Treasury even before the oil was discovered, and has continued to plough billions into the UK economy, specifically the London economy, ever since.

The real reason that the Scottish Government wants a currency union has nothing to do with wanting the UK Treasury to continue underwriting Scottish debts, and everything to do with ensuring that Scottish independence does not provoke a crisis in the rUK's economy once it is deprived of the billions it sooks in from Scotland. An economic crisis in the rUK would not be good for Scotland's economy. But the bottom line is that it's not Scotland which requires underwriting, it's the UK Treasury.

It's not Scotland's economy which is unbalanced and risky, Scotland hasn't put all its eggs in the basket of the City of London - which is considerably more volatile than Brent crude. Standard and Poor's recent report into the credit status of an independent Scotland pointed out that it only considers reliance on a single economic sector to be overlarge when it exceeds 20% of the total economy. Oil and gas make up just 16% of Scotland's GDP, and even without the oil Scotland's economic output per head of population is greater than that of all UK regions except London and the South East. The Standard and Poor's report characterised Scotland's economy as "rich and diversified".

But try pointing that out to yer average Unionist commentator in the pages of UK newspapers, and you'll be answered with a snort of derision, some very predictable comments about deep fried Braveheart welfare junkies, and accusations of anti-English racism.

It's not really their fault, having arrived late at the independence debate party bearing no gifts but a tin of bile concocted by the Sun, the Telegraph, the Mail and the Guardian. All they have to go on are their stereotypes and prejudices reflected through the distorting prism of UK media coverage of the debate. They've been told for decades that Scotland is poor and depends upon cash transfers to keep us in free education and prescriptions for methodone. They're not going to be shifted from that view by people they are already convinced are anti-English racists, no matter how many economic papers or citations you give them.

This weekend Davie Cameron will make another of his flying visits to Scotland to add some fuel to the fires of Unionist prejudice, and will doubtless run away again before he can be challenged. Not that the assembled media hacks are keen to challenge him. The comments sections of the papers will rise to 10 tolans.

I'm not saying we shouldn't engage with these people, I have nothing but admiration for those brave souls who engage in missionary work amongst the benighted. But we should only do so in the knowledge that it is a waste of time and energy. They don't have a vote and they're not going to change their minds anyway. We need to concentrate our efforts on persuading people who do have a vote, and who experience the reality of Scotland - not the caricature of our country found in the pages of the Telegraph and in David Cameron's speeches.

The independence campaign has moved into a new phase. On the Unionist side there is a barrage of negativity, fear, hatred and odium. These are distraction tactics. The correct response is for us to focus our efforts where it makes a difference. That's a lesson Father Tolan never appreciated.

16 March 2014

Nailing the Common Travel Area to a plank

Theresa May, who presides over the dysfunction that is the Home Office, came to Scotland this weekend to make a wee speech to the geriatrics and the odd middle class student who make up the dwindling band of Scottish Tories. As she vowed to erect barbed wire fences all along the border, complete with G4S security guards and sniffer dogs specially trained to catch Irn Bru smugglers, the wee bunch of Scottish Tories clapped and applauded. They were soon joined in their cheer by random Unionists crowing on the interwebbies. I've not seen anyone collude in their own misery with such enthusiasm since having the misfortune to witness a stage show featuring a happy masochist getting his scrotum nailed to a plank. But even that evening was less surreal than the Scottish Tory conference.

Onieweys, the substance of Theresa's threat, such as it was, was that she would consider imposing border controls if Scotland becomes independent. The foundation of this threat is Theresa's belief that Scotland will freely open its doors to all and any asylum seekers, benefits tourists, and people who won't vote Tory, who will take one look at the rain stoating down at Embra airport and enquire if the trams go to Berwick. Theresa thinks that life on income support in a run down council estate in Tory ruled Britain is more attractive to people who cross the planet in order to better themselves than a decent paid job in Dundee.

Scotland is just a tad further away from Europe than Dover, anyone seeking to use Scotland as a back door into England isn't going to hitch a ride on the back of a lorry. They're certainly not about to stow away on a high speed train, since Westminster has no plans for it to reach Scotland anytime soon. But perhaps Theresa is planning for the eventuality that a flotilla of canoes may set out from Denmark for Aberdeen, laden with asylum seekers bent on reaching London. It's because of forward thinking like that that she rose so high in Tory ranks.

The Republic of Ireland is a part of the Common Travel Area with the UK. The Scottish Government proposes that after independence,

Scotland will remain a part of the Common Travel Area like the Republic of Ireland. It makes sense. At least to everyone but Theresa May.

However Theresa is insistent that Scottish independence will undo all the "good work" the Home Office has been doing contributing to the hysteria over immigration, and the only way it could possibly keep doing good work in pandering to Daily Mail columnists would be for the Scottish Government to submit its immigration policy to Theresa for prior approval.

Entry into the Common Travel Area is dependent upon the foreign minister of an independent Scotland offering up his bollocks, or in the case of a female foreign minister the bollocks of a nominated male relative, so they can be nailed to a plank by Theresa. Following careful consideration by Theresa, the bollocks will have to be displayed on an advertising van round the streets of Birmingham, under a banner headline screaming SHOP A JOCK ILLEGAL IMMIGRANT. Otherwise Theresa couldn't possibly countenance allowing the border to remain open.

I'm quite sure that Irish government ministers past and present will be thrilled to learn that they are in fact unpaid lackeys of the UK Home Office whose duty is to implement Theresa's will on pain of bollock planking. But I don't recall seeing the bollocks of an Irish foreign minister ever being displayed by Theresa, and that's the sort of image that would tend to stick in the mind. The Irish Republic may very well have its fair share of masochists, however begging for more punishment as a matter of public policy is restricted to Scotland's Unionist parties.

Ireland has its own immigration policy which is tailored to its own needs. Dublin does not need to get the nod from Theresa before deciding to issue more green cards for those Ireland considers to be suitably qualified migrants. Perhaps they do in the imaginations of Unionists, where Westminster is a colossus which strides the globe punching above its weight and bowing all the little people to its mighty will. But in the real world the views of the UK Home Secretary have as much bearing on the immigration policy of the Irish Republic as

Prince Charle's views on architecture influence the choice of venues of the Radical Independence Campaign.

What does exist however, is an agreement negotiated between Dublin and Westminster to uphold one another's immigration decisions. This arrangement dates back to the establishment of the Common Travel Area in 1923. The British were not inclined to impose border controls along the newly established border between Northern Ireland and what was then the Irish Free State, and the Irish were happy not to deliberately sabotage British policy on immigration from third countries in return for the guarantee of freedom of movement throughout the island.

So the agreement that the Unionists claim would mean an independent Scotland surrendering its immigration policy to Theresa May is in the public domain - at least the equivalent agreement between Dublin and Westminster is. It was revealed in answer to a question in the Dáil in 1980.

A member of the Irish Parliament asked Brian Lenihan, the Irish Minister for Foreign Affairs if there was any agreement between the Irish authorities and Great Britain "concerning dealings with aliens or immigrants", and enquired whether the Irish Government was considering changing the agreement.

The minister replied that there was an agreement, and gave the following reply:

Since 1952 there has, by agreement, been no immigration control on the movement of persons between Britain. Northern Ireland and the State. A necessary concommitant is a measure of co-operation between the two immigration services. This is recognised formally in Article 5 (2) (j) of the Aliens Order 1946 (at present inserted by Article 3 of the Aliens (Amendment) Order 1975, (S.I. No. 12B of 1975)) which empowers an immigration officer to refuse leave to land to an alien coming to the State from a place not in Britain or Northern Ireland if he is satisfied that the alien "intends to travel, whether immediately or not, to Great Britain or Northern Ireland and the officer is satisfied that the alien would not qualify for admission to Great Britain or Northern Ireland if he arrived there from a place other than the State".

The Government have no proposal for any change in the arrangements.

This arrangement quite specifically does not mean that Dublin must submit its immigration policies to Westminster for approval, neither does it mean that Dublin cannot seek to attract skilled and qualified migrants into an independent Ireland. It means that Ireland agreed to prevent the entry into Ireland of anyone who, in the opinion of the Irish immigration officer (and not, please note, in the opinion of Theresa May) intended to travel onward to the UK, but who would not be legally admitted there.

That's it. That's the onerous condition imposed by membership of the Common Travel Area. You can see why the Irish Government didn't see any need to change it. And note also that both the questioner and the Foreign Minister know that the Irish Government has the right and ability to negotiate changes in the agreement, or even end it, as and when it sees fit.

If Scotland seeks to attract new residents, we want them to stay here and contribute to our economy. We want them to become a part of the fabric of Scotland. We do not seek to open our borders to absolutely anyone who might ever have expressed an interest in settling in England, Wales or Northern Ireland and immediately pack them off on their way south, just to annoy Theresa May and the Daily Mail. We could maybe sell them a packet of crisps and a tin of bru as they made their way to the English border, but other than that they're not going to do a great deal to help grow the Scottish economy - which is after all the point of encouraging immigration into a depopulated land.

So when we distill away the froth, boil off the alarmism, and chisel away the disgusting wee crusty bits that cling to any Tory statement on Scottish independence, what we find is this: Theresa May has just warned Scotland that she may have to impose border controls if an independent Scottish Government is even more vindictively stupid than a Tory Home Secretary.

I don't think we need to worry about that Theresa. But even in the unlikely event that it was as vindictively stupid, Scotland could always vote it out. The Union doesn't give us that option with Theresa. We've only got one way of voting her out.

The BBC's credibility, the big loser in the independence debate

Andrew Marr is supposed to be one of the BBC's leading interviewers. It's true that he is recovering from a stroke, and his mind may not be as sharp as it once was, but that's no excuse for bringing his personal views into an interview. That is directly in contravention of BBC guidelines which state that the viewer should not be able to discern the personal opinions of the interviewer when a politician is interviewed. Yet we see this sort of behaviour time and time again when the BBC's London Scots contingent present programmes dealing with the referendum.

I met a lot of London Scots when I lived in the city for a decade. Many of them had left Scotland because there were few opportunities in their chosen careers. They remain of the opinion that Scotland is a bit of a basket case, and want Scotland to remain a basket case as it validates their decision to leave. Andrew Marr displays many of the same symptoms.

During his interview with Alex Salmond on Sunday's Politics Show, Marr asserted that it would be very difficult for Scotland to gain EU membership, saying: "I think it will be quite hard to get back in, I have to say."

Challenged by Alex Salmond, Marr tried to backtrack, saying this wasn't his opinion or the BBC's. But it was clearly a personal opinion coming from the same man who sat quietly and nodded when José Manuel Barroso made his controversial statement that Scotland would be out on its ear. The statement was roundly condemned by a diverse range of European politicians from both the left and the right, and dismissed by real experts in EU law, none of whom thought Barroso even had the right to express his opinion in such a way, never mind agreeing with his dubious assertion.

Yet Marr did not even raise a quizzical eyebrow. Which can only mean that either Marr hadn't done his research, or that Barroso's comments chimed with Marr's own beliefs. Or indeed both, since these are not mutually exclusive scenarios. In either event, Scotland was shortchanged and the independence debate was distorted. And we pay this guy's wages with our licence fees.

This is also the man, let us not forget, who came to Edinburgh and asserted that anti-English racism underlies much of the demand for Scottish self-determination. Again Marr distorted the independence debate. At least on that occasion he did not make the remark in his capacity as a BBC interviewer, but his status as one of the BBC's leading on-screen presenters ensured that his views got wide coverage in a UK media which is eager to depict independence supporters as swivel eyed racists.

A BBC staff member expressing his or her support for independence during an interview with a Unionist politician would be equally objectionable. This is not a partisan point here. However it's obvious to one and all that the bias expressed by the BBC's staff is entirely in one direction. And I don't mean Harry Stiles. I don't think the boyband has ever given its views on the Scottish debate, although if they were against independence you can be sure it would rate a mention on the main news at 6.

The bias on the BBC has now got beyond parody. It is so bad that when the excellent BBC Scotlandshire site was launched, some people thought it was the real BBC. Derek Bateman, in his thoughtful and unfailingly informative blog posts, says that there is no conspiracy amongst BBC staff to campaign against independence, and I believe him. However what there certainly is is an ethos of British nationalism which runs throughout the BBC, and it is written into its DNA.

When that is combined with the fawning nature of BBC Scotland's management towards its London bosses, and organisation's clear hierarchy in which London based reporters are considered a cut above mere provincials, you get a toxic mess where those who do have Unionist bias are free to express it. Especially if you're a star performer called Andrew Marr, Andrew Neil, James Naughtie or Kirsty Wark.

We are after all talking about a broadcaster that can describe a sewing programme as "Great British". If an organisation is prepared to lay claim to needlework for British nationalism, it will have a tendency towards British nationalism in other respects as well. And when we're dealing with the Scottish independence debate, British nationalism is pretty much all we see on the BBC.

There are some things which happen above Derek Bateman's paygrade. It was reported last year that the Foreign Office had been contacting English language publications in Spain, requesting that they publish items favourable to the stance of the UK Government in the independence debate. If the UK Government has being doing this with publications in foreign countries, then what exactly has gone on in private communications between - say - the former Tory cabinet minister Chris Patten, currently chair of the BBC Trust, and the UK Government which is the BBC's sole shareholder? That's not something we're likely to be told for 30 years. And that's without getting into the question of whether a former Conservative cabinet minister can ever be an unbiased arbitrer in a highly politicised debate.

Have the top levels of BBC management decided to foster British nationalism and a sense of Britishness as it became apparent that Scotland was going to hold a referendum on independence? There's certainly been a plague of Great British this and Great British that on the BBC of late. In the context of an independence referendum, even the title of a sewing competition looks like it is being politicised by the Unionists. We should be told. we pay the BBC's bills. But we won't be told.

So what to do? I'm not going to call on people not to pay their licence fee. Due to my partner's age and health condition, we get an exemption and don't have to pay. It would be hypocritical for me to call on others to take the legal and financial risks involved with non-payment. That's a decision that individuals must make for themselves.

When this independence campaign kicked off, we all knew that the independence cause would find precious little support in the mainstream media. That opinion was however the preserve of those who already supported independence. Now that opinion has gone mainstream. Scots are becoming increasingly aware of the bias in our media, and especially the shocking disservice provided by BBC Scotland. That awareness helps the independence campaign, and we must do all we can to ensure that the awareness grows and spreads.

Whatever the outcome of the vote in September, the BBC is going to be the big loser. Their credibility is in tatters. There will be a reckoning with Scottish licence fee payers, one way or another.

18 March 2014

Labour's devo deception

They're here. Labour's long awaited proposals for devolution have arrived, splashing into the independence debate like the tsunami created by tossing a pebble into Loch Lomond - a pebble conveniently attached to a length of elastic so Johann can howk it back out again, the Westminster crew insisted on safeguards. Dropping a pebble into the watter might rock Jim Murphy's boat. It created such a little splash that it only rated 30 seconds on the BBC lunchtime Scottish Och Aye the News, and Brian Taylor still managed to find time to mention David Bowie.

The proposals are an incoherent mess, but to be fair, so is the Labour party in Scotland so what did you really expect? Even Severin Carrell of the Guardian, who on Monday's Newsnicht expressed the opinion that his Unionist rag's coverage of the indy debate was fair and unbiased, wasn't able to put much lipstick on the pig.

The headline news was that Labour wants to allow Holyrood powers over income tax, including the power to vary the top rate by up to 15p in the pound, up from the 10p variation allowed by the Scotland Act due to come into force in 2016. What they're not saying is whether Westminster would claw back any increase in Scottish revenues by reducing the block grant, which is the case with the unused and useable tax powers granted in 1997. They're hinting they won't, but aren't making a commitment, so we can take that as a "yes they would".

Labour will allow Holyrood to vary individual tax bands, but not control over any other taxes which effectively makes the income tax powers unusable. The unusability of the tax powers is not a bug, it's a feature. Labour likes it that way. It stops Ian Davidson giving Johann grief, which is a far more important consideration than any demands for greater self-government from Scotland.

So we'll get more unusable powers. That's really going to stop the independence juggernaut in its tracks.

Neither is Labour saying why 15p in the pound is the correct figure to, in the words of Johann, "bolster, defend and energise" devolution, and not 20p, or 35p, or 100p. What criteria did Labour use to arrive at the 15p figure? I suspect it was "what we can get past Ian Davidson and Jim Murphy without causing too much of a strop", which isn't exactly the same as "what is in the best interests of Scotland".

Labour is also prepared to grant Holyrood greater powers over Housing Benefit, but the remainder of the benefits system will remain firmly under control of Westminster, and Holyrood will not get any extra funding to ammeliorate the ill effects of Westminster's benefit cuts. It couldn't be that they're only making this tiny wee concession in a nakedly political attempt to neutralise the outrage over the Bedroom Tax now would it?

Labour will also concede some limited control of the Crown Estates - but not to the Scottish Parliament. They want these powers to go to local authorities. It keeps Gordon Matheson happy. They also want to devolve control of the Work Programme to local authorities, giving Labour cooncillors more ALEO boards they can sit on.

We are told that this devo package represents the maximum devolution Scotland could possibly need or want, but what is far longer than the wee list of wee things that Johann is prepared to concede, hedged about with caveats as they are, is the list of things that Labour refuses to consider devolving to Scotland. Scotland won't get these powers, not now, not ever. For a devolution journey, we're on a very short ride.

- Financial and economic matters
- Monetary policy
- Currency regulation
- Debt management
- Employment law
- Foreign affairs
- International development
- Defence
- The welfare state
- Pensions
- Benefits
- The constitution

- Immigration
- Drugs, drug trafficking and related laws
- Betting, gaming and lotteries
- Broadcasting
- The civil service
- Abortion and analogous issues
- Air passenger duty
- VAT
- National insurance contributions
- Corporation tax
- Alcohol, tobacco and fuel duties
- Climate change levy
- Insurance premium tax
- Vehicle excise duty
- Inheritance tax
- Capital gains tax
- Tax on oil & gas

So forget about getting rid of Trident, forget about control of benefits and taxation. You can even forget about control of broadcasting - a power granted to just about ever other autonomous administration under the sun. We can be sure that Scotland's current affairs will continue to be refracted through the distorting mirror of the BBC, and there will be nothing we can do about it. Labour prefers it that way.

But there is not even a guarantee that Scotland will actually get the highly limited powers proposed by Labour this week. It depends on whether the party adopts the proposals in full in their 2015 Westminster manifesto. It depends on whether the proposals will not be filleted and gutted in the same way that the timid measures of the Calman Commission were deconstructed - and in some respects the new proposals don't even go as far as Calman, which recommended the control of air passenger duty and corporation tax. It's odd that these powers no longer form a part of the maximum powers that Scotland could need or want, when Labour itself thought they should be devolved just a few years ago.

And of course it depends on whether Labour will form a majority government after 2015. That's not looking too likely the way the polls are currently going.

Labour's just blown its last chance. Too little, too late, a lot of words saying nothing at all. Vote no and get nothing. Vote yes and get all the powers Scotland could ever need - for real.

21 March 2014

Strictly come Ed

Ed Miliband is coming to Scotland to stick it intae Alicsammin. Can you feel the frisson? Are you getting a thrill? Is there not just the tiniest wee damp patch in yer knickers? There is in mine, but I've been sitting on top of the washing machine when it's on its spin cycle. Ed's spinning gets no one moist, not even the damp paper bag he can't punch his way out of.

Ed comes to Scotland fresh from triumphantly making no impression at all after Osborne's budget promised more austerity, more cuts, more making the poor pay for the avarice of the bankers, and some giveaways for "hard working families and pensioners" - Westminster code for "people who could be persuaded to vote Tory", and the fact they are so persuadable is also the reason both the Tories and Labour spend so much time courting them. Ed can only carp about the details, about Johann Lamont's wee things, because when he's in power he's going to implement the same cuts and reward the same Tory leaning constituency.

Ed's in Scotland to give a wee speech to the demoralised band of fratricidal comrades at Labour's Scottish conference. He wants Scotland to vote no to honour the legacy of the late John Smith. Perhaps he mean honouring it like Tony Blair honoured it when he went to war in Iraq. Or like Gordon Brown honoured it when he abolished boom and bust and encouraged the bankers to get rich quick. Introducing the bedroom tax on private tenants was honouring John Smith, who knew? Privatising, and PFI, they honoured his legacy too. Giving ATOS loads of juicy contracts was a socialist act that would have made John Smith proud.

If the leadership of the Labour party can't honour John Smith's legacy they have no business expecting it of anyone else. Least of all people who understand what his legacy really was. John Smith's legacy lies buried on Iona, and Labour's leadership danced on the grave. Ed's not in Scotland to honour John Smith's legacy, far less to build on it. We need no lessons in what John Smith stood for from a man who was a government minister under both Blair and Brown. Ed danced with the worst of them.

Apart from the unseemly appeal to the dead, Ed's big idea is to revive the SNP are Tartan Tories trope. That might have worked back in the 1960s, when my Irish Republican grandfather was convinced that Scottish independence meant surrendering to Presbyterians - who according to him would always be Tories even if they dispensed with the Unionist bit. But my grandfather has been deid for 40 years. Even so, he's not buried as deep as Ed's chances of reviving the fortunes of the Labour party with his tacky sequins and torn ballgown.

But credit where credit is due, at least it's not quite as behind the times as the Tories' Victorian era One Nation slogan which Ed believes best represents the aspirations of the British centre left in the 21st century. Ed's catching up, and if he keeps going at this rate he'll be starting to grasp the real issues around the independence debate about the time that HS2 finally gets to Scotland.

Ed claims that Alicsammin apes Tory policies. He'd know a lot about that then. Margaret Thatcher taught Tony Blair the steps of Westminster's dance to the seat of power. Ed has every intention of following in their footsteps. Labour is happy to ally itself with the Tories when it comes to screwing over Scotland, Ed Balls and George Osborne practised the choreography for their currency routine for ages. But the voting panel of Scotland's Strictly judges was not impressed. The dance did not wow the audience and was received with an arched eyebrow and bitchy comments. They should have got Eric Pickles to do it, the overweight comedy turn may screw up the dance steps but at least it gets the sympathy vote.

Ed's basic problem, and it's not really giving succour to one's opponents by pointing out the fatal flaw in their thinking when the fatal flaw is bleedin' obvious, is that he thinks Alicsammin is a word meaning "Scottish independence". All this time we thought Westminster was personalising the debate and making out that the future of an entire nation is entirely the same as a single individual, but it turns out it's just Westminster politicians getting confused by the Scottish vernacular. That's what happens when you rely on Magrit Curran to translate.

However there are a number of problems with the attacking Alicsammin approach to the independence debate, not the least of which being that a not insignificant number of people who intend to vote yes don't give a toss what Alicsammin thinks about Corporation Tax, or indeed anything else. At this stage in the proceedings, we should take it as read that the yes campaign has already hoovered up all the SNP voters that it's going to get, but the yes campaign cannot win on SNP votes alone.

SNP supporters are unlikely to be moved in their opinions of Alicsammin by anything Ed says. The very large number of non-SNP voters who have decided to vote yes have already realised that they're voting for independence, not for Alicsammin, so they are scarcely any more likely to be discouraged from voting yes when Ed attacks Alicsammin. It's not going to shift the poll movement back towards no. But in lieu of any deeper comprehension of what's happening in Scotland, it's all Ed's got to go on.

It wouldn't be the first time Westminster politicians have been confused by what Scotland is saying. In 1997 when Michael Forsyth led the Scottish Tories into the General Election and lost every one of the party's seats, Scotland's verdict was the most definitive "away you tae fuck" it's possible to achieve in an electoral system. But Westminster thought we'd said "Give this man a seat in the House of Lords so he can keep influencing our laws." Easy mistake to make.

But it's not Scotland's accent. It's their ears. Ed has come to Scotland to make a speech, not to listen. Westminster's ears are still not working.

28 March 2014
Thrilling with Nick

This weekend it's the Lib Dems' Scottish conference. Had anyone noticed? Does Scotland care? At least these questions have answers, which are "damn few" and "dae we feck" respectively. And these are also the answers to the questions "Who's going to vote Lib Dem?" and "Does Scotland trust any promise made by Nick Clegg?" There is however no answer to the question - where is this positive case for the Union then hmm?

Fresh from getting his arse kicked by Nigel the Bawbag of UKIP in a debate about Europe, Nick Clegg's speech to the conference will be used to make a call for a positive and "thrilling" case for remaining in the UK. The Lib Dems and thrilling are not two concepts which are usually found in the same sentence, and most people will be struggling to comprehend what a thrill from a Lib Dem might consist of. Perhaps using Danny Alexander as a human cannonball and shooting him over the Thames would do it. Especially without a safety net. Danny's made it his career to rip up the safety net for the poor and low paid, so it would only be fair.

Not that Nick's making a positive case for the Union himself mind, he's just asking someone else, anyone else, to do it - even Nigel the Bawbag would do. But the only public figure that's attempted it recently is Kermit the Frog, and his heart wasn't really in it. And I'm not even going to make the obvious joke about how it's only a muppet that will speak up for the Union. Only I just did. But if Nick can say one thing and then do the exact opposite, it's only fair if we can too. So aye Nick - I'm going to make a solemn vow to vote no, and will trot along to a university and sign it in front of a load of students.

We can be kind, and let Nick off from providing a "thrilling" case for the Union, a positive case would suffice. We've already seen what the UK has on offer in terms of emotional excitement, there's the edge of yer seat tension of a televisual diet of Great British Scone Baking and Great British Macrame competitions, the soap opera of Willnkate, the drama of near constant wars in far off lands, the tasteless celebrations of the start of a world war, and the vertiginous thrill of plunging towards economic ruin every time the UK's cycle of London property booms hits bust. And a tiny number get very very rich, which is extremely exciting for them, while millions struggle in poverty and low pay, which is also extremely exciting but not in a good way. These are thrills which most people, whether living in Scotland or outwith Scotland, could do without.

Charlie Kennedy and David Steele, Nick's predecessors as leader of the Lib Dems, made a similar call the other week. But they didn't make the positive case themselves either. Unionist politicians are like schoolweans who haven't done their homework, each pushing someone else to the front of the queue to see the teacher while they desperately jot crib notes on their shirt cuffs. But all they can think to scribble down is "Mummy, help me" and the recipe for Mary Berry's jam sponge cake they saw the previous evening on the Great British Bake Off. Sadly the tuck shop is out of jam, and has been as long as anyone can remember.

Since they don't have a real positive case, Unionist politicians have been reduced to claiming that threats and scare stories count. They are well versed in telling us that black is white, up is down, and austerity is economic success, so it's not too much of a stretch to make out that the claim that an independent Scotland would be a bankrupt basket case is actually a glowing recommendation of the benefits of Westminster rule. This is why any speech in which a Unionist sets out to make the positive case for the Union ends up in a litany of scare stories from the Project Fear song book.

But Cleggie wants Better Together to set out proof that Scotland "will have new and exciting opportunities if they vote against independence". That would be a new opportunity like a zero-hours contract, or the excitement of waiting to see if ATOS have rejected your claim for disability benefits. Then there's the thrilling excitement of going off and making a new life down in London or further afield because there's no work back home. UK elections are also far more exciting than anything an independent Scotland could offer. In an independent Scotland the people will, boringly and predictably, get the government they vote for, only the Union can offer the high-stakes risk and thrill of gambling your future on the voting decisions of people who think that Nigel the Bawbag is worth listening to. Pity the odds are stacked against us then. In Westminster the bawbags always win.

The Tories, the Lib Dems, and Labour all promise the same thrills, the same circus of victims being devoured by the ravenous beasts of the City of London. So aye, the Union is dead thrilling, destruction and devastation often is when you're viewing it in safety from a political sinecure. Roman Emperors were experts in providing thrills too. But I don't want thrills from my government. I want decent government and accountability. I want political parties which make manifesto commitments that they keep. Cleggie isn't going to give us that, and neither are any of the rest of them. Under Westminster, there's bugger all we can do about it.

So no Nick. The thrill of the Union has long gone. And very shortly, so will you. There is no positive case for the Union. If there was we'd have heard it a long time ago. All you have to offer are scare stories and threats dressed up in lies. We've had enough of them, we've had enough of you. In September we can wave bye bye to you, to Danny, and to Nigel the Bawbag. You won't be missed.

29 March 2014
Truth and consequences

According to the Guardian, a UK Government minister who the paper claims would play a major role in negotiations following a yes vote - so not Danny Alexander or Alistair Carmichael then - has admitted that a currency union would happen. According to some reports, the person in question is an "uncomfortably senior Tory". Which rules out Vince Cable, who would otherwise be the likely suspect.

The truth is it doesn't really matter. What matters is that our Westminster masters are beginning to realise that the independence campaign is not drowning under a tsunami wave of scare stories. Scotland has learned how to surf. The more they throw in, the higher yes rises.

It was another lost in translation problem with the Scottish vernacular, the UK Government didn't understand at first that when Scotland responded to Osborne's threat with "aye, that will be right", we were not in fact agreeing with him. The penny has now dropped, along with Better Together's poll ratings. Meanwhile the independence campaign keeps surfing higher.

The minister even admitted what many north of the Border have been saying for a while, that the no to a currency union is a tactic in the referendum campaign, but after a yes vote everything changes and there will be less of the foot-stamping petulance and more of the reasonable discussion on matters of mutual interest. He hinted that Westminster might be willing to enter a currency union, but only if Scotland will negotiate on, say, Trident removal. Which is bound to provoke another "aye, that will be right" from a considerable section of the Scottish populace. Getting rid of the weapons of mass destruction sitting 20 miles from Scotland's largest population centre is a moral question. A currency union is a matter of money. I know which is more important because I'm not a Tory MP.

But the main point is that Better Together's currency claims have been debunked, not by a pro-indy blogger, not by an economist, not even by a rogue backbencher. They were debunked by a UK Government minister at the very heart of the anti-independence campaign. Better Together has been sowing a minefield of lies. With a few words in the shell-like of a Guardian journalist who isn't Severin Carrell, the anonymous minister deliberately trod on the biggest landmine in Project Fear's armoury. The damage limitation squad was rapidly deployed, but the corpse of the currency threat has exploded into a pink mist. There's nothing left to put back together.

Of course that hasn't stopped Better Together's bitter enders from trying. It's just people being emotional, as Alistair Carmichael was trotted out to blubber, and as one insider said to the Guardian's reporter:

"We went early with the currency union announcement in the hope that a rational, rather than an emotional, judgment will prevail among voters," one Better Together source said. "But people have got to believe we mean it."

And there's their problem right there. People don't believe Better Together on the currency, nor about anything much else. They've been caught out too many times in the past. These are the people who brought us the economic crisis, the war in Iraq, the expenses scandal, the lack of accountability in just about every UK institution you care to mention, and on and bloody on... You'd think they'd have realised that their credibility tanks contained nothing but a nasty smell.

In a referendum where the central question for the Unionist campaign is "does Scotland want to give Westminster another chance", the low esteem in which the public hold the political classes demanded their truth and candour from the beginning. It required the renegotiation of public trust. It meant listening and learning. And if they'd done that they'd have realised that they should have snapped up the offer of a question on the ballot about enhanced devolution, and come up with a credible and meaningful proposal. We'd be in a whole different campaign, and Alistair Darling wouldn't be knotting his distinctive eyebrows.

Instead we got a promise to conduct a positive campaign followed by a barrage of fear and scares. The entire premise of the Better Together campaign strategy is itself a lie. Disnae bode well for the rebuilding of public trust does it. And now one of their insiders has more or less admitted they've been lying on the currency all along.

Better Together is paying the price for relying on lies as a campaigning tool, even when you can trust a friendly media which won't probe too far into uncomfortable questions - at least if you can maintain a semblance of keeping a lid on things.

It starts off with a promise to be truthful. But then you tell a little lie. Then you have to tell a big lie to keep the wee lie sounding plausible. Then the lies run away with you and you begin to sense that people don't believe you any more. So you tell a really big lie, or three. Yet this only causes people to doubt you even more. And so the lies grow more colourful and fantastic and contrived. By this time you have lost track of your lies and no longer know what's the truth and what's the lie. As the contradictions slam into one another like Eric Joyce in a House of Commons bar, in your panic you end up exposing your own lies, and your stories lie shattered around your feet amidst the wreckage you've created from the lives around you.

By this time you're left with as much credibility as a devolution proposal from Johann Lamont. And even a friendly media finds it difficult to ignore, because now their credibility is on the line too.

Like many gay men of my generation, I spent quite some time in the closet. My straight friends and family didn't know I was gay. For much of my 20s I lived a double life and got very good at lying. I know a lot about lying. And I know that lying takes its toll. There's a heavy price to pay for lying, even if you're not found out. When you spend your life trying to pretend to be something you are not, you lose sight of everything that has real meaning and value. Which is why one day I woke up and something just snapped. I thought "och fuck this", and came out and started living truthfully. It was the best decision I ever made.

Westminster lives a lie, a not very important European power trying to cling on to former glories, pretending the Union is something it is not. They've lost sight of everything that has real meaning and value, and can't tell the difference between truth and lies any more. And the lives that suffer the consequences are mine and yours and the disabled auld guy along the street, the lassie on the zero hours contract waiting by the phone as the electric meter counts down to cold, the lad who can't find a job and has to think about leaving.

I was much better at lying than Better Together, because I never got found out. They've been found out. And I fervently hope that come the 18th of September, Scotland will wake up, muse on the condition that this country is in, and think "och feck this" and vote yes.

Then Scotland can live truthfully.

30 March 2014

There is nothing that you could ever say to me now that I could ever believe

On the weekend when Project Fear ought to have been gloating about a plummeting yes vote after Osborne's currency veto, Barroso's intervention on the EU, and the announcement of Labour's devo proposals, they are instead searching for the Tory minister who crapped all over a stumbling no campaign and destroyed what little credibility they have left. Well I say stumbling. Like when you stumble off the edge of a 300 foot cliff onto the jagged rocks below. The last couple of weeks couldn't have been worse for them.

Labour is sinking into the quagmire of devo proposals that not even their own front bench can understand, the arguments and recriminations have barely started. The party's UK poll lead over the Tories has shrunk to 1%, making it unlikely that they will form the next government, so their devo-nothing proposals are not even likely to get as far as being eviscerated in Westminster committee hearings. Johann has gone back into hiding, leaving Jackie Baillie to attack Alicsammin at FMQs for "standing shoulder to shoulder with the Tories" only for him to helpfully point out that Labour sits down and dines with them. Jackie is going to be a speaker at a Cowal Conservatives lunch.

The Lib Dem conference was notable only for the fact that a couple of leading party members announced their intention to vote yes while the Lib Dems continue to plummet in the polls. The European elections are looming, and the anti-Scottish UKIP looks set to do well, giving voters in the referendum another reason to reject Westminster politics.

Yes campaigners have been chuckling away all weekend at the self-inflected wounds of Better Together. Schadenfreude is the evil twin of a good laugh, it is wrong to take pleasure in the misfortunes of others. Fortunately there is a special dispensation when the misfortune is suffered by people who have engaged in underhand and deceitful behaviour, only to learn a very hard lesson in Buddhist philosophy. Project Fear's bad karma ran over their currency dogma and Danny Alexander's annoying wee yap lies pancake shaped on the A9.

Translated from the original Pali, the law of karma says that if you spend your days throwing turds, everything you touch will get covered in crap. Following the news that even a Tory minister doesn't believe Osborne's sterling threat, Better Together makes the lavvy in a dysentry ward look hygienic.

The currency threat formed the centrepiece of Project Fear, the big scary story that all the other little scare stories hang from like dangleberries on an unwiped arse. It lived up to Better Together's expectations in one important respect. They wanted a game-changer, and it was. It just didn't change things in their preferred direction.

We now learn the currency threat was the invention of Alistair Darling, who was one of the main players presiding over the last

Labour government's economic implosion, and a Scots Tory advisor called Andrew Dunlop who had a big hand in that other Westminster success story, the Poll Tax. They're Proud Scots but. They're only trying to threaten, bully and scare Scots shitless because they love us so much. They call it tough love, the rest of the world calls it abuse. If Westminster was a parent, social services would have swept down and taken Scotland into the safety of a foster home.

Tory backbenchers are beelin that a former Labour Chancellor is influencing Tory Treasury policy. It's not that they have any greater understanding of the nature of the Scottish debate, they're just annoyed that they didn't get the chance to screw Scotland over first. But the cracks in the no campaign's fragile façade are now wide open, exposing the nasty germs on the dirty toilet seat they want Scotland to sit on.

The Secretary of State for Scare Stories has had a busy weekend on janitorial duties, rushing from tv studio to tv studio with a bottle of Osborne own brand mind bleach and doing an impression of bog paper, denying that the leak came from anyone important and the person doesn't know what they're talking about anyway. The problem is that the person he's talking about is a senior Tory minister. Better Together's defence of their discredited currency threat rests on persuading Scotland that Coalition ministers don't know what they're talking about, which we had kinda already figured out for ourselves.

Demonstrating only that there may be some truth in the theory of nominative determinism, Karmamightkill delivered the message with the look of a man who knew that his excuses were on a par with "the dog ate my homework", only with less chance of being believed by the teacher. Although to be fair, that's the look he's always got, but now he's covered with suspicious brown stains as well.

It's too late. From now on in, every claim from Project Fear, every scare, every threat, can be countered by pointing out that even their own inner circle don't believe them, so why should anyone else. Scotland switched off when the threat was first made, and with every attempt to retrieve the situation, Alistair has only made it worse. Karma has killed.

You can only lie to people so often before they stop listening. The leading lights of the naw campaign ought to understand that better than most. Gordon Brown's words to Tony Blair in 2004 have come back to haunt the Better Together campaign, and will set the tone from now until September.

"There is nothing that you could ever say to me now that I could ever believe."

31 March 2014
Blinking for Britain

Alistair Darling has been blinking for Britain in interviews again, as he tries to haul his credibility out of a bottomless pit with a length of string he's spun out of frayed press releases. The Tory minister's admission to the Guardian that Westminster's sterling zone veto is merely a negotiating tactic has left Ali as exposed as transvestite with a 6 o clock shadow and his size 12 feet in his mouth, refusing to believe that people know he's really a man. A small and discredited man.

Ali clutched his handbag containing all that's dear to his heart, his Commons expense claim form, the draft chapter in his memoirs where he takes credit for saving the Union, and the invite to the Tory party dinner. With a toss of the hair on his Better Together fright wig he tried to maintain that the pretence was not a pretence. He's really a 60 year old woman called Brenda who won't be allowed to use the pound to buy her train ticket to visit her newly foreign grandweans in England. He now insists that in their manifestos for the 2015 General Election the Westminster parties would include a promise to veto any currency zone encompassing an independent Scotland, and accused the yes campaign of clutching at straws. He knows a lot about clutching, and grasping. "We're not lying!" he lied.

It was entirely predictable that he'd say this. What else is he going to say - "Oops, you caught me. I have in fact been lying from the start." It might be the truth but they are not words that will ever fall from Ali's Boots Number 11 painted lips. The no campaign rests upon the plausibility of the currency threat which Ali and his pals have chosen to make the centrepiece of their referendum campaign, a strategy which the media have enthusiastically followed like a wee dug sniffing a trail of pee. All is won or lost on persuading Scots that he's a man of his word, yet now he sees a future where he's not the saviour of the Union on a red bench, he's a disgraced stranger in a strange independent land. The man who conspired with the Tories to damage his country's prospects, then lied to his own people. I almost feel sorry for him. Almost. Not quite.

Attempting to crowd out the many and varied non-economic arguments for independence has been the core of Ali's strategy, because he has no answer to these other arguments. And now the currency threat lies shattered and broken like Ali's dreams of winning the Miss Better Together beauty parade, his hopes of an ermine gown and a coronet becoming as implausibly ridiculous as a BBC news report on the Royal family.

It's a non-economic argument which is also at the centre of Better Together's currency credibility, or rather its lack of credibility. The real point is that it doesn't actually matter who the Tory minister is, and it doesn't even matter whether he is wrong and Osborne really is prepared to damage the UK economy in a fit of spite.

The damage has been done by the fact that the source of the Guardian's story is a Tory minister, and an "embarrassingly senior" one at that. A senior Tory minister who does not believe what his own party are saying about Scotland. A senior Tory minister who knows that his party is lying through their back teeth to the Scottish electorate in order to court popularity amongst UKIP leaning voters in the south.

Say what you like about Tory ministers, but they're not going to admit - even anonymously - to lying if they honestly believed it's inconceivable that their party might lie. Even if the minister in question knew nothing about the currency veto, which would raise a whole lot of questions by itself, he knows they've lied on other topics. He knows they will continue to lie. And so does Alistair.

Which brings us straight to the biggest non-economic argument for independence - how can it be in good for Scotland to be governed by people who will lie to us and damage Scottish interests in order to secure elections in the rest of the UK. Scotland's interests are not their top priority, we already knew that. Now we know that Scotland's interests don't even figure in their calculations, they can be sacrificed to the minor demons of UKIP on the altar of appeasement.

It goes to the very heart of the Union - what sort of Union is Scotland in? We're constantly told it's a partnership of equals, that Scotland benefits immensely from throwing in its lot with its neighbours, yet in the corridors of Westminster the bottom line on the balance sheet is that everything belongs to them. It's their pound, not ours, it's their army, not ours, it's their membership of the EU, not ours. After 300 years we're Better Together with nothing of our own.

Everything that issues from Better Together is based upon the assumption that after Scottish independence Westminster and Westminster alone will be the parliament of the sole successor state. Westminster believes that the Union was not created when the Kingdom of Scotland and the Kingdom of England signed the Treaties of Union. It was England all along. That's the legal position adopted by the UK Government, that's the position adopted by Alistair as a route to a red bench and a fur trimmed retirement. Yet it's not a legal argument that has solid foundations. They only appear solid because no one in the mainstream media has ever examined them. But you don't need to be a constitutional civil engineer see that they are made of sand and built on fervent wishes. Scotland's case is strong.

Scotland will not be walking away from the United Kingdom, Scottish independence will bring the Union to an end, and when it ends Scotland will take what Scotland is due - which includes the pound. Otherwise Westminster gets to keep all the debt. That's the reality that the terrified Alistair doesn't want to acknowledge. That's the reality that doesn't alter even if Westminster keeps calling itself the United Kingdom and keeps using the same flag.

When the Soviet Union collapsed in the early 90s, Russia became the sole successor state, and Russia took on all the national debt and inherited the USSR's seat on the UN Security Council. But this only happened because the other Soviet republics agreed to it. Westminster is assuming that after a yes vote, it can accede to the status of sole successor state, that all other states will accept this unquestioningly and Scotland can't challenge it. But they want us to take on the debt anyway, even though it is in Westminster's name, even though there are no financial institutions possessing government bonds saying, "IOU squillions of quid, xx Scotland".

Think again. Scotland could internationalise the dispute. As a sovereign state we don't need Westminster's permission to make our own approaches to other states and governments. There are a number of routes by which the government of an independent Scotland, or even a private Scottish citizen, could mount a challenge to Westminster's claim to sole successor status. And that's without considering whether other states will refuse to recognise Westminster's claim for reasons of their own.

The opportunistic Putin or the Chinese government would happily grasp the opportunity to block the rUK's seat on the UN Security Council if Scotland were to raise objections to the seat being occupied by a Foreign Office bum. Russia and China have no interest in fighting Scotland's corner, but they do have a big interest in reducing the influence of Western powers. Does Westminster want to risk giving them the chance? It seems they do.

The European Courts would also provide a venue for the airing of Scottish legal complaints. The Scottish Government could challenge Westminster's claim to be sole successor state and sole inheritor of the UK's EU membership. Any Scottish citizen who was affected by Westminster's purloining of sole successor state status could mount a legal challenge, arguing that their rights as a European citizen were being breached.

And while all this was going on, Westminster would be faced with EU partners on one side who wanted a quick and speedy resolution, while facing down Nigel Farage on the other. It's an uncomfortable bed they are making for themselves.

That's what Alistair is desperate to avoid. He's desperate to avoid his own constituents and his own country having the power to fight their own corner, to make their own decisions. He's desperate to avoid a retirement spent in ignominy. But it's too late. The truth is out and Better Together's flushed face is busted, their threats exposed.

Blink your way out of that one Alistair.

April 2014

1 April 2014
April fuel

It's the first of April, and the newspapers traditionally publish a spoof news story, and just as traditionally they're about making fun of Scottish people and their silly pretensions. The idea that Scotland might govern itself better than Westminster can do it for us is apparently the biggest April fool of all. The Guardian tells us that Scotland will be driving on the right, while the Telegraph insists that Alicsammin's heid's going on the new Scottish pound coin. Meanwhile the Independent warns that in the event of a Yes vote Scotland will be occupied by UN peacekeepers, and from behind its paywall the Times says that some German prince is aiming to become king in an independent Scotland. Such larks.

In the interests of research, I even looked on the Daily Mail website so you don't have to. They did have a piece about parking signs discriminating against men and being a part of an EU feminist plot, but it turned out that wasn't a spoof, it was just the Mail being swivel eyed again. I couldn't tell their April Fool spoof from the rest of the guff that litters their pages, but there's bound to be some joke about the "poond" in there somewhere.

I'm not sure who says "poond", apart from people trying and failing to use Scots words, folk from "Glazgie" - that mythical Scottish city just south of Millengavy and east of Grennock - and columnists in the

UK media. Whenever someone in the last category uses the word, it's done in a contemptuous and dismissive way. It must be, because if the person using it wasn't intending to be contemptuous and dismissive they've have been arsed enough to find out what the real Scots word for pound is. Poond isn't a real word because Scotland can't have a real pound. But I digress.

Eventually I found the Mail's spoof. It's an article claiming that after Scottish independence the blue bits will be bleached out of the Union flag. Only that's a story that the Guardian did some months ago.

Anyway, it's all just a laff right, and humourless nats can't take a joke. And in isolation, that would be true. But it's not in isolation. It's all the time, and the jokes are generally directed against the Scots as a whole, and make use of the same set of limited set of stereotypes. There's no real difference between them and Jim Davidson's jokes about black people. They're just a laff as well, at least if you're a gin swilling golf club member in Surrey.

If Scottish publications published similar jokes about the English, their silly pronunciations and inability to say the letter R, their daft belief that they can manage their own affairs, and their ridiculous notion that England punches above its weight and isn't just a lackey of the Pentagon, there would be howls of outrage about evil Scottish anti-English racists from the very same people who say Scottish nationalists have no sense of humour. Andrew Marr would present a special programme on the BBC about it, with lots of concerned commentators probing into the deep dark recesses of the Scottish psyche and its supposed seething hatred of all things English. When English people do it about Scots, it's just a bit of banter and touchy Scots with a chip on their shoulder read far too much into it.

It's not the unfunny jokes we object to. It's the double standards. But don't expect the UK media to get it.

The UK media's April fool efforts weren't even original. We've already been told we will have to drive on the right after independence, Labour's Andy Burnham said as much a few months ago, only he was being serious. Or rather, as serious as it's possible for Labour to be when they have only a tangential relationship to reality. Labour's claim to be returning to its socialist roots is the real joke.

Scotland has also had threats of military occupation. Just last month the Independent published a warning that an independent Scotland might end up at war with itself like the Ukraine. Now they've republished the same story as an April fool spoof. A possible Scottish currency is the regular butt of jokes and contemptuous dismissal from UK media types, the Guardian has already run a "light hearted" feature asking what the new Scottish currency should be called.

Writing in the Telegraph a few weeks ago, Tory commentator Peter Oborne suggested that Cameron should advise Liz not to be queen in an indy Scotland and Scotland could get some random person called Stuart instead. So the Times duchy original duke joke has already been done as a proper threat too. There's fresher and more topical humour on 1940s seaside postcards.

Who needs a Tory minister to admit that the currency threat is a bluff? When the threats and scares issued by Better Together start appearing in their own newspapers as April Fool spoofs, we have conclusive proof that the entire No campaign is a poorly thought out joke. And their strategists wonder why Scottish people don't believe them any more.

But we shouldn't complain too much. It's all April fuel for the yes campaign.

2 April 2014

A dictionary of Unionese

Alicsammin: The UK press believes the referendum question is "Do you want Scotland to be an alicsammin country?" It's all about Alicsammin. Alicsammin is the only person in Scotland who wants independence, no one else had ever thought of the idea before he did. This is why the press constantly attacks Alicsammin, because if people don't like him they wouldn't dream of voting yes.

Anglophobia: Any sentence uttered by a supporter of Scottish independence which contains the words "England" or "English".

Banter: A racist slur directed against Scottish people in the UK media. It's just a bit of a laff.

Barroso: An EU mannikin, a Portuguese Tory with pals in the Spanish Partido Popular - but he's still a neutral voice of authority because he's foreign. Barroso is the latest technological advance in talking dolls, no more having to pull a on a string to hear a selection of rote comments - if you offer to support his candidacy for the post of chief of NATO, you can get him to say anything you want.

BBC: The neutral, unbiased and utterly impartial broadcasters of Great British News Bake Off, a light hearted competition presented by Andrew Marr in which contestants vie to cook up scare stories against independence from sour dough.

Big Beast: A Westminster dinosaur with a well padded bank account and an enormous sense of entitlement.

Bullying: Criticism of Westminster, any Unionist, or any Unionist media outlet, by an online supporter of Scottish independence. The British Government is regularly bullied by an arthritic granny in Fife whose grandson bought her a laptop for Christmas. She keeps sending Alistair Darling messages telling him his tea is oot.

Currency union: Mentioning a currency union will provoke a temper tantrum, foot stamping, and "But you can't make me! It's not fair!" - which results in being put on the naughty debt step.

Cybernat: An independence supporter with an internet connection and an attitude. According to the Unionists, cybernats are controlled by Alicsammin's mind control waves and form part of an organised and highly disciplined army of robots which Alicsammin can switch on an off simply by sticking his tongue in a filling. This is sadly mistaken, cybernats think independently.

Devo Journey: The process by which the Labour party ensures it has power in Holyrood and Alistair Darling gets a seat in the House of Lords.

Devomax / Federal Britain: A unicorn, occasionally glimpsed by wishful thinkers, fantasists, and David Torrance.

Difficult questions: Questions where the answer is withheld by the questioner, like a magic trick performed by an end of the pier conjurer but with Johann Lamont instead of a cute fluffy bunny. The process works by a combination of distraction techniques and ensuring that the audience don't have enough information to be able to work the trick out for themselves - like the UK Government's trickery over

Scottish EU membership, or Labour's devo-diddlysquat proposals and hints of possible jam. Better Together are believed to have employed Paul Daniels as a consultant on difficult questions. Sadly they ignored his advice to get rid of the fright wig.

Foreigner: A state of alienation and abandonment which prevents you from laughing at British comedy shows. Citizens of the Irish Republic are immune, and are also immune from being brought up by Unionists as an example when they assert Scots will become foreign.

Galloway: An ego on stilts and the true saviour of the Union. Galloway will save the Union by asking everyone to wait for a properly socialist Labour party. He doesn't know when it will arrive, he doesn't know how to create one, but he thinks it's a good idea because it keeps him on the telly. His flag is a red flag, and in order to make sure his flag keeps on being the red flag, he wants Scotland to have a red white and blue one.

Hatred: The misguided belief that a country is best governed by the people who live there.

Naughtie: Unit of measurement for anti-independence bias on the BBC. One Naughtie is worth ten Reporting Scotlands and five Sally Magnussons.

Nationalism: The root of all human evil, but thankfully Westminster is immune which is why they've never done anything bad, ever. British nationalism is the only non-nationalist nationalism on the planet because it stops people in the UK from being foreign. And being foreign is bad, but it's not nationalist to say that if you're British.

Negativity: Any expression of confidence in the future of Scotland which doesn't include a high profile post for Jim Murphy.

Positive case for the Union: A species of jam tomorrow, always promised but never arrives.

Proudscotbut: A defense mechanism employed by Unionist politicians when making statements or adopting policies which are damaging to Scotland. As a small reluctantly Catholic child I made use of a similar strategy in order to avoid getting penance when my mammy dragged me to Confession. Simply recite a list of made up minor sins, and end them with "And I tell lies" so you are covered for all of the above. Proudscotbut has the same effect in the independence debate, and covers up for a multitude of mortal sins that Unionist politicians won't admit to. Neither God nor the Scottish electorate is going to be fooled.

SNP: The only political party supporting Scottish independence, but only because they're controlled by Alicsammin's mind waves. They don't really support independence, they're just blinded by Alicsammin's halo.

Thinking it through: What independence supporters haven't done during the past 50 years or so that independence, the constitutional question, and the Scottish identity have been debated and discussed in Scotland. People from south of the border who have just arrived at the debate and know nothing about it are able to think things through in the 10 seconds it takes them to leave an irate comment in the Guardian complaining that Alicsammin hates English people.

Uncertainty: The only uncertainties are what happens after independence. The Union gives Scotland the certainty that it will continue to get Tory governments and things will stay as crap as they are just now forever. The Union also gives us the certainty that things will get much much worse after Westminster has pissed away the last of the oil revenues without investing them in Scotland's future.

3 April 2014
Wibble wobble

All is well, nothing to worry too much about, just a little wobble that was entirely to be expected. Wibble wibble went the Unionist press as it tried to minimise the effects of eight little words from a senior Tory minister on a campaign which is neither better nor together. "Of course there will be a currency union."

Sadly for Alistair Darling these words did not come as a heroic but minor wound to a Naw campaign that has been confidently carrying Scotland into a red white and blue future, words that could be shrugged off manfully like John Wayne insisting it's just a scratch before single handedly defeating the entire Commanche nation. Project Fear had already received so many kicks in the bollox that they'd swollen up and are being used as a space hopper.

Tragically for them this must be the only form of transportation they possess - because every time they attempt to move, they only do themselves further damage. Alistair's assertion that there would have to be a referendum on a currency union in the rest of the UK was quickly squashed by a Downing Street that will not countenance the idea of a popular vote on a policy they've spent the last few months making unpopular but which they know they'll have to implement in some form if the independence referendum goes against them. So in that sense, aye, they're wobbling. Alistair Darling has turned into Buster Gonad.

According to the Telegraph there is no sign in London that the No campaign is about to change its strategy. They plan to keep digging themselves into a hole, confusing the quagmire into which Better Together has sunk with undermining the Yes campaign. They've put all the family jewels in Buster Gonad's wheelbarrow. There is no Plan B, there can be no Plan B, because Plan B could only mean making a positive case for the Union. The Unionist parties can only come together when Alistair tells them he has a wizzard wheeze for killing Scottish nationalism stone dead, again.

Alistair was the architect of the Balls, Osborne and Alexander plan, the BOA which is currently the star of their unconvincing Unionist drag act, the BOA their Unionist fathers woah. The knives are out for him, as the realisation dawns on Westminster that the BOA isn't the colourful neckwear at the centre of their campaign, the highlight on their dowdy frocks, it's a noose that's choking them.

In the absence of anything that looks like it will gain purchase in the referendum campaign, Project Fear can only ramp a failing strategy up another notch. Now they're trying to create fear not just about independence, but also about those campaigning for it. Evil cybernats who insult and abuse - that would be me, you, and thousands of others then.

But Scotland isn't Kenya during the Mau Mau rebellion, it's not Ireland when the IRA were bombing their way to Irish independence. Now Westminster is reduced to turning law abiding citizens into demons as they desperately try to pretend they are the underdogs in this campaign. The might of the all powerful British state, reduced to a quivering Help Me Rhona by a granny with a laptop, a carer with a computer, and the ancient Scottish tradition of mocking those who lie, dissemble and deceive. It's a strategy which works well south of the Border, but in Scotland where people live the reality of this campaign no one is fooled, except the Unionists who fool themselves.

It raises an interesting question. If the British state can be bullied, threatened and abused by a bunch of ordinary citizens with nothing more than wit, humour, and the truth as their weapons, just how do they expect to convince Scotland that our country can't survive without their protection and stewardship? If they're threatened by a pensioner with an ipad, just how would they cope with a real threat? Not well, is the only possible answer.

Meanwhile Westminster's focus has shifted to the more pressing issue of May's European elections where it is looking increasingly likely that Nigel Farage and UKIP will perform strongly, forcing the Conservatives to tack further to the right and giving Labour wriggle room in the so-called centre ground of British politics. Which means clearing a space on the right for Labour to occupy, and removing the party even further from the aspirations of Labour's traditional voters.

So the flooding of fear continues, today the engineering and defence company Weir Group made their predicted and predictable claim that independence would damage jobs and their business, citing a paper they had commissioned from an economic think tank with close links to the UK Treasury. In 1997 the company made similar claims about the doom and gloom that would befall Scotland if the country voted for devolution.

Few listened then, few will listen now. Scotland has had enough of being lectured to by voices of self-proclaimed authority, tied to Westminster by an umbilical cord of patronage and contracts. The warnings didn't work when they were issued by other think tanks and other companies. Better Together has no more hope that they will work now. Poor Alistair, nothing but spin while he's not for turning and the BOA wraps itself ever more tightly around his neck.

4 April 2014
Antisocial history

Hello world! Welcome to the Commonwealth Games. We're your hosts, Glesca Labour Cooncil, watch us blow up our city and sell it off to private developers!

Gordon Matheson, leader of Glesca Cooncil's Committee for Secret Rendevouz in Car Parks and Pretendy Architectural Competitions, thinks demolishing the Red Road flats as a spectacle to celebrate the opening of the Commonwealth games is a great idea, a brave idea, one that highlights Glasgow's social history. But however batshit insane anyone might think the idea is, Gordie is correct, and the city faithers are only continuing in a long and proud tradition of demolishing the city in the name of supposed regeneration, then crowing about it crassly. Well that and having suspiciously friendly connections to property companies.

It's Glasgow's social history. It's the social history of a Victorian city council that demolished a 15th century university building to make way for a railway goods yard, then in the late 20th century demolished the railway goods yard to build new office spaces. It's the social history of Parliamentary Road, once one of the city's main thoroughfares and the heart of Toonheid, which is now lost under multi-story blocks and a motorway. It's the story of the Gallowgate, once a thriving bustling street of shops, the aorta of the East End. Now the Gallowgate is empty and dead, a through route but not a destination. Glasgow's social history is the history of council vandalism in a city run for the powerful, not the people who form its soul and who breathe its life and vitality.

Social history is the history of the people and the communities they create. But communities are organic, they grow naturally out of settled groups who form relationships and connections. A mature community takes generations to evolve, and forms a rich rain forest (well, it is Glasgow, of course rain is involved) sheltering a diversity of family ties, bonds of friendship, places of work and leisure. Community regeneration Glasgow style involves blowing up the rain forest, selling off the valuable timber, and replacing it with spindly saplings tied to poles in a wasteland of cheaply constructed buildings which have to be demolished 30 years later, before a community ecosystem has a chance to regrow.

In Glasgow, the social history clock is reset to zero every generation. The result is disconnection and disorientation, alienation and deprivation. The distinctive flora and fauna of the Glasgow cityscape is driven away, never to return. The windae hinging wummin, the weans playing in the street, the auld boys smoking fags outside the pub, they go the way of the Amazon's rare and precious creatures, preserved only in books of tastefully shot photographs that cost half a weekly benefits payment. The wee guy in the bunnet on the page facing the chieftain with the lip plug, gazing out the pages of a book that neither can afford. Dignity preserved in sepia, but not allowed to flourish. That's what Gordon Matheson thinks of when he thinks of social history.

The Red Road flats were another one generation long experiment in social engineering, an experiment that failed. Glasgow is full of those. The flats are damp and unsuitable and need to be demolished, but at least they provided social housing. If the flats were being levelled in order to give the residents of Red Road the chance to rebuild their community in new and better social housing, perhaps that would be something to celebrate. But Glasgow Council is blowing up the 11,000 Glasgow Housing Association flats to make way for 7000 low rise housing units. Most of the new houses will be privately owned, just 500 new social housing units are slated to be constructed in the redevelopment plan. The social history clock is being reset to zero again.

One tower block is still inhabited, mostly by asylum seekers. Many of them came to Glasgow to escape those who wanted to blow up their homes. Now they're getting to witness explosive destruction again, as the buildings around them are cleared for a redevelopment that they don't earn enough to live in.

In the Glasgow North East constituency where the Red Road flats stand, 43% of children live in poverty. The same week that the announcement was made to blow up part of the constituency to thrill and enthrall visitors to the Commonwealth Games, the local Labour MP, Wullie I-Stay-With-Ma-Maw-But-Not-In-Red-Road Bain, voted in favour of the Tories' benefits cap along with 31 other Labour MPs representing Scottish seats. As a local dignitary, whose dignity is not to be confined to the pages of a book of tastefully shot black and white photies, Wullie will get an invite to the opening ceremony.

Tickets for the opening ceremony cost £40 each, how many of the kids living in poverty in Glasgow North East will be able to afford that? Probably about as many as will be able to afford one of the new private homes that will go up where their tower blocks used to stand.

When the Games were announced, Glasgow was promised all sorts of goodies. The legendary East End Subway extension was to be constructed, bringing a vital public transport link to a part of the city where car ownership is the lowest in the UK. The East End has been waiting for it longer than we've been waiting for a positive case for the Union. But the plans were quietly dropped, just like they were quietly dropped when an East End extension was first mooted in the 1940s. Instead we're promised a new expressway for the cars few can afford. It's going to run along an old railway line that's now a public green space where the local dogs are walked and foxes and squirrels make their home. They'll become more refugees as the cooncil lets Glasgow flourish in a fog of car exhausts.

This is the city that Glasgow Labour wants to show to the world - one that destroys social housing to make way for the market, one that ends the social history of a community in order to celebrate it. It builds houses that those cleared out cannot afford to buy. And it wants us to rejoice.

"People make Glasgow" is the Council's marketing slogan. It's rarely rung more hollow. Glasgow's legacy from the Games will be opportunities for property developers to make money. It's Glasgow's antisocial history. So no change there then.

4 April 2014

Thank you Margo

Margo MacDonald has lost her battle against Parkinsons. She was a rare and precious gift, a politician who was warm, likeable, truthful and passionate. No matter how brightly her star shone - her feet remained firmly planted on Scottish soil. She embodied a great paradox, a miracle even, despite being an extraordinary woman Margo was always one of the ordinary people.

Margo made me a into supporter of independence. I only met her once, very briefly, when she was standing for election as rector of Glasgow University back in the early 80s. I was shy and tongue tied in the presence of my hero, she'd already worked her magic on me long before when she won the Govan by-election. With that victory she showed a confused wee boy in the East End that working class Scottish people could take on the powerful and win with wit and intelligence as our only weapons. Margo taught us that Scottish independence was not just for beardy men with an obsession with ancient history. It was about social housing, about jobs, and above all about democracy. It was about us, our stories, our voices, our future.

And Margo had a voice that rang true and sang the song of self-determination. Margo taught us that self-determination begins with yourself. Set yourself free, break the mental chains that bind, see through the fear, don't defer to self-proclaimed authority. Margo taught us that if you live in the light of truth, if you feel the strength that comes from within - you can do anything. Margo didn't just preach that message. She lived it.

The fates dictated that Margo would not make it to the promised land, but she showed the rest of us the way. She was one of the greatest Scots of her generation, of all generations. She will be remembered, she will be missed.

Today I'm shedding a tear for Margo. I've never before wept when a politician has died. But Margot wasn't just a politician. She was far more than that. Her song lives on in the hearts of the thousands she reached out to and touched. Margo is gone, but her song will never be stilled. On the 18th of September we'll vote yes in her memory - and Scotland will make her proud.

Goodbye Margo. Thank you.

5 April 2014

Project Fear's letter to the McCorinthians

Let the love bombing begin! Well not really. It consisted of Eddie Izzard in union flag nail polish appearing at a Better Together fundraising concert in Edinburgh, paying his dues to the Labour party so they'll let him stand as their candidate for London Mayor. Eddie is a very talented comedian whose heart is in the right place, it's just a pity his understanding of Scotland is up his arse. Still, it was a sell-out event, just not in the sense of selling all the tickets.

Better Together events are always stage managed, and this one come came with a proper stage. It should have dominated today's Scottish news coverage but was pushed off top billing by the sad death of Margo MacDonald, having a last laugh at the contortions of a wealthy elite trying to manufacture a grass roots movement.

Eddie's appeal to Scotland consisted mainly of expressing the view that without Scotland, there would have been no London Olympics. This was a fine and emotional call, let down only by the fact that few in Scotland give a toss about the London Olympics, other than the fact that our taxes helped to pay for them, and the Olympics are awarded to cities, not countries. It's an appeal that might have worked on Chris Hoy, but the rest of us know that riding bikes really really quickly is merely a form of entertainment, it's not a strategy for governing a nation.

One of Eddie's funniest sketches is the Corinthians' Letter back to Saint Paul, in which he describes the reaction of citizens who wish only to decide their own rules for governing their city to a series of interventions from an interfering and self-important busy-body who doesn't have a clue. Amongst other imprecations, St Paul told the Corinthians that they should never put jam in a toaster. St Paul wouldn't approve of the nail polish, but apart from that Eddie's impersonation was spot on - although we can't put jam in a toaster as Scotland's jam never arrives. Eddie should ask Johann about that.

His comedic sketches might be a riot, but Scotland doesn't want to live in them. The joke isn't funny when Conservative governments are the punchline. In Eddie's letter back to St Paul from the Corinthians, the Corinthians told St Paul to fuck off. Perhaps Better Together was hoping for a similar reaction from Scots, giving them more grist to their evil cybernat mill. But it didn't happen. There were no heckles from the audience, which is hardly surprising since there aren't many independence supporters who are going to pay £25 towards Better Together's funds just so they could should fuck off at a distant stage. We can do that at TV screens for free.

Johann Lamont opened the proceedings, and received a huge cheer from an audience who thought they were in the presence of the UK's most surreal transvestite. But then she opened her gob. It's a shame really, with Labour's shambolic devocontradictions she's got some extremely good material for comedy, but Johann has no sense of. All she does is slag off Alicsammin, poorly. Timing. If she'd been a real comedian she'd have been howked off with a stick.

Meanwhile another wannabe stand up comedian was making his pitch to an audience at a Tory party gathering in London. Davie Cameron was again hoping that someone, somewhere, would make a positive case for the Union. But it wasn't going to be Davie, who trotted through a list of achievements that belong in ancient history. There was precious little about the future, which is where the rest of us will be living while Davie lives in the past. Even so, it might have counted for something if Davie and his crew were not hell bent on destroying the legacy of the United Kingdom that he hopes might appeal to Scotland.

In lieu of a positive case, Davie had to rely on the old stand up material, personalising the debate and making out it's all about Alicsammin. Alicsammin has no independence plan, said Davie, although he still won't come to Scotland to debate the Eck. Davie can't risk his assertions being challenged, since Scotland knows that he's about as plausible as St Paul in an Eddie Izzard sketch.

The only plan Davie has ever had is to continue to treat Scotland as a cashcow, a source of skilled labour, of resources to be pillaged, and along with everywhere outside London as an internal colony in the service of the City. To be fair, that is a plan. It's just a rubbish one. If Davie wants to tell Scotland not to put jam in a toaster, it might help if he provided some jam.

There is only one plan that's required for Scottish independence, and that's the plan to vote yes in September. The rest isn't up to Alicsammin, it's up to the people of Scotland. That Davie, is the only plan we need.

Monstering for independence

Monstering for Independence

OMG. If we'd only known. All this time we thought we were putting a positive case for an independent Scotland and pointing out the misinformation and machinations of a duplicitous Westminster, but no, we're just being nasty and getting Alistair Darling all upset. It's wrong to make Alistair sad, he cries himself to sleep at night and it puts him off his cornflakes of a morning. And that in turn means that when he grants an audience to a fawning Andrew Marr he's feeling a bit tired and run down which could very well bring about the end of democracy as we know it. Or at least as Alistair knows it. And that's your fault cybernat person. And you at the back, sniggering. And mine. I feel so awful.

Sometimes, when they've just come out with a truly spectacular piece of pish, which is more or less every time Blair MacDougall tweets something, we even laugh at them. Laughing at people is worse than talking pish. It's perfectly fine for unionists to collude with one another in private, then to come out with made up stories to scare folk, scare stories which promptly fall apart under the weight of their own contradictions - but don't you dare mock them for it. It's bullying. Mocking is what Nessie would do. And she's a monster.

Alistair has an image of himself as the Ambassador whose staff hand out the Ferrero Rocher while Scotland goes "ooh you are spoiling us Mr Darling." Alistair is handing out confections after all, but they have a sour and bitter taste. He's aggrieved that he's not being deferred to, because everyone ought to treat him like Andrew Marr does. That's not a monster coming over the hill Alistair, it's a chartered surveyor from Banff who thinks you're talking nonsense.

Anyway, the word "monster" now has a new usage as a verb, it means "criticising the arguments of unionists". Darling also has a new usage as a verb, it means "unwittingly revealing a lie by frantic blinking", as in "He said wasn't seeing George Osborne in secret, but he was darling sexting messages in morse code."

Demonising independence supporters has been ramped up a notch of late. It's part of Better Together's so-called wedge strategy, the one that was meant to drive a wedge between the supposedly tiny minority of nailed on yes voters and everyone else. But all it's produced is the wedgie in Project Fear's liar liar pants on fire, which may explain why Alistair was sitting so uncomfortably while he was smooching with Andy Marr.

Since the currency fearbomb went off like a fart cushion instead of a small thermonuclear device, the demonisation of yes supporters is the only part of the wedgie strategy that Better Together thinks there's a chance of howking out the deep dark skid mark where the rest of their campaign resides. The people they're trying to reach are not yes voters, they're trying to persuade the don't knows that yes voters aren't the kind of people that sensible ordinary folk would want to be associated with. Yes voters are the kind of people who use words like skid mark with reference to politicians, and Jim Murphy wants that sort of thing banned.

There's a big problem with this strategy however. It's what I call the Catholic relative conundrum. Back when being gay was a bigger sin than being a Tory, the Catholic relatives of gay people were confronted with a problem. On the one hand the authority of the church taught them that gay people were "intrinsically disordered" and were doomed to a life of misery and transient sordid affairs. On the other hand they were confronted with the reality of gay family members getting on with life and being perfectly happy in stable relationships. So who to believe? The evidence from authority, or the evidence of your own eyes and ears? The eyes and ears invariably have it.

Better Together now face the same problem the Catholic church did. Demonising a group only works when your parishioners have little or no first hand experience of members of that group. It's not Better Together which has the active, lively, and extremely numerous volunteers on the ground. But that's not the worst of their problems, when support for independence reaches over 40% in the polls, everyone in Scotland knows a yes voter. Most know several. Many know a lot.

People who have yet to decide how to vote already know yes voters. They are family members, friends, work colleagues, acquaintances. They will not form the opinion that yes voters are people you wouldn't want to associate with on the basis of what they are told by a political class which is already held in disrepute. The tactic will not shift the polls back towards No. It's more likely to have the opposite effect, providing more evidence in the ears and eyes of people who already sense the disconnect between Westminster and the lives of ordinary people in Scotland.

The demonisation of yes voters, the accusations of monstering, they're unpleasant - and are likely to intensify - but they are the sign of a No campaign which has lost its way.

Project Fear has been gulped down by its own imaginary monsters. Nessie's having a good laugh at that.

8 April 2014

Not a legend, an epitaph

The Labour party, after the currency union veto which left its credibility as sound as the Zimbabwean dollar, and the devobuggerall which not even their own leadership understands, has now announced a new strategy which is going to save the Union and kill nationalism stone dead. No don't mock, this time it will, honest. Anas Sarwar said so, and his dad thinks Anas is a first class politician.

The new killer strategy to put the fear of god into the monsters of independence is to summon up the Legends of the Lords. It sounds more like an episode of He-Man Masters of the Universe than a strategy, but Labour's been trading in cartoon fiction for decades, so it's really quite appropriate. And Jim Murphy blagged the role of Skeletor years ago. The marketing opportunities are obvious, in its assortment of lordy troughers, Labour has already got a surplus of overpriced plastic inaction figures. You can have your own in return for a part time directorship and a six figure salary.

It's a sub-Tolkienesque fairy tale, piss poor dialogue complete with goblins, intellectual dwarfs, and George Foulkes doing an impression of Gollum, on a quest to defeat the Wizard of Bute House who wants to slay the gold grubbing trolls of Westminsteron. Sadly, what with austerity and everything, the special effects budget is very limited, but Johann Lamont and Ian Davidson will be in it, so they're saving a fortune on orc costumes.

They got the lords, or at least people who were given pretendy titles by their pals in the party. The legend in this instance is the legend that Labour's lords are heavyweight statesmen and women who command respect, as opposed to them being a bunch of pensioned off troughers whose snouts are firmly buried in swill.

Gordie Broon is going to step up to the plate and save the day, which at least means he'd have to do a proper day's work in Scotland instead of jetting off to give highly paid speeches in conference centres in the Azores where he can insist that he saved the world. I'm sure Gordie stepped up to the plate and saved the day a couple of months ago, and then again a few weeks back, at least if stepping up to the plate and saving the day is defined as giving a speech in front of an invited audience of Labour loyalists and media representatives.

But there's a lot of other legends too. There's the legendary rightward trajectory of John Call Me Doctor Reid, the holiday companion of Radovan Karadžić, apologist for the Iraq war, and close ally of Tony Blair, who will put aside his differences with just about every single other person in the Labour party and pretend he's better together with people he loathes. He was once famously described by Henry McLeish as a "patronising bastard". He's got a PhD in pissing people off. John's a very clever man you see, but not clever enough to realise that people don't like it when you rub your intelligence in their faces like it was a custard pie. Or not possessed of sufficient empathy to care, which is a lot worse.

There's Helen Liddell, who was the local MP during the Monklands scandal when Labour was mired in accusations of sectarianism, and who once followed Robert Maxwell into a toilet. She will also happily give up her well remunerated time to condescend a wee bit to the little people. It will be just like presenting Reporting Scotland all over again, complete with the hysterical denunciations of alicsammin. She's even prepared some photies of some cute furry animals. Oh look a squirrel.

And then there's the old stalwarts. George Robertson will step up his efforts to persuade his business pals to issue statements against independence while telling Scotland we can't have independence because we have no culture. George Foulkes will do a wee dance with a polis and claim that independence supporters are being positive on purpose.

Sadly for Anas, big daddy, the emeritus MP for Govan, His Sarwarness himself, won't be able to make it as he's too busy fending off Islamic fundies in Punjab who've found out he made his money flogging alcohol to Scottish people and are not at all happy he's their new governor.

South of the border Labour is frantically hoping that voters will forget the dinosaurs of its previous terms in office, just in case the voters remember that Eds Miliband and Balls were up to their neck in it as well.

The architects of New Labour are one of the main reasons we're having this independence debate in the first place. They were the people whose terms in office finally put rest to any hopes that a vote for Labour was a vote for progressive and social democratic change. Labour gave us privatisation, PFI, ATOS contracts, ruinously expensive attempts to introduce compulsory ID cards, the security state and foreign wars. We got a financial sector that ran amok, and a government that rushed to rescue the banks while insisting the poor had to pay for the sins of the rich.

Anas's call for a Jurassic revival is Labour's equivalent of calling all hands to the pumps as their leaky ship hits the rock of devo-ye're-havin-a-laff. The gilded princes and princesses in first class have to go back to pumping bilge because Labour's natural support base has deserted them in droves. Anas isn't for saying why he thinks the disaffected will be enticed back by the very Labour figures who disaffected them in the first place. Which probably means that this latest wheeze has been as carefully thought through as Darling's currency scare and anything Johann Lamont has ever said in her entire life.

It's certainly just as desperate, and just as doomed to failure. It's not a Labour legend, it's an epitaph.

8 April 2014
Clatty jizzum

I know we're not supposed to go in for personal abuse, what with it being monstering and everything. But sometimes - well OK, daily - a Unionist politician utters something so gob-smackingly arsewipiferous that yer average human being turns into a special effect from Jurassic Park and is overcome with an urge to bite his head off. Dear reader, that politician is George Robertson.

Within 24 hours of Anas Sarwar calling on the Legends of Labour to save the day, Georgie has demonstrated his legendary ability to make idiotic statements which will come back to haunt him - like his claim that devolution would kill Scottish nationalism stone dead, or his belief that Scotland doesn't need independence because we have no language or culture of our own.

Georgie's latest is a warning that Scottish independence would be a cataclysm for the West. It would collude with the forces of darkness, make only Vladimir Putin happy, and he called on the US government to intervene and tell us to say naw. Like we're going to listen to American politicians. Independence would indeed be cataclysmic, but only for George's career and his rapidly plummeting public standing.

He repeated the lie, and he knows it's a lie, that NATO would refuse membership to an independent Scotland if we get rid of Trident.

First off, I should say that along with many in Scotland, I'd be delighted if NATO wouldn't let us in. I'd prefer Scotland to be neutral.

We are a nation which is blessed by geography in many ways, nature has seen fit to put Scotland on top of an ocean of energy resources, and blessed us even more by putting us in a quiet corner of the planet. We don't need to be a member of a military alliance that is as offensive as it is defensive.

That's my opinion, but unlike George I recognise that my opinion is not necessarily the one shared by most of Scotland. An independent Scotland will have choices. I choose for Scotland not to join NATO, but that may not be the choice of the government elected by an independent Scotland. The policy of the current Scottish Government is to join NATO. And despite what George says there is no reason NATO will refuse us membership.

The claim is frequently repeated, and was repeated again by George, that NATO would veto Scottish membership if we get rid of Trident. This is bollocks. And George knows it's bollocks. He reason he knows it is bollocks is because he was once the secretary general of NATO, and as such ought to know the organisation's history. He should know that an almost identical scenario played out before. Another country got rid of nuclear weapons and another country's nuclear submarines from its territory, then went on to join NATO. That country is Spain.

During the 1950s, the dictator Franco was isolated in Europe. In an effort to make friends in a continent which was now dominated by democracies and not the fascist dictatorships he was more comfortable with, Franco agreed to sook up to the US and allowed America to base Polaris nuclear missiles and their submarines at a naval base in Rota in Andalusia. Spain could not become a member of NATO, because Spain was not a democracy. Hosting US nukes was the next best thing for Franco.

The decision was unpopular in Spain, and only grew more unpopular after a series of accidents and incidents - the most serious of which occurred when a US plane carrying nuclear warheads crashed into the sea off the Spanish coast. After Franco's death in the mid 70s, a key demand of the pro-democracy parties in Spain was the closure of this base and the removal of US nuclear submarines and their missiles.

As Spain began the transition to democracy, negotiations were opened with the US for the rapid removal of the nukes. A treaty to this effect was signed between Spain and the USA in 1976, and the missiles were gone within a couple of years.

At the time, Spain did not want to join NATO. But just a few years later a Spanish Government went back on its election promise to keep the country neutral, and held a controversial referendum on NATO membership. Spain joined the alliance in 1982, just a couple of years after the American nukes were evicted from the country.

Spain rejected another country's nuclear submarines, then went on to join NATO. It's happened before George. Now explain to us why it can't happen again. The former secretary general of NATO is either ignorant of the organisation which he once led, or he's lying through his teeth in a transparent effort to save his own sorry airse and that of his pathetic bunch of fellow travellers in the Labour leadership.

The only forces of darkness in this referendum campaign are those which George represents.

11 April 2014
Diplomatic message

Oh dear. People in Scotland don't believe Project Fear's currency threat. A series of economists don't believe it, and have popped out of academia to challenge Better Together's threat in erudite sentences which include economic buzz words like 'quantitative easing', 'balance of trade deficit', and 'see that George Osborne, whit a balloon'. Tory cabinet ministers don't believe it - and they're so gullible that they believed Maria Miller's excuses. And now even that bastion of reticence and tact, people who have diplomatic in their job description, the representatives of foreign governments based in the UK are saying they don't believe it either, according to a report in the Guardian.

But it gets worse for Alistair Darling's master plan. In the estimation of these furren diplomats, Scottish independence looks likely. You can be certain that this opinion will have been reported back to capital cities all round the globe, where governments will now be preparing for the very real possibility of a 19th of September when Scotland reappears on the world stage after a 300 year absence billed below the Krankies in an austerity panto at the British Empire theatre.

And despite what Project Fear tells us, the world will welcome Scotland back into the community of nations. Because one of the things about being a small country out of the way on the corner of a continent, with pretty scenery, a rich history, and culture by the bucketload, is that we have never actually pissed anyone off seriously enough to make them hate us. Apart from Tories and UKIP voters, but they don't talk to furreners anyway. EXCEPT LOUDLY AND IN ENGLISH.

Take Spain as a furrexample. Project Fear's recurring ibero-meme is that Spain might block Scottish entry to the EU in order to discourage the Catalans, or even just to express their disapproval of what ABC, aka Franco's Favourite Newspaper, calls *los movimientos rupturistas*. I've already argued in previous blog posts why that's not going to happen, so won't repeat it here.

But I have every confidence that the Spanish government will change its tune after a yes vote. I lived in Spain for 15 years and am fluent in Spanish. I have many close friends of varying political opinions on the Catalan question. People I consider family. I know a range of former work colleagues and associates. So I think I know more than a Better Together press release writer about opinion in Spain regarding *la independencia escocesa*.

The truth is that irrespective of their views on Catalonia, people in Spain are overwhelmingly supportive and enthusiastic about the idea of Scotland returning to take her place amongst the independent nations of the world. This is true even of people who vote for the Partido Popular, the right wing party of Mariano Rajoy.

It's certainly true that many people in Spain have a highly romanticised, and even stereotypical, view of Scotland - but their romanticised stereotypes are highly positive ones. My favourite romanticised stereotype was the view that Scotsmen are deeply romantic. A view which can only be held by those who've never slept with one.

Both sides on the Catalan question hold the Scottish referendum debate up as a model of democratic legitimacy and reasoned argument. Both sides fully accept that Scotland is a nation in her own right, a nation in every sense of the word. *Unionistas* point to Scotland and say "Scotland was an independent state until historically recent times, they can be a state again", while *independentistas* point to Scotland and say "Scottish Unionists recognise Scotland's right to self determination, why can't Spanish Unionists recognise ours?"

By the way, it's far easier to express some political concepts in Spanish than in English. In Spanish you don't constantly have to have annoying arguments about all independence supporters being nationalists and just the same as Hitler. Spanish has the useful word *independentista* - which means a person who supports the right to self determination, and nationalism doesn't come into it. English just has the word "nationalist". Unfortunately the English version, independentist, makes you sound like a tooth puller for independence, or someone who does freelance fillings. Perhaps those are the ones we use to receive the secret signals from Alicsammin's underground lair... hmmm... But I digress...

Yet according to Project Fear, Spain is the country that is the ground zero of international naw-ness to Scottish independence. Spain ought to be hoatching with people who object vociferously to Scottish independence. And it's true that in the columns of right wing Spanish newspapers you will find the occasional OBE Juan. But go speak to Spanish people, and you find very few objections and a whole lot of positivity. That's a picture that repeats itself all over the globe, just ask one of the hundreds of thousands of Scots who've made their lives in furren pairts.

Foreign governments - at least the democratic ones - by and large reflect the views of their people. It's only Scotland that gets lumbered with governments which are completely unrepresentative of the popular will. And people in foreign countries, especially European countries, have positive views about Scotland. Foreign governments take the idea of Scottish independence in their stride. This doesn't mean there will be no problems or issues. But if there are issues foreign governments will be open to negotiation, and they will negotiate in good faith and with good will.

Better Together has shrugged it off. It's just a wee flush in the trajectory of a campaign which has already negotiated several toilet

U-bends, and descended down the sewer some while ago. They're not worried, because they say they haven't actually started campaigning properly yet. No, they really did say that, or at least Severin Carrell reported in the Guardian that they're saying it in private.

Which does kinda make ye wonder whit the feck they've been doing up to now, if they've not actually been campaigning properly yet. Has all of Project Fear just been an improper campaign then? It's nice to see that Better Together finally recognise what most of Scotland has seen for quite some time. It's a pretend campaign of togetherness involving people who would cheerfully send each other's grannies off to the tender mercies of an ATOS interview, and which spouts pretend threats and invented warnings. But in a little while, they'll be properly pretend threats. And they will pretend that it will make all the difference. They'll lay astroturf and pretend they're growing grassroots.

There's only one real campaign in Scotland. That's the yes campaign and its army of ambassadors who are out chapping on doors and changing opinions one by one - and it's only just beginning. There's 160 days to go. Let's use them well. There's a whole lot of don't knows and wavering no voters out there. Let's show them that independence means giving Scotland back her voice, being welcomed back into the community of nations, and sending a diplomatic message of our own -

Hello world! We're back!

13 April 2014
Labouring the point of independence

Alicsammin has made an appeal for Labour voters to remember something that Better Together and the Unionist media are desperate for them to forget - the referendum in September is not an election and no one is voting for alicsammin.

Like hundreds of thousands in Scotland, I am supposedly a natural Labour voter, but over the course of my lifetime the Labour party has migrated ever further removed from its roots and is no longer recognisable to most of us. It's a party which preaches austerity and practises privatisation. It's a party which even voted against free school meals.

No free school meals for Scottish kids living in poverty, but subsidised champagne for the princes of the party in Westminster. The radioactive contamination of Westminster took a working class movement for social justice and mutated it into the flesh eating zombies who sit in the Lords and a Commons populated by careerists and placemen whose sole concern is persuading Tory leaning voters in Labour-Tory marginals that the party has signed up to a Conservative agenda. The working class movement for social justice remains only as a tattered and neglected shop display in premises which have long since been occupied by a pay day loan shark.

There are no Labour-Tory marginals in Scotland. But the only way the party can win a General Election is to secure the votes of those Tory leaning voters in marginal constituencies - which are overwhelmingly located in the south of England - Tory voters who are increasingly attracted to the right wing populism of Farage and his bunch of homophobic meteorologists. That's the vote Labour has to attract, not working class voters in Scotland - or in Wales or Northern England or the impoverished inner city boroughs of London for that matter.

Labour isn't about to reform itself. For Labour's hierarchy, meaningful reform is whatever helps them win General Elections. Labour's leadership put their own careers first, then the interests of their party, then the interests of Westminster. The people of Scotland rank far below the need to tackle UKIP, a party with zero representation in Scotland. Compare and contrast the coverage in the UK media of the rise of UKIP with their coverage of the independence debate. It's obvious which they regard as more important. Even the most momentous democratic decision in Scottish history is considered less important than the antics of swivel eyed loons who blame flooding on gay marriage.

Labour won't address the concerns of its traditional voters, so it's up to Labour's traditional voters to force it to change. In politics, as in life, you can't sit back complaining about the jobby that's been deposited on your carpet. A pile of jobbies doesn't clean itself up. It will sit there steaming away until you clean it up yourself, and the longer you leave it the more it stains. With their obsessional hatred of alicsammin, Labour in Scotland have turned into a dirty protest, content to fling jobbies like chattering monkeys in red rosettes, cheering when Tories talk Scotland down, and standing on the same platform as bosses, barons and bankers to deny Scotland her assets and potential.

By bringing about a change in the electoral dynamic, a reform of the voting system for Westminster elections might have brought back to a Labour party that's worth the name, but electoral reform has been off the agenda since the failure of the AV referendum. That leaves Labour voters in Scotland with just one way of creating the radical change to electoral dynamics that can bring about reform of the Labour party - voting for independence.

Independence shatters Labour's Westminster shackles. It makes Labour in Scotland independent too. That doesn't mean that the party will instantly transform into the force for social democracy and progressive politics that many in Scotland long for, but it breaks the stranglehold of Westminster and opens up new opportunities for what will become a Scottish Labour party - a real Scottish Labour party, not a marketing brand for a Westminster bandwagon.

For too long Labour has called itself the people's party, and thought that this meant it could tell the people what to do. Labour will only be the people's party when the people take charge of their own destiny, and with it the destiny of Labour. So let's show them what the people can do - we can grasp Labour by the scruff of the neck and force it, kicking and screaming, into change. We are the people, not the Labour leadership.

Vote yes, and we might just get a Labour party that's worthy of the name. That's worth a yes vote all by itself.

14 April 2014

Project Fear's gumsy midgie

Another day, another scare story. Now we're told (copyright Justine Greening the Tory International Development Secretary) that Scottish independence will rip the bread from the mouths of the poorest people in the world. See those starving babies in the charity campaign advert? That's alicsammin's fault that is.

Justine says Scottish independence will reduce the UK's aid budget. Won't anyone think of the children? Justine thinks Scotland won't be giving anyone any aid of course, on account of us needing UN food parcels full of mars bars and lard.

Och, I cannae be arsed. Can you be arsed? Sometimes Better Together's scare stories are just so needledicked they're less consequential than a gumsy midgie. Let's just file this one under "too poor" and move on. Project Fear's embarrassed itself enough for the time being. Ignoring it is an act of kindness. And just to demonstrate that people in Scotland are in fact deeply charitable, more and more of them are ignoring Project Fear every day.

Instead, I'm going to list some of my top reasons for independence, just to prove that cynical auld gits can do positive too. Or at least as positive as some of us can get, which, to be honest, isn't very. So in no particular order ...

1. Getting rid of Trident

A weapon which can evaporate a city is worse than an obscenity. But it's not enough for some power crazy weapons fetishists to have the ability to wipe out the entire human race, oh no, they want to have the ability to wipe out everything that's more evolved than bacteria. Possibly because that's the only way they won't feel threatened by any intellectual superiors.

Trident has no redeeming features. It's not even a weapon of mass destruction that serves any purpose, other than allowing British politicians to make like they're important. They can't even use it without US permission. Trident is the viagra of the decrepit ruins of the British Empire, and we're all being screwed. We're going to have to pay hundreds of billions for the privilege.

I want it gone. Westminster governments have shown not the slightest inclination to get rid of Trident. Instead they want to spend vast sums on a new version, so British governments can have viagra with go-faster stripes and join in circle jerks with the Pentagon.

Independence means Scotland will be rid of Trident. I'd vote yes for that reason alone.

2. Politicians cannae be trusted

People who want to make a career out of making laws for other people to follow are people who need to be kept on a short leash. Scotland's Westminster masters are not on a short leash. They're on an infinitely long elastic which passes with ease through wormholes in the fabric of space and time. They call it the UK's unwritten constitution. What it really means is that the Westminster Parliament can do whatever suits itself, and that's exactly what it does, and is exactly the way the Unionist parties like it. Vote yes and we snap the elastic, leaving Westminster's knickers around its ankles.

Independence would give Scotland a written constitution. There would be rules, there would be checks and balances. There would be no infinitely long elastic. There would be a short leash. I want people with power close enough so my foot can reach their arses, metaphorically speaking, of course.

3. Did I mention that politicians really cannae be trusted

They never do what they say. Aye right, hordes of SNP supporters are going to tell me that the SNP Government has done what it said it would do in its manifesto - but being a cynic I'd just say that's what I'd do too if I was trying to persuade people I was responsible, even though I'm basically an irresponsible person who's only responsible when it suits me. Which is pretty much the same as the rest of the human species.

Anyway the point is you can't always rely on it suiting people to be responsible. So you need some means of showing them your displeasure when they aren't. Being able to vote them out of power would be a nice start. Under Westminster, we can't vote them out of power. We have to hope that our neighbours vote them out of power. The neighbours don't always oblige. But even when the neighbours vote out a government, the individuals in the party sail on regardless. If they've got their bum on a safe seat they're there for life.

And when we do manage to get rid of them at the ballot box, like in 1997 when Scotland put a stake through the heart of Michael Forsyth, his manifesto, and his entire Scottish Tory party they only get bitten by their fellow vampires and get a coffin in the House of Lords along with thon Labour guy whose Native American name is Dances-With-Polis.

There are no consequences for failure in the Westminster system. Voting yes shows them that there are consequences. Then we can replace Westminster with a Parliament whose representatives the electorate of Scotland can get rid of all by themselves. And some garlic for Michael Forsyth.

4. Broadband or modem?

There ye go, wanting to Skype with your cousin in Waiwhakamukau in New Zealand. Would you like a shiny new superfast broadband connecting you directly to the world wide webbies, or would you settle for one of those whirrbuzzksheeetttttwhangtwang thingies that blocks up your phone line and takes 4 days to download a 20 second video of a cute kitten that you're desperate to see because they never ever show that sort of thing on Reporting Scotland?

As far as Scotland's communications with the wider world are concerned, we don't even have the creaky old modem. Scotland is represented on the world stage by the UK Foreign and Commonwealth Office and the British Government. Naturally they represent the interests of the UK, which is most commonly interpreted as the interests of the UK Government, which in turn is the interests of whichever bunch of unaccountable politicians happens to have the biggest gang in Westminster. They'll quite happily sell out Scottish interests if it suits them, and all too often that's what they do. Fishery quotas anyone?

Scotland has no international voice. We do not punch above our weight as part of the UK, because being part of the UK makes Scotland invisible. The unfortunate truth for Better Together's grandiose claims of vast Scottish influence is that Scotland is part of a Union which is usually known abroad as *Inglaterra*. Folk like former NATO Secretary General George Roberston confuse their own public profile with that of Scotland's. And we really wish he'd stop, because he's a total embarrassment. When my Spanish speaking friends refer to him as a *político inglés* I don't want to correct them any more, and that makes me a cataclysmicly bad person.

We need our own broadband connection to the world. Our own representation in international bodies. It's not like I expect Scotland to have a massive influence in world affairs. I'd be content with the rest of the world realising we exist.

5. A normal country

It would be nice to live in normal country, where people had normal political arguments about the kind of stuff that Johann Lamont keeps saying she wants to have a debate about, just as soon as she's finished working her way through the 36000 long list of Chinese character insults for alicsammin, because the 26 letters of an A-Z just aren't enough for her. But we can't have that, because Scotland is not a normal country. Johann's patter is proof of that.

More precisely, Scotland is a normal country stuck in an abnormal situation. Scotland is a normal country which isn't allowed to act like a normal country. Normal countries get the governments they vote for who implement the policies the electorate preferred, and if they don't they get voted out. Normal countries have a national broadcaster. Normal countries, at least the democratic ones, have a press and media that reflects the diversity of voices and opinions in that country. Normal countries forge ties and alliances with other countries according to their own national interests. Normal countries are able to take steps to tackle their own problems - and Scotland has a lot of those.

But Scotland can't do any of the things a normal country can do. Being a part of the UK condemns Scotland to an eternity of devo navel gazing while the inequalities remain unchallenged and more food banks open. And Scotland's sense of itself gets battered into the Cringe.

The remedy, if you are truly fortunate, is to remove yourself from the abnormal situation. We can do that by voting yes to a question which really ought to read "Do you want Scotland to be a normal country?"

Then we can concentrate on solving our problems and making Scotland a better place for everyone who lives here. Even grumpy auld sods, who will, if we screw things up, have no one else to blame -

though that probably won't stop them trying. And no one is going to have interminable discussions about whether Scotland really needs the power to vary one tax band or two and by 10p or 15p.

6. A referendum on the monarchy

We're not voting to abolish the monarchy in September. More's the pity. Even worse it's not a referendum on whether to abolish Nicholas Witchell from the telly. He does for the Royals what George Osborne does for the Better Together campaign.

This is not the opinion of the current Scottish Government, which wants to keep Liz as head of state and refuses to make jokes in public about Nicholas Witchell. If Liz is head of state in an independent Scotland then they can insist that she's to be Elizabeth I and not Elizabeth II, although there are very many in Scotland who'd prefer she was known as Elizabeth the Last. However there are also those who love the romance and drama of fancy costumes and the whole ruler and ruled schtick, even though there are nightclubs for that sort of thing.

I'm not a gambling man. In my drug fuelled youth I once put a bet on a horse called Roll A Joint, thinking oh that's the nag for me. Only it fell at a fence and they had to shoot it. I took that as A Sign. It is however a safe bet that a stoned dead horse with a broken leg has a better chance of winning a steeplechase than there is of the Westminster Parliament ever offering us a referendum on the monarchy.

There are very different odds with an independent Scottish Parliament. It's far more likely that there could be a majority in a Scottish Parliament in favour of a referendum on the subject. It's a question which is definitely going to come up when we're faced with King Charles and Queen Camilla. Or WillnKate, the AntnDec of monarchy. I'll be making it come up, and I strongly suspect I won't be alone.

So I'm voting yes in September for the possibility that one day we can get rid of the monarchy. Vote no and it's a vote to keep it forever.

7. A Labour party

It would be nice to have a Labour party wouldn't it? A Labour party that didn't want to privatise things, and developed policies aimed at meeting the needs of ordinary working class people, one that was opposed to nuclear weapons, and kept equality of opportunity and access for all as its central goal. You know, an actual Labour party. The kind that the current Labour party mythologises, but for real. The kind of Labour party that George Galloway says he wants only if it really was that kind of Labour party it wouldn't let George Galloway in. That kind of Labour party. The one we were promised but never got.

Labour won't change itself. It can't change itself. Independence will change it. It's Labour in Scotland's only chance to become the party it was supposed to be, the party it claimed to be. A party which is actually a Scottish Labour party. Then it might even become worth voting for.

So there's six of my own reasons. There are many many more. And every single yes voter has a list of reasons of their own. Few of which involve ancient history or caring about currency unions. No doubt I'll get round to the rest of mine in due course. The best response to a Unionist politician like Justine Greening grabbing a cheap headline with irrelevant pap is to ignore them and talk about more important things instead.

15 April 2014
Hysterical history

Rory Stewart MP's Unionist propaganda thinly disguised as a BBC history documentary has provoked the ire of SNP MSP Steward Maxwell, who has attacked the BBC for yet another of its exercises in compulsory Britishness. But we all know that's the BBC's bread and Scottish butter. He ought to have attacked the programme for being risible history, a melange of cherry picked factoids whipped up into the wrong conclusion by a Tory MP who kept reminding us that he is Scottish. He didn't actually say he was a Proud Scot, but you know he wanted to.

Being interested in ancient history, I watched the first episode, expecting it to be propaganda seeing as how it was made by a Tory MP, but even propaganda can be done with art and a sense of style. Instead we got Rory, who wanted us to know he was Scottish, mugging his way through a series of interviews with ordinary folk and posh folk and the occasional nutter, mixed with the usual long shots of Great British Scenery. Rory, who's actually Scottish, was telling the story of the "lost Middleland", the Uhu of the UK. Which seemed to be mostly Welsh, or Danish, but that bit was sort of glossed over.

His thesis, as far as I could tell, was that Scotland only wants independence because we've been seduced by a transient and tribal identity. That would be the Scottish one. Britishness encompasses all in Rory's view, and everything else is a temporary aberration in the glorious march through history of a single British people. And he's Scottish so he wouldn't just make stuff like that up. But as history goes, it's still bollocks. It's Britishness which is the temporary aberration in the story. Rory chooses to confuse what anthropologists call a cultural province with a single national identity.

A cultural province is a region where neighbouring political, social, linguistic and ethnic groups share many aspects of their culture in common. Cultural provinces are not home to single national identities, quite the reverse. One of the best defined and distinctive cultural provinces in the anthropological and linguistic literature is that of the native peoples of the Pacific North West, the coastal area of Washington state in the USA, British Columbia, and the Alaskan Panhandle. The people of this region shared a distinctive art style and religion, they had similar economies, and many cultural practices in common. But it was also home to many different nations and languages - and just as many identities - which were shifting, kaleidoscopic and ever changing.

The islands of Britain and Ireland and their associated islands are a cultural province within Europe. And just like Pacific North West, this group of islands in North West Europe has always been home to diverse peoples, cultures, languages, and traditions and a shifting kaleidoscope of identities. It's the ever changing and dynamic relationships between these groups which creates the cultural province. Whatever you care to call the cultural province they've created, it's not the same as a modern British identity - however that's defined. It can't be called British, because it encompasses Ireland too.

Rory, did he tell you he was Scottish, was attempting the classic appeal of nationalism in the name of the British nationalism which is trying to persuade us it isn't nationalism at all. Validation by appeal to an ancient past. My Britishness is older than your Scottishness, and therefore it's more authentic. It's a highly dubious argument for many reasons, not the least of which is that the modern sense of Britishness is historically a very recent development. Its seeds were sown with the Union of Crowns in 1603, but it wasn't until the Scottish bourgeoise enthusiastically adopted the English language and North Britishness in the 18th century that it caught on, yet even then it was just a plug in, the preserve of the Scottish elite. We kept using the Caledonian browser. In England it never caught on at all, British merely became a synonym for English.

The ancient Britons didn't have any concept of themselves as Britons. Their allegience was to their tribe. However it is true that before the arrival of the Romans it's likely that a single language was spoken throughout the island of Britain, and that language is known to linguists as Brittonic. The problem for Rory, who even has a Scottish name, is that Brittonic is merely a convenient term for those parts of a pan-European Celtic dialect chain that were spoken on the island of Britain.

Dialects forming a part of the same Celtic language complex were also found in Ireland, France, Germany, Spain... all the way across Europe into modern Turkey. Roman historians make it clear that Britons and Gauls understood one another without the need for translators, and some Celtic tribes had lands in both Britain and Gaul. Including tribes living in the supposed "Middleland" like the Parisi of Yorkshire, who also held lands around the city of Paris which was named after them.

So really it was a European identity then, not a British one. We spoke the same language as people in Paris. We're really French, or possibly Belgian. Only that probably won't go down so well with the more Eurosceptic party colleagues of Rory the Tory, who's Scottish you know.

Not that the antiquity of a national identity is relevant anyway. The modern Macedonian national identity dates to the late 19th century and the early parts of the 20th. Previously the Macedonians had been considered Bulgarian, but in the 19th century as the Christian Orthodox Slavic speakers of the Balkans gained independence from Ottoman Turkey, the new Bulgarian literary language became established on the basis of the eastern dialect of the city of Tarnovo. Western dialect speakers found this too far removed from their own speech, and created their own Macedonian literary language based on the usage of the region south of Skopje. Macedonia then found itself a part of the Kingdom of Yugoslavia, and the combination of a distinct literary dialect and the political history of the 20th century created a Macedonian national identity. It's not any less valid just because it's historically recent.

It's really stupid arguing with people about their identity anyway. Because the thing about personal identity is that it's personal, which means another individual is far more of an expert in their own identity than you can ever be. Otherwise you end up like a German lassie I met on holiday on my first foray into properly furren pairts, who when hearing I was from Scotland assured me: "I'm sure you'll find you are in fact English." And I was just as sure that she would find she was talking shite.

So Rory's attempts were doomed to failure even before he began, even if he is Scottish, because this isn't a debate about identity at all, never mind one about whose identity is the oldest. Although it is definitely the Scottish one. The Scottish national identity dates to - at the very latest - the Scottish Wars of Independence and arguably a lot earlier. So it predates a British national identity by a good few hundred years, just to rub it in and go nyah nyah nyah. Because if that's how David Starkey and Rory the Tory, who's Scottish you know, can do history then so can the rest of us.

Scotland exists as a nation, a nation with a distinctive political culture and national institutions. We already know what our identity is, and we don't need to be told we're victims of false consciousness by an Eton educated Tory. Because however Scottish he considers himself to be, he's still doesn't understand what this independence debate is all about. And you don't even need to be Scottish to understand it Rory. You just need to live here and listen to what people are talking about.

It's not even a debate about nationalism. Accepting the existence of a distinct polity known as Scotland and recognising it is a nation doesn't make you a nationalist any more than visiting Las Vegas makes you a vegan. The debate is about what to do with Scotland's distinctive political culture. It's about achieving the means and methods of tackling the serious problems Scotland faces - land reform, Trident missiles, inequality, social exclusion, an ageing population. It's about whether we trust in Westminster to use the resources of Scotland's land and the talents and skills of her people to make a better future for Scotland and to tackle these problems - and its track record in that department does not inspire confidence - or whether we trust a Scottish Parliament with the full powers of the parliament of any normal nation. A parliament that's beholden to the voters of Scotland and no one else.

It's about the future Rory, not the past. If you hadn't been too busy planning a torchlit human chain the length of Hadrian's Wall you might have had a lightbulb moment and worked that out for yourself.

But ask a Unionist for a positive case for the Union, and the past is all you get. Independence offers a positive case for the future Rory, where's yours?

16 April 2014

Rum, sodomy, and the lash

It's another of Project Fear's carefully coordinated frightnights. It's another drive-by Tory. This time it's Tory Defence Minister Philip Hammond, again. Phil has come to Scotland to make a positive case for the Union, which consists of positively telling defence workers in Glasgow that they're positively going to lose their jobs. Phil represents a Parliament which has already cost Scotland some 10,000 defence jobs. 40% of UK defence cuts have hit Scotland. But these were positive unionist cuts, so don't really count and it's just negative nationalist scaremongering to call attention to damage which has already happened.

Phil was supported in his headlong retreat from answering questions by covering fire from First Lord of the Admiralty Admiral Sir George

Zambellas, who's been needing something to do as he's one of the 40 admirals in a navy which efficiently has half that number of warships and he keeps getting his socks wet when he sets sail on a desk. So George decided that it was a jolly roger of an idea to stick his oar into a political debate, and to tell the people who pay his wages and who therefore outrank him - that would be us - how to vote. Admiral George warned that Scottish independence would "weaken the effectiveness" of the Royal Navy, possibly by creating a situation where the navy's 40 admirals have only 18 ships which would be ridiculously inefficient because then they don't even get a half a boat each. And to make matters worse the cost overruns and delays on the MoD's Amphibious Desk project are horrendous, but there are plans to use a couple of aircraft carriers they can't afford planes for.

You can be certain that a military man didn't invade a subject outside his job description without orders, or at the very least some strongly supportive suggestions nods and winks, from someone higher up the foodchain.

Many of us on the pro-independence side had already accused the No campaign of politicising the armed forces with their celebrations of D-Day and WW1 flag waving jamboree only to be told that we were being insane conspiracy theorists or deeply cynical miserabilists. And that last part would be true, because we've seen plenty in the way of cynical miserabilism from Westminster, so we've learned on the lap of the masters. But they can't deny it now. With Admiral George's intervention, there can be no argument that the British Goverment and Better Together will cheerfully politicise and subvert any institution in an effort to keep Westminster's gravy boat afloat, up to and included the armed forces. And as such, it's yet another reason why Scotland needs independence. I don't want my public institutions perverted in this way.

Admiral George said Scottish independence wouldn't be good for the rest of the UK although they'd get over it just as soon as the desk was watertight - but it would be dire for Scotland with the protection of no naval patrol vessels at all until the Scottish government could acquire some. Though how this would be worse than the situation we have under the Union where there are no naval patrol vessels based in Scotland and little prospect of getting any, George didn't elucidate.

George thinks that Scotland's independence would be a direct threat to the Royal Navy, which the First Lord of the Admiralty assures us has an unparalleled reputation and tradition. You won't get that anywhere else apparently. Although Winston Churchill, who was also once First Lord of the Admiralty, reputedly once summed up these traditions as rum, sodomy, and the lash, which aren't really that hard to find at all. As I recall, all are freely available on bondage nights in a number of the more niche market clubs and bars.

But in the case of Scotland, the equivalent would be taking our whisky revenues, shafting us, and threatening us with abuse if we try to leave. Now we know where Better Together got its navigation skills from, which explains why their campaign is now going full steam ahead like an Astute class submarine stuck on a rock off Skye.

Phil Hammond, who's on drive-by duty this week, and who is looking more and more like the anonymous clype who shot his mouth off to a Guardian reporter and holed Better Together's currency threat below the waterline, wanted to assure us that if there is a yes vote, absolutely nothing would be off the table in subsequent negotiations. Which was a not so coded way of saying "Please please please don't do a bedroom tax on Trident, because we'll pay more rent so it can stay. Look, here's a shiny currency union." Although he later swore blind that he didn't mention a currency union as he was away in America at the time. And Alistair Darling had been on the phone again.

Naturally, being a Tory and a Unionist, Phil thinks any negotiations with Scotland would be immensely complex and difficult. We shouldn't be surprised by that, Tories find everything to do with Scotland complex and difficult, as they are demonstrating with their ham fisted attempts to reach out to a Scottish electorate. Phil, who wasn't scaremongering at all, said:

"Because if they insist that [Trident] has to go, there would have to be complex talks about the costs and timescales involved. Any notion that it would be quick and easy is just plain wrong."

Saying it would not be quick or easy is a half truth, as Phil knows all too well because he may be many things, but he's not that stupid. Spain negotiated the removal of the US Polaris nuclear missiles and subs from the American naval base at Rota in Andalusia. Agreement on removal was reached in 1976, not long after the death of Franco, and the nukes were adios by 1979. It took just 3 years from the opening of negotiations with the USA to the removal of weapons of mass destruction from Spain. So the process of removal is indeed relatively quick and easy, or at least it will be for Scotland.

Of course the USA had somewhere else to put their nuclear strap on dildoes, sorry, defence assets, the rUK doesn't. So it's not actually going to be quick and easy after all. It's just that it's the rUK that's it's not going to be quick and easy for, not Scotland. Scotland's negotiating stance is easy to articulate. It's: "That's your problem pal".

Talks about the costs are equally quick and easy for Scotland. They're Westminster's nukes, and if Westminster wants to keep them then Westminster can pay the removal costs. Otherwise we just make a wee call to the UN's version of the cooncil binmen, and tell them we've got some nukes we'd like collected on Thursday. They were left behind by an antisocial lodger who we evicted.

The cost of a new base comes under "that's your problem pal" too. Although no doubt a Unionist politician will pop up sooner or later to insist that Scotland has a moral duty to contribute financially to the most immoral weapon in the history of humanity. They don't really do self awareness in Westminster.

However notionally some 8.4% of Trident belongs to Scotland, so theoretically Scotland could offset its share of any removal costs by giving Westminster the 8.4% share. But there will be the costs of cleaning up the mess the MoD will leave behind at Faslane and Coulport, so we'll be expecting some compensation. Our 8.4% share of Trident may cover it, but it may not. The clean up afterwards may take years, but that depends on just how much radioactive contamination the MoD will leave behind. Currently they're not for telling.

After independence we'll find out just how much damage they've done. Since the MoD managed to contaminate a beach in Dalgety Bay for hundreds of years to come with just some glow in the dark paint, it's sobering to consider just how much dangerous waste they may have spilled or lost track of when they've been dealing with yer actual nuclear warheads and nuclear powered submarines.

The current anger over Trident will be a wee tsk and an indulgent "och whit are you like" compared to the particle-storm of gamma rayed fury which will explode against the MoD when Scotland finds out just how much glow in the dark crap they've left in our land and our seas. The present bunch of Westminster incompetents are in no small part motivated by a desire to keep Trident in Scotland at least until they've safely retired to a seat in the Lords and some cushy directorships. Then they can escape the fall out.

So it's not Scotland that's been got over the barrel of a Trident missile Phil, that would be you. What dirty little career ending embarrassments is the MoD hiding under the cover of national security? Independence means they'll be found out.

That said, there may be the glimmerings of a deal. But it's not a question of how much Scotland is going to have to pay Westminster for the removal of Trident, it's a question of how much Westminster is going to have to pay Scotland. For starters, Westminster can stop pissing us around with currency union threats, EU threats and Eurovision threats, see sense on debts and assets, and Scotland might just give Westminster a short, limited, and tightly supervised period of grace in which to move its WMDs. But only if they start acting like grown ups and not like petulant pettit lipped weans who've been too used to getting their own way. Or we can get rid of the nukes the day after independence. It's your call Phil.

But there are very many in Scotland who would not be at all happy with even the shortest period of grace - like me for starters - so Phil and Admiral George can rest assured a Scottish Government will be expected to extract a very high price for it. Because it will be the people of Scotland who are holding the lash. Won't that be a novelty.

18 April 2014

The Great British Bake Off

It's going to be easy, everyone says so. You're a top chef, you're pals with the owners of the TV channel and the owners of the newspapers. They're all on your side. The food critics agree to pick holes in the other side's offerings or leave them ignored on the side of the plate. You can't lose.

So you get together with some other TV cooks and you come up with a recipe that can't fail. You test it round the dinner table with Nigella's friends. The metrofoodies love it. You'll win the Great British Bake Off, and you'll be everyone's favourite contestant. You'll be loved. You'll get your own series. And it's as easy as boil in the bag.

So you carefully measure out the heavily refined starch from which you've removed any specks of uncomfortable truth, a generous helping of sour cream, a liberal helping of E numbers, add a dash of bitter and lavish topping of froth. Stir it vigorously to mix things. You whang it into an oven that your friends have carefully preheated to the correct accusatory temperature. Sorted.

You've followed the recipe to the letter, it's looking great. You're cruising to victory and it feels so good. The food critics have already started printing their stories of your mastery of the art of cooking. You're the saviour of the Great British dish, you've created a masterpiece from the crumbs off the table to offer the Scots.

But your Positive Cake for the Union refuses to rise, it's an indigestible mess. You test it on some polling panels. But however much you stuff it down their throats, it only gets vomited up back in your face. Some tweaks must be needed. Nothing to worry about. Just a hiccup.

You carry on regardless, but the results don't change. The hiccups get worse. It's puzzling, it should have been an easy gig. You want a make a dish that gives Scottish voters salmonella, so they'll never be able to face a referendum again without feeling queasy, but you've got to make something they'll swallow first. And they're not swallowing it.

You go over the steps in your mind again, and again, and you just *know* you did everything exactly according to the recipe. It ought to have worked. Why isn't it working? Everyone said it would work. Proper serious big city people. People you thought were experts said it would be a piece of cake. Yet something's missing, something's not right. Something's gone wrong, but you don't know what. The kitchen clock is ticking.

You try again. You redouble your efforts and you put everything into it. You add extra bitter, try a dash of bile. You call on Phil Hammond for some alien ingredients. You get George Roberston to cook up a cataclysm. But now the judges are sniggering and looking at you with a mixture of disgust and pity. They won't even touch the plate.

The harder you try the worse it gets. So you scream, and wail, but no matter how much you hurl abuse and shout and swear, you're still no closer to finding out why the supposedly sure fire recipe went so badly wrong.

And time is running out. Mel Giedroyc and Sue Perkins are hovering in the background getting ready for their piece to the camera, ready to show the world how idiotic you've been. You can see your reputation before you, a sugar spun confection arching gracefully through the air on a trajectory for the floor.

The judges are assembling and they look in your direction. Some of them are laughing.

But it can't be right. Don't they know who you are? Have they no respect for your reputation? The judges can't really choose a granny from Anstruther with her home baked offerings over you. How can people prefer those? You can't charge £120 per serving in a posh London restaurant for that amateur stuff. You won't get into a French restaurant with that, you say, and the Spanish will veto it.

The granny must be lying. She must be deceiving. Her scones must be full of a nasty addictive chemical that causes cancer and everyone will die a horrible lingering death while you sit smugly by. If people eat them they'll probably turn violent. After all, those scones are explosive, they're blowing you out the water.

The cameras are on you and you feel that it's all a bad dream. The one when you were giving a speech to a crowd and you didn't realise you were naked apart from your socks. How can you possibly be beaten by an amateur? She must really be in the pay of Alicsammin Inc, the evil international pie conglomerate. They've contrived all this in a kitchen buried deep within a secret underground lair.

The judges must be a bunch of provincials. They're just acting emotionally. It just takes time for the subtlety and nuance of the bitterness to be replaced by common sense. Give it a bit longer and the revolting taste of your puke inducing offering will be forgotten, and the judges will realise that you are after all a chef with an international reputation and this is punch above your weight cuisine. They love it in the expensive restaurants in London.

But there isn't much longer left. The kitchen clock is ticking.

People are going to mock, and you know it. You'll never make a soufle again. You're the triple A rated chef who's going to be stuffed by a granny from Anstruther with her home made scones of destiny. They're just so moreish.

Tick tock. Time's up. You lose.

The bastards have put real jam in them. And they did it deliberately. Why didn't you think of that?

20 April 2014

CBBye Bye

In news which was as big a surprise as the revelations that Davie Cameron is a posh Tory, Johann Lamont hates Alicsammin, and Danny Alexander is on work release from the Muppet Show, the CBI's North Britain branch has come out as an official supporter of the No campaign. Stunned Yes supporters the length and breadth of the land who had hitherto looked to the CBI's colonial governor Scotlandshire for words of wisdom and pats on the head for pro-indy puppies were shocked, shocked I tell you. Who knew?

In 1979 during the Home Rule referendum campaign, the CBI described the very limited powers on offer as the greatest threat to Scottish industry since the Luftwaffe - because in the 70s no one had heard of Godwin's Law and hysterical comparisons with the Nazis were still a novelty. The CBI has continued in a similar vein ever since.

In the 80s they were hailing Thatcher as the best thing since square slice. In the 90s they warned that devolution would bring about the end of civilisation as Michael Forsyth knows it - and said that like it was a bad thing.

Finding that civilisation hadn't ended after all, they spent the naughties trading Alicsammin insult pokemon cards with Labour and the Tories. So absolutely no one expected the CBI to oppose independence this time round. Except the 4 million people in Scotland registered on the electoral roll and everyone who has ever met, heard of, or read a press quote from, Iain McMillan, the heidbummer of CBI Scotlandshire.

The CBI did not consult its members before announcing its decision. Which was a bit rich coming from an organisation which has severely criticised trades union leaders for not balloting their membership. And even richer if the rumours are true, and CBI's North Britain branch membership consists of just a handful of companies. There wouldn't have been any need for a ballot. It wouldn't have taken Iain that long to visit them all personally and ask.

Miffed that Iain didn't pop round with a packet of Peek Freans empire biscuits to ask them over a cuppa what they thought about indy, a succession of companies have announced that they will be leaving the CBI.

First out the door was Balhousie Care Group, but since its chairman is Tony Banks, a leading light in the pro-independence Business for Scotland, the resignation was about as shocking as learning the CBI supported the No campaign. Colour us unsurprised. However Business for Scotland has been pushing for months for the CBI to fess up and either put its No credentials where its mooth is and drop the hypocritical pretence that it's a neutral body - or keep its nose out. As an organisation BfS are in the same business as the CBI, and they've just given Iain McMillan a lesson in boardroom tactics. Business for Scotland weren't engaging so much in a hostile takeover, as being hostile undertakers. They handed the CBI a loaded gun and helpfully showed Iain how to shoot his own foot off. He pulled the trigger.

But the real blast was the way the CBI went about it. It's supposed to be a members' organisation. It represents the views and interests of its members. But it's never been arsed enough about those views and interests to ask its members what they are. Since a goodly number of Scottish businesses are either in favour of independence, or believe that commercial organisations have no business trying to influence democratic decisions, Iain's now finding out the hard way. He's not just shot himself in the foot, he's blown his legs off.

The resignation of the Balhousie Care Group was immediately followed by Aquamarine Power, and yesterday STV also announced it would be leaving the CBI with immediate effect. Both companies stated that they wished to remain neutral - Aquamarine Power said that it was for individuals to decide how they wish to vote in a democratic ballot, as a company Aquamarine Power is obliged to respect their decision. STV issued a statement saying that as a broadcaster, they are obliged to remain politically neutral. This is not possible if they are members of an organisation which has explictly affiliated itself to a political position.

By today the Sunday Herald revealed that the dam was bursting, as one public body after another resigned from the CBI. Public bodies must also maintain political neutrality. You know, like the BBC ... oh. Try again. Public bodies can't be overtly associated with political bodies, and by registering as a No campaign supporter, the CBI has become a political body. Difficult legal questions may arise if funds from public bodies are used for a political campaign.

The Herald reports that other businesses will leave the CBI as a result of its decision to decide on their behalf. And yet others are rapidly trying to distance themselves from the CBI as fast as the legs of their pinstripe troosers will carry them.

The CBI has just proven Business for Scotland's point for them, in what is, when you think about it, a beautifully elegant fuck you to Iain McMillan. The companies leaving the CBI are not doing so because they're overt supporters of independence. They're leaving because of legal and commercial considerations. If the CBI had bothered to consult its members, they might have found that out. Yet amongst the first rules in any successful business is know your market, and be aware of potential legal pitfalls. If Iain was appearing on Dragons Den, even No voting Duncan Bannatyne would be telling him he's out.

Business for Scotland have just made the CBI demonstrate that the CBI has no business sense - it's not even capable of doing what's in the interests of the CBI, never mind its members, and the wider interests of Scotland don't enter into their calculations.

What business wants to be represented by an organisation that doesn't know what good business practice is? Answers on a postcard to Iain McMillan.

And in new news, and further confirmation that the No campaign is increasingly living up to its name, and is no campaign at all - a new poll shows that when undecideds are excluded Yes is just 4% behind No. There's a lot more work to do, but thanks to folk like Iain McMillan, it's getting easier for the Yes campaign every day.

21 April 2014

Pensioning off the Union

The Naw Ye Cannae campaign is sending Gordie Broon to Glasgow on Tuesday to lovebomb us. Because sending Gordie to show his neoclassical endogenous growth theory to an invited audience of Labour loyalists and media hacks worked so well for them in Kirkcaldy.

Gordie doesn't do public meetings, in part at least because there's a good chance that the public won't display the required degree of anally-retentive reverence - if the public can even be arsed to turn up. Gordie may, for unexplained and inexplicable reasons, command huge fees for making speeches, but the rest of us are more likely to find a reliable provider of endogenous growth by buying viagra from a website based in China. They're quite helpful when vaguely creepy looking men offer you a lovebomb in a darkened room. Lots of alcohol helps too. So does being bereft of any self-respect.

The topic for Tuesday is pensions, like it was in Kirkcaldy. At this point a proper journalist would give readers a potted summary of what Gordie said about pensions the last time. But like 99.9% of the Scottish population I wasn't paying any attention, although I do seem to recall thinking that asking Gordie for advice on pensions was like asking Goldilocks for advice on burglaries. She fell asleep on the job too.

However, to save time, it was something along the lines of "You'll all be screwed if you vote for independence and will have to work until you're 112." But he said it with a smile, so it counts as a positive case for the Union. Or it may not have been a smile, it may have been gas, with Gordie it's difficult to tell. He's like a wee baby that way, they pee in their own beds too.

During the last Labour government, Gordie infamously screwed everyone's pensions. In 2006, the Institute of Actuaries estimated that the tax changes Gordie introduced in 1997 had reduced the UK's national pension pot by at least £100 billion, and probably by much more. Many companies used the increased costs as an excuse to wind up final salary schemes for their employees. Even on the Treasury's estimates, Gordie cost workers contributing to employee pension schemes an average of £300 per year and forcing them to delay retirement in order to make up the shortfall. The true figure could be as high as £5000.

Pensions expert Dr Ros Altmann said at the time: "Gordon Brown saw pension funds as an easy target - so he raided them. He either doesn't understand private pensions or he doesn't care about them, which is hardly prudent."

Gordie, who was more interested in pursuing his internecine warfare with Tony Blair, got some minions to issue a statement pointing out that he'd also cut Corporation Tax which would stimulate growth and make up the shortfall in pensions. This was before cutting Corporation Tax became Labour's totemic symbol for surrender to evil capitalists. That only happened when Alicsammin said he wanted to cut Corpie tax too.

Gordie's mismanagement of the economy and his enthusiastic conversion to the notion that letting the financial sector do what it liked with a minimum of supervision was the reason that the UK was so vulnerable to the effects of the economic meltdown in 2008. Any benefits which might have arisen from cutting Corporation Tax vanished along with the last shreds of Gordie's reputation for prudence.

Not that Gordie noticed, he was too busy throwing Nokias at Ed Balls and Ed Miliband when they'd failed to brief journalists with a sufficient amount of dirt on Gordie's opponents. Gordie, like many politicians, has a wild bird egg collector's attitude towards political office. All that matters is getting your paws on the pretty prize, you don't care if you drive the species to extinction in the process. And that's why final salary pension schemes have gone the way of the Great Auk. But Gordie got the shiny prime ministerial egg locked away in his collection cabinet, which is all he ever wanted to do with it.

However for the purposes of persuading Scotland to remain in the Union, Gordie has transformed into Caledonia's leading expert on income maximisation after retirement. And he does actually have some credentials there. Since losing power in 2010, Gordie has devoted himself to income maximisation, and now has a lucrative career in expensive after-dinner speeches for companies which can't afford the fees of anyone more entertaining, or indeed capable of retaining the audience's attention until the end of his opening sentence.

Gordie described himself as an ex-politician during one of his highly paid after-dinner speeches to some bunch of executives in a posh hotel in a warm climate. He's an ex-politician who is still the elected representative for Kirkcaldy, but he's got no plans to resign even though he can rarely be arsed to represent the people of Kirkcaldy in the Parliament that is allegedly so influential and all-powerful that Scotland will be screwed without it. But if Gordie stands down from Westminster he'll bugger up his MP's pension. MPs are only entitled to their full pension rights if they stand down at a General Election, or are voted out of office. That's why he's pretending to represent Kirkcaldy in a Parliament he rarely bothers to attend. So Gordie is really an expert in endogenously growing pensions, at least his own.

Gordie's last attempt to scare the bejeezus out of Scotland with pension threats didn't work. It's not clear why they think it will work this time, although it may not be unrelated to the fact that they don't have any other ideas.

To coincide with Gordie's positive pension blitz, Better Together has embarked on a billboard campaign of positivity. It shows a pair of miserable looking pensioners who've just come from an audience with Gordie, and a warning that if they vote yes they won't be able to afford cat food. Starving moggies will attack and eat them as they doze in front of the telly - which has been switched off because there's no electricity in an independent Scotland. It's that special sort of positivity that only Better Together can do - see they do so have a Unique Selling Point.

However according to the recent opinion poll published by the Scotsman, only 25% of Scots believe that pensions will be negatively affected by independence. Most think it will make no difference, or that pensions will improve. The Republic of Ireland, regularly trotted out as a basket case economy by Better Together activists who hope that no Scots go there on account of it being foreign, pays its pensioners a basic state pension of €219 (approx £180) a week. The UK manages just £113.10. Unless of course you're a former MP.

Pensions would be secure in an independent Scotland. The Scottish Government has already released a detailed paper explaining the likely situation. The truth is that Scotland currently pays a lower share of its GDP on pensions than the rest of the UK, and with new Scottish spending priorities and freedom from the UK's punching above its weight expenditure - like Trident and the bloated MoD - Scotland will be in a position to pay its pensioners a decent pension, to continue to pay them, and eventually to increase the basic pension to a level more like that found in other rich and developed EU states.

That's not a guarantee we'll get with the Union. The only guarantees you'll get from Gordie and his Westminster pals is the guarantee that they personally will have a comfortable retirement. The job of the rest of us is to pay for their mistakes, and that's not a job we're allowed to retire from.

The Union is not fit for purpose, it's time we pensioned it off.

23 April 2014

The Messiah by the Squinty Bridge

If devolution is a journey, can Dougie Alexander please tell us the destination? Otherwise we're on a mystery tour. I went on a mystery tour once. It was all very exciting. We got on the coach and were taken to a mock historical tourist trap to be fleeced by vendors of overpriced tat, before being taken back to where we started and being dumped at a bus stop after the last privatised bus of the day had already gone. And then I had to walk home in the rain, poorer, pissed off, exhausted, and considerably more cynical than I had been at the beginning. Which anyone who knows me will tell you is quite an achievement. So exactly like Dougie's devolution journey then.

Dougie's been taking the Proud Scot But pills again in an article in the Scotsman. He loves all sorts of stuff about Scotland that's not going to change whether we're independent or not, like the scenery, and things that happened 200-odd years ago. He cites a pair of Scottish Enlightenment philosophers, and their contrasting views on the human condition.

Francis Hutchison's [sic] argument that humanity finds its contentment in the contribution we each make to the well-being of our neighbour contrasting with Lord Kaimes's [sic] view that our human condition is to crave what the other owns, and the structures, and so the peace, of society are built on the laws we create to protect what we possess.

Dougie prefers Hutcheson's Better Together caring and sharing over the implied selfish materialism of the Lord Kames Nats. It's the lookit my ProudScotBut intellectual credentials intro into the main gig. Which would have been more convincing if Dougie had spelled their names right, but still, points for trying. The wee sowel's been making one of his plaintive pleas for solidarity again. He does that because half the Labour party hates him, and the other half is his sister.

Mind you, Hutcheson was born in Ireland, and is buried in Dublin where he spent much of his life. His work was influential to the later foundation of the Society of United Irishmen, an early forerunner of the Irish republican movement, which sought to unite Catholic and Protestant in the goal of an Irish state for the benefit of all. Kames was yer actual diehard Unionist who had Benjamin Franklin as a penpal. He tried to persuade Franklin of the benefits of Union, but Franklin was unconvinced. Perhaps Dougie ought to have thought his examples through a bit more carefully before citing them like IQ baubles. It's Wendy that's the one with the galactic intelligence, isn't it?

The Scotsman helpfully illustrated the piece with a photie of Dougie in a Christ-like pose with the Squinty Bridge forming his halo. He's a martyr for the Union, offering himself for sacrifice to the vinegar tipped spears of the cybernat centurions. He's the saviour of devo and will redeem Scotland's sinful worship of the devil of independence. He's the walker on the waters of Better Together's effluent. Yea, verily, he is the forgiving son of the vengeful Gord. And he will die a death, but will rise again, and again, as often as the Scotsman keeps printing his solidarity sales pitch. Which appears to be weekly from now until September.

But at least he's trying to pitch a positive case. It's just a shame he's got such poor material to work with. He's reduced to saying that no is positive, and getting anyone to believe that is a bigger miracle than entertaining a wedding party in Canna when all you've got is the bitter water of crocodile tears.

Dougie, what with him being an expert on solidarity and everything because he likes Irish philosophers, tells us:

Solidarity, if it is anything, is about never giving in or simply giving up. There's nothing positive or progressive about walking away from the ideal or the practice of solidarity.

Only no one is suggesting that, except maybe in Dougie's head. Solidarity, if it is anything, is about doing more than making meaningless gestures, it's about more than being the moral compass that Gordie lost. Scotland remaining within the union is meaningless gestural solidarity. It cannot protect the poor and marginalised of the rest of the UK from Conservative rule, and it subjects Scotland to decades long bouts of Tory governments that we didn't vote for.

No one, least of all supporters of Scottish independence, is proposing to "give up" on the struggle for social equality, for the fair distribution of wealth, for opportunities for all. Solidarity, if it means anything, means recognising that some strategies are not working, have not worked for a long time, and show no signs that they'll start working within the lifetime of anyone alive today. The British Parliamentary Road to socialism was crucified a long time ago, but it will take more than a miracle to bring it back from the dead. And looking at the front bench of the Labour party it's difficult to discern anyone with godlike powers. It sure as hell isn't Dougie.

Scotland, as Dougie points out, contributes 10% of the UK's income with just 8% of its population. He tells us that this is something to be proud of, and it is. He tells us solidarity dictates that we should share our good fortune, because he has the moral authority of Christ by a Squinty Bridge. It's just a terrible shame who we're sharing it with. If we were sharing our good fortune with the poor and the marginalised in the rest of the UK that would indeed be just fine and dandy and supersolidaritocious. But we're not sharing it with them though, are we. Dougie's not the Messiah, he's just a very naughty boy. Which I only wrote because a Life of Brian reference is obligatory in this sort of context.

We're sharing our good fortune with London transport infrastructure, with bank bailouts, with tax cuts for millionaires, with defence contractors, with ATOS and G4S, with Trident and with the Westminster gravy train. And for those people, Scotland, along with Northern England, Wales, and just about everywhere outside boardrooms in the south east and the corridors of Westminster, are the gift that keeps on giving. We've been giving so long they now see it as an entitlement, and they take a bigger slice of the pie with every passing year. The UK is now one of the most unequal countries in the developed world. Social and economic inequality in the UK is now worse than at any time since WW2. The UK only got less equal during Labour's 13 years in office, when Dougie held various cabinet posts.

It probably counts as monstering to point out that Dougie and the Parliamentary Labour party are amongst the recipients in this deal. Calling upon others to make a meaningless gesture which keeps you in a job at great cost to those making the gesture is the exact opposite of solidarity. It's the liquidisation of hope.

I don't think that's what Jesus would do Dougie. Unlike Dougie, I'm not a Christian, but I seem to recall the teaching that Jesus died for our sins. Dougie wants Scotland to die for the Labour party's.

<u>24 April 2014</u>

Lies, Damned Lies, and Iain Duncan Smith

Today Scotland got a stern warning from Iain Duncan Smith, who runs a department where the admin costs of his new pet benefit vastly exceed the amount actually paid out to claimants, that Scotland will have to find £1.5 billion to set up and run its own benefits system. He also warned that he won't let the Scottish Government share the rUK's IT systems if there is a yes vote, which means the money we save not paying for Iain's admin overruns ought to cover everything we need.

The effectiveness of Iain's threat depends on a number of things. It depends upon the reputation of Iain for producing reliable faces. So we're not off to a good start. Let's quickly gloss over the embarrassing episode in 2002 when the BBC's Panorama revealed that Iain's claim to have attended a series of prestigious educational establishments really meant he'd dropped by while on a day trip and he'd confused it with an ice cream parlour.

And it's really best to draw a discreet veil over the Epiphany in Easterhoose, when having been booted oot as Tory party leader on account of being crap, Iain went on a pilgrimage to Shandwick Shopping Centre where his eyes were opened to the reality of poverty in modern Britain. Whereupon Iain realised in a blinding flash of divine inspiration that rebranding himself as a compassionate conservative could refloat his sunk reputation. He would be ever so umble, at least until the Tories were re-elected, then it could be back to vindictive business as usual. Iain came to Easterhoose with nothing, and left with a highly lucrative career, a means of cowing the poor, a luxury motor and considerable political influence. A trick previously pulled off only by certain local heroin dealers.

Accusations that Iain has misused statistics don't leave much room for margin of error, except on Iain's part. Over the past 12 months Iain has been found to have abused, misused, misrepresented, or just made up, statistics on numerous occasions, each of which is comprised of a galaxy's worth of the twinkly untruths which orbit Iain's brain. Here's a statistically representative sample of the articles which crop up when you google "Iain Duncan Smith statistics". None of which praise the man's numeracy. That's statistically significant when it comes to rating your credibility Iain.

In March this year the Huffington Post reported that Iain had been accused of misusing statistics for the fourth time in twelve months. In June last year, the pressure group Disabled People Against Cuts produced a report detailing 35 examples of the misuse of statistics by Iain's department, which it said "demonstrates a consistent pattern of abuse of official statistics by Ministers of the present Government." The same month the Guardian's Zoe Williams accused government ministers, and Iain in particular, of "going off the scale on the spectrum of deceit"> over their misrepresentation of statistics. Meanwhile the

BBC was reporting that the UK Statistics Authority had criticised Iain over his claims that the benefits cap was working. And in November last year the Mirror reported that an online petition calling for 'Iain Dodgy Stats' to be held to account for his dodgy use of statistics had received over 100,000 signatures within a couple of weeks.

Presumably the statistics Iain is giving us today are the same ones conveniently, ahem, "leaked" to Gordie Broon the other day. And equally presumably the thinking between the leaker and the leakee was that another set of dodgy Conservative statistics were better presented to Scotland by a Labour figure with a reputation for misusing statistics than a Tory with a reputation for misusing statistics. Still the same auld lies, still the same auld liars.

No doubt Iain's claims will be analysed, chewed over, found to be indigestible, and spat back out by statistical carnivores. Because it's pretty obvious they're imitation steaks made out of a fungus that grows in the dark feeding on crap. Iain's claim that Scotland will only be able to fund its benefits system by raising taxes or spending cuts rests upon the assumption that an independent Scotland will continue with the exact same spending priorities as our Tory led Westminster government. So Iain thinks an independent Scotland will still be providing 10% of the billions Westminster plans to spend on a high speed railway between London and Birmingham, and will still be footing 10% of the bill for the rest of the UK's nuclear energy programme.

He also asserted that he would not share the DWP's IT and payments systems with the Scottish Government during the transition period after a yes vote if the Scottish Government introduced any changes to the benefits or pensions systems in Scotland. Which is a first, until now Project Fear scares were about what would happen after independence. Now Iain's saying that if Scotland votes yes, he'd refuse Scotland access to public services while we're still part of the UK and still paying taxes to the UK Treasury and paying 10% of Iain's department. That's probably against the law. But then Iain could always get his pals in Parliament to introduce a back dated bill denying cheated benefits claimants the money they were illegally denied, and get Labour to support him.

And all this without even mentioning the bedroom tax.

But Iain's just going through the motions. Unlike his cabinet colleagues he's got a note from his maw excusing him from drive-by duties, and won't be coming to Scotland to refuse to take questions. He just sent a note saying he was refusing to take questions. Because it's statistically the case that Iain is one of the top ten reasons for Scottish independence all by himself.

They no longer seem to care whether people in Scotland believe them. In the absence of any other bright ideas, going through the motions is all they've got left.

25 April 2014
Transformational Generative Glamour

Noam Chomsky has announced his support for Scottish independence. It's news which hasn't made much of an impact in the avowedly anti-intellectual UK media, which on the whole prefers to cater for a readership which thinks Chomsky was one of the baddies in Planet of the Apes. However Chomsky's support for the Yes campaign is highly significant. He's yer actual heavyweight intellectual. The best the No campaign can manage is the confused meanderings of the lost marbles of Gordon Brown.

Chomsky is perhaps best known for two things - his academic work in linguistics and philosophy, and his criticisms of US foreign policy. In both fields he's made a reputation for himself as one of the leading thinkers of our day. In the meagre coverage of his thoughts on independence for Scotland, the focus has been on his political views - anti-nuclear, pro-peace, in favour of social equality and freedom of speech. Views which are considered controversial in a warped world.

Chomsky is widely regarded as the father of modern linguistics. He revolutionised the discipline in the 1950s with Transformational Generative grammar, a theory which attempted to explain the mental and developmental processes underlying children's acquisition of language. Until Chomsky, linguistics had been descriptive, studying the external manifestations of language - the languages, dialects and accents, and the use of language in society. Chomsky's work opened up new fields in the research and study of the internal manifestations of language, how language works within the human brain, its interface with thought, learning, and psychology. It transformed linguistics from a purely descriptive discipline into a theoretical one and created whole new fields of study. Chomsky is to linguistics what Einstein is to physics.

Chomsky developed his theory on language in response to the work of the psychologist FB Skinner, the man who famously claimed that he could teach a pigeon anything. For Skinner, it was all about positive reinforcement and negative reinforcement, reward and punishment. The mind, Skinner argued, was essentially a blank slate at birth. The child's environment and rearing were the chalk which drew in the adult, and the child learned by responding to positive and negative stimuli.

Chomsky disagreed, pointing out that children acquire language without being explicitly taught it. Human children acquire language seemingly by accident, whereas animals reared amongst humans fail to acquire language at all.

Dogs don't learn to speak, even though they're often reared and live as part of a human family, like the Dug, who's currently sprawled over the sofa with his head on my lap and getting in the way of typing. Animals learn to understand a number of words and phrases, but often we misperceive their ability to read our body language as an ability to understand our words. Our minds focus on the words, the dog's mind doesn't. And we can't always be sure that the dog understands the same thing we do when we utter a particular word. We call the dog's name, the dog hears, "Here's something interesting".

With children however, it's very different. Young children absorb words like sponges. They master complex and difficult grammatical rules - and do so without anyone explictly teaching them. Because very often the adults aren't even aware of the rules themselves.

Ask your average working class Glaswegian if they can tell the difference between a transitive and an auxiliary verb and if they're a smart arse, as so many of us are, they might say "Ah jist done it. Ah did so." Which is just what happened there. In the first sentence done is a transitive verb taking a direct object. In the second it's grammatically an auxiliary. While you might hear Weegies saying "Ah jist did it. Ah did so." because of the influence of standard English, you'll never hear a Weegie saying "Ah jist did it. Ah done so." If they were using the two in a slovenly and careless way, they'd be just as likely to say one as the other. But they're not, so clearly something else is going on.

There is a rule in the grammar of Weegie that demands that the past tense of *dae / do* is *done* when the verb is used as a transitive verb, and *did* when it's an auxiliary verb. Far from being taught this rule, its users were told it's slovenly and incorrect, but it's not. And when they choose to use the standard English rule, they do that correctly too. It's complex and grammatically sophisticated behaviour. It obeys rules. Just different rules from standard English. But its speakers don't know its a rule, and neither do those who criticise them for using it.

It was Chomsky who first pointed out the weirdy weirdness of this. How do you learn rules if no one realises they exist? And that's the difference between a truly great and influential thinker, and an ex-politician who milks the lecture circuit and whores himself round directorships. The great thinkers ask the interesting questions, and offer the inspirational answers.

Chomsky argued that the only way to account for the fact that children learn these unteachable rules was for the deep structures of grammar to be already hardwired into the human brain - like Windows 8 on your laptop, which like the mental hardwiring of language also has the side effect of causing the occasional outburst of swerrie wurds. These deep structures were transformed by the language or dialect the child was absorbing from its family and community, which is like the programmes you have installed on your laptop. And this in turn generates the child's production of language - all the stuff you create with your laptop, like the cute photie of the kitten you just emailed to your cousin in New Zealand, the angry Twitter exchange, and your attempt to win £100 quid in Bella Caledonia's indy poster competition that turned out not to be such a great idea when you looked at it the next morning.

Chomsky's ideas did not enjoy universal support, and set off a whole chain of other research seeking either to prove or disprove his views, including the famous experiments to teach sign language to chimpanzees and other great apes - which produced mixed results. It also sparked off investigations into Universal Grammar, and the commonalities behind the rich diversity of human languages. Research and study based on Chomsky's contributions to linguistics, or research based on critiques of Chomsky, continue to this day.

Arguments rage on, because academics like disagreeing with one another - it's their job. But in one important sense Chomsky's once controversial opinion is now universally accepted, everyone agrees that the human ability to acquire language is hardwired into the brain before birth - although there is still little agreement about what exactly this hardwiring consists of. And everyone also agrees that whatever your take on the current incarnation of Chomsky's theory of grammar, his opinions cannot be ignored.

The point of this over extended discussion of Chomsky's contribution to linguistics, philosophy, and psychology is to show that he's not just some obscure academic best known for his trenchant criticisms of American foreign policy. Chomsky will go down in the annals of history as a figure comparable to Sigmund Freud or Charles Darwin. He changed the way we think about things.

And when you've got one of the world's leading intellectuals on your side, it knocks wee Dougie Alexander's and Rory the Tory's attempts at pseudointellectualism in defence of the Union into a U-KOK'ed bowler hat.

But there's another reason Chomsky's approval appeals to me personally if to no one else. In older Scots the word grammar came to mean a magical incantation, and then mutated further in sense and in sound to become the word glamour, meaning "enchantment" - which Walter Scott introduced into English whereupon it further shifted in meaning to signify fabulosity. Scotland's transforming itself, generating new possibilities, and we're changing the world with words. That's real magic. It's the transformational generative glamour of independence.

No wonder Chomsky approves.

26 April 2014

Contractual obligations

May 2011

Dear Westminster,

As an enthusiastic proponent of the privatisation of governmental services, which you have repeatedly promoted as a means to cost savings, greater efficiency and accountability, we trust that you will wholeheartedly embrace the fact that our board members have, after considerable consideration, resolved to take your views to their logical conclusion.

You will appreciate that we have already made numerous complaints via your call centres, which are conveniently open once every five years, to express our disapproval of a number of aspects of your service delivery. However your automatic dialing system permits only a choice between 4 shades of approval - press blue for enthusiastic austerity and privatisation, press red for austerity and privatisation with a sad face, press yellow for a ministerial motor for Danny Alexander, or press purple for swivel eyed lunacy.

Therefore, following intense discussions amongst the 4 million voting members of the board of the Scottish National Cooperative, the decision has been reached to put our contract with you for parliamentary services provision out for tender.

We feel it is appropriate to advise you that the board has received a bid from an alternative supplier, which promises significant cost savings, greater efficiency, and vastly improved accountability.

However, as our parliamentary services provider for 307 years, we hope that you will embrace this opportunity to demonstrate that we are, as you repeatedly claim, better together, and that you will submit a new bid to retain your existing contract. In turn, we anticipate your exciting proposals for service enhancements going forward.

Please rest assured that we will consider your application carefully and sympathetically. We look forward to hearing from you.

Yours faithfully

Scotland

******

February 2014

Dear Westminster,

Thank you very much for the reply from your Chief Executive, Mr David Cameron. We are disappointed that he chose to deliver his presentation to the Olympic Velodrome in London, and did not present it in person to members of our board. Indeed for a number of our board members the subliminal message of being told to get on yer bike by a Conservative in London provoked a reoccurrence of a distressing medical condition - PTSD (Post-Thatcher Stress Disorder).

While we are heartened that Mr Cameron expressed his deep affection for all things Caledonian, we could not fail to note that he did not give details of the improvements to service delivery which had been requested. We are hopeful that you will remedy this omission in future communications.

Please note that we have now received a detailed proposal from an alternative supplier, and look forward to your bettering this offer. We trust that this will not be problematic for your organisation, as we are, in your words, better together. However we cannot fail to note that until now you appear to have interpreted "better together" as "you'll be doomed without us". We are sure that this is merely a temporary lapse, and that you will shortly present the positive case for the union which you promised on receipt of our letter of 2011.

Yours faithfully,
Scotland

******

March 2014

Dear Westminster,

Thank you very much for the joint submissions from Mr George Osborne, Mr Ed Balls and Mr Danny Alexander. However you must appreciate our distress that your sales team's pitch was based on the surprising premise that your organisation has sole rights to a currency and central bank which we were under the impression we already owned jointly with the rest of your service users. This is a situation which we consider comparable to receiving a notification from our electricity supplier that they own our tv set, toaster, and the plug in spa foot bath we got as a Christmas present from Auntie Magrit, which now lives in the cupboard under the stairs along with the last remnants of the Scottish Lib Dems.

It is however regretable that none of the three gentlemen submitted themselves to questions from the floor after making their presentations. We can only assume that they are taking their cue from Mr Cameron and his repeated assertions that he is not getting involved in the debate while telling us we would be nothing without him.

We would also like to express our thanks for Mr José Manuel Barroso's communication, in which he was so ably enabled by Mr Andrew Marr. We have since discovered that following in the long and venerable tradition of Portuguese right wing politicians, Mr Barroso's intervention came in response to your offer to write him a letter of recommendation for a lucrative post with another organisation, and we would like to remind you that our board considers that a parliament which goes behind our back to make secret deals with foreign companies is a parliament which is unlikely to prove trustworthy. Indeed we have since received a number of communications from experts in the field of EU enlargement, who assure us that Mr Barroso's intervention was, if you will forgive our employment of technical EU bureaucratic jargon, a pile o pish.

We have therefore passed on your communications to Edinburgh resident JK Rowling, who is, as you are aware, a leading exponent of the art of fantasy fiction. We believe she may be able to make productive use of them now that she's killed off Voldemort.

We continue to await your positive case for the union with excited anticipation.

Yours faithfully,
Scotland

******

April 2014

Dear Westminster,

Thank you for the presentations from Mr Gordon Brown, Mr George Robertson and Mr Philip Hammond. They have indeed made a deep and lasting impression on our board members.

Mr Brown has now made three interventions on your behalf, each of which was apparently his first intervention in the discussion. We shall be charitable and assume that he forgot the first two. We must also bring to your attention another memory lapse on Mr Brown's part - it may not have been a good idea to present a warning on the future of pensions by a man who is perhaps best known for wrecking the pensions of millions of workers and whose moral compass is stuck on a permanent spin cycle. However his intervention does prompt us to put a question to you in return - did you actually think this one through? Indeed, have you thought anything through at all?

We are especially grateful for the entertaining impression of Dr Strangelove provided by Mr Robertson, who we are informed prefers to be known by the name Baron Robertson of Port Ellen KT GCMG FRSA FRSE PC. Mr Robertson warned of an apocalyptic scenario should our board choose to reject your services. Having been told for the previous two years that we are an insignificant nothing, poorer than Rwanda and with an international presence considerably less than that of San Marino, it was heartening to learn that our contract with you is all that stands between world peace and the end of civilisation as we know it. Who knew we possessed such influence? However we should advise you that in Scotland, we prefer to refer to Mr Robertson by the name "Psychotic Walter Mitty Wannabe".

We had not considered the eventuality of an invasion of lizard aliens from outer space, and are grateful to Mr Hammond for bringing this important matter to our attention. However we are of the view that a civilisation which possesses technology allowing it to successfully navigate the vast distances of interstellar space is unlikely to be deterred by a submarine which is incapable of making a successful orbit of the Isle of Skye.

We would also like to point out that, contrary to the impression given by your representatives, lizard aliens from planet Alicsammin are not the rival bidders for your existing contract. We are in fact proposing renationalisation, and intend to supply parliamentary services ourselves.

We cannot escape the impression that you do not in fact have any concept of what a "positive case for the union" might consist of. Please note that given you have now had some 2 years in which to make this presentation, we have little confidence that you will do so before the formal meeting of our board on 18th September.

Yours faithfully,

Scotland

******

26 April 2014

Dear Westminster,

You are running out of time until your contract is up for renewal, and we are running out of patience.

We have now come to the inescapable conclusion that your organisation is not in fact the world beating parliamentary services provider detailed in your glossy but misleading leaflets, but rather you are a bunch of clueless shysters who are only interested in furthering their own careers.

Please be advised that there are now less than 5 months until our full board meeting, and it is now looking increasingly unlikely that we will vote to continue with your services.

However should our board vote to cancel your contract, we are confident that following the market principles which you repeatedly promote, the cancellation will inspire you to remedy the deficiencies in service provision for your remaining customers in England, Wales and Northern Ireland. We consider this our lasting legacy to the union, a legacy which will have considerably more positive and lasting effects than anything you've done yourselves.

Yours faithfully

Scotland, your friends in the north

28 April 2014

The charge of the shite brigade

Alicsammin loves Vlad, who's currently impaling Ukraine on a pointy Russian stick. It's all over the media, so it must be true. Alicsammin just loves Crimean kebabs with a spicy oligarch sauce. Labour and the Tories, naturally, are outraged. Appalled. Shocked. Mortified. Unionist politicians would never do anything like that.

The remarks were made during an interview for GQ magazine, the interviewer was Alistair Campbell. Yes. That Alistair Campbell. He of dodgy dossier fame. Of course Alicsammin's comments about Putin were hedged about with enough qualifications to keep the dugs out the garden, but that didn't stop certain yappy wee Labour and Tory MSPs digging their way through the mud and crapping all over the lawn. What he said was that Putin had successfully restored the shattered pride of the Russian people, which had been ground into powder by the dissolution of the Soviet Union. He didn't say he approved of Putin's methods of doing so, in fact he explicitly said he didn't. The only gushing approval in his comments was of the Russian people. Not their political masters.

Of course Alicsammin didn't ask for Putin's help in the referendum campaign, that would be David Cameron who did that.

First things first. Alicsammin's opinions on foreign politicians are not relevant to the independence debate. We're not voting to express our approval or disapproval of Russian policies. We're voting to express our approval or disapproval of UK policies and the Westminster system of government. Unionist attempts to work a few anodyne comments by Alicsammin about an irrelevant issue into a reason for Scotland remaining under the Tory and Tory-lite governments of Westminster are a symptom of the poverty of their own arguments.

But they can't help themselves. They rush to criticise Alicsammin because they still believe that the referendum question is "Do you want Scotland to be an alicsammin country?" They're hoping no one will notice the even more gushing approval of a whole list of nasty dictators, oligarchs, strongmen, and out and out gangsters sprayed like a sewer outfall from the mouths of an even longer list of Labour and Tory politicians. Their attack on Scotland's First Minister boils down to - see that Alicsammin, he's just as bad as we are so he is. Which isn't exactly a glowing recommendation of the Westminster system.

But Alicsammin isn't as bad as they are. He's never accepted money or favours to promote an oligarch's interests. Which is more than can be said for certain Unionists. And that is a whole lot worse than highly qualified approval voiced in a magazine interview months before the object of their admiration invaded Crimea.

In 2012 the Guardian newspaper reported that Tony Blair had accepted US$13 million from the dictatorial government of Kazakhstan to whisper good words about President Nursultan Nazarbayev in the ear of Western governments. The Guardian article was titled "Blair's moral decline". Which is a bit misleading as it assumes that Blair occupied some moral high ground to fall from. But the man was always in the gutter. Meanwhile Peter Mandelson accepts lucrative fees for giving speeches and presentations to the Kazakh state enterprise Samruk, a wholly owned subsidiary of the Nazarbayev family. And according to the same Guardian report, Blair's media attack dog Alistair Campbell acted as go between for Blair, and was spotted on a visit to the Kazakh capital of Astana. That will be the same Alistair Campbell who interviewed Alicsammin for GQ magazine.

Nazarbayev's regime has been criticised by Human Rights Watch for its repeated abuse of human rights, imprisoning political dissidents, torture, disappearances, and closing down critical media outlets.

In May 2012, former Blairite cabinet minister and current BBC director of strategy James Purnell went to a dinner organised by Portland Communications, the Russian Government's publicists. He was accompanied by Andrew "Lord" Adonis, who now advises Ed Miliband on industrial policy. Adonis had a number of high profile posts in both Blair and Brown's governments - although he was never elected. He's a lardy lord. Portland Communications, which is a paid shill for an impressive list of repressive regimes, was founded by Tim Allan, formerly Blair's media advisor.

John Reid, who has been touted in some circles as the man to save the ailing Better Together campaign, is notorious for his contacts with unsavoury foreign politicians. Now that he's left politics he's touting himself as a performing artiste. You can book him for your wean's birthday party, and he'll blow up some balloons and advise on how best to get your dogs of war to perfom some tricks for the MoD. For a hefty fee or course. He infamously accepted a holiday invite from the Bosnian Serb war criminal Radovan Karadzic in 1993. Perhaps we should be kind, and concede that John just isn't a very good judge of character. According to respected journalist Iain McWhirter, John Reid is "an aggressive and unstable character who thrives on confrontation and conspiracy". So not a very nice human being then.

George Cataclysm Robertson is a board member of the Cohen Group, a US lobbying organisation founded by the right wing former US defence secretary William Cohen. The group uses its contacts with governments to promote the interests of some seriously dodgy points of view. The Cohen Group has reportedly provided invaluable assistance to the Turkish government in its attempts to deny the Armenian Genocide - for the fee of US$100,000. By their friends shall ye know them, eh George.

And that's just with a bit of light trowelling. I haven't done much in the way of digging into the numerous contacts between Unionist politicians and people you wouldn't want to invite round for tea.

Hypocrisy much? It's the charge of the shite brigade - into the valley of the death of their careers.

29 April 2014

Preparation Hate

I'm sick of this mince. Heartily pissed off, fed up, and growing increasingly angry. A short while back there were reports that the Better Together campaign was having meetings to rethink its failing strategy. A few weeks have passed, and it turns out that the new strategy is the same as the old strategy, just more of it. Fears, scares, slurs, threats, hypocrisy, attacks on alicsammin, and transparent psychological projection. The same as before, just at greater volume and with greater frequency.

Project Fear is not talking Scotland's language. They're the stereotypical British tourist abroad, thinking that they can make the natives understand English by speaking in a loud voice. Their blank incomprehension is met with SHOUTING MORE LOUDLY.

Already this week we've had Alicsammin being besties with Vlad, the accusation he's threatening to block international access to Norwegian waters in a fit of pique, wee Wullie Hague warning - again - that we'll be thrown out of the EU, accusations that Alicsammin is lying about the living wage, an allegation that the Yes campaign is illegally using front organisations to get around campaign spending limits, which conveniently merges with the warning that the Yes campaign is funded by homophobes, the warning that consumers in the rest of the UK would boycot products from an independent Scotland, yet another borderline racist cartoon in the supposedly liberal Guardian, and the claim that an independent Scotland would have to implement deep austerity cuts and won't be able to afford free education or health care.

And it's only Tuesday. We've still got Danny Alexander's speech to come. He's due to repeat his warnings of economic meltdown tomorrow. So that's something to look forward to.

We shouldn't complain really. It's still a failing strategy. More of the same will merely guarantee that it fails more comprehensively.

But I'm fed up with it. Because there's one thing I hate above everything else, and that's being patronised by duplicitous self-admiring morons who cherry pick facts in order to scare and intimidate. These people, our governors and directors, our leaders and would-be opinion formers, they're not clever, they're not big, and they are possessed of less insight than you find between the covers of a Ladybird Jack and Jill storybook.

Tomorrow's announcement from Danny Alexander will go the same way. See Danny. See Danny wave. See Danny tell off naughty Alicsammin. See Danny warn we'll all be poor. See Danny ride in a ministerial motor. See Danny fall flat on his smug overpaid over-promoted face.

Will this week's barrage of fearbombs convert any yes voters to don't knows? Will it persuade any don't knows that Westminster and the UK media really have our interests at heart. I wouldn't bet on it. Westminster is betting everything on it.

When this campaign started, the Union thought it was going to win handsomely. Alicsammin was just a minor irritation, soon to be salved with the balm of Westminster authority and a demonstration of their power. Scottish independence was going to be brushed aside, and everyone could return to business as usual.

I sigh in resignation every time another scarebomb bursts. And I'm actually interested in the debate. Project Fear never considered the effect of their tactics. They thought that a tidal wave of toxicity would deter the less involved from taking the question of independence seriously. Instead it's made them stop taking Project Fear seriously.

Alicsammin was jut a wee haemorrhoid in the arse of the Union, but the Project Fear couldn't help scratching it. The more it itched, the more they scratched, and the bigger their piles got. Now they're impacted and bleeding. If it wasn't for the Preparation Hate so lovingly concocted by the media, two parts bile three parts lie with a dash of venom in a litre of contempt, the arse would have fallen out of Better Together's campaign months ago. But their medicine has a toxic side effect. It exposed them for the incompetents that they really are. It exposed their disdain and arrogance. Who wants to be governed by people who know little about us, and what little they do know they hold in contempt?

They're not sitting comfortably now. We're getting it up them.

30 April 2014
Making plans for Nigel

Wee Michael Crick, political correspondent for Channel 4 news, could hardly contain himself. "This could be the most exciting by-election in my entire career as a political reporter," he gushed, after a Tory MP bearing an alarming resemblance to Ann Widdecombe in man-drag announced he'd be leaving parliament.

There was nothing honourable in the honourable member's announcement. Patrick Mercer, Eurosceptic MP for the constituency of Toryville in Toryshire, had been caught selling political influence to lobbyists and had been suspended from Westminster for six months in punishment. But he was going to fall on his sword, or rather, stick it into Davie Cameron, and provoke a potentially embarrassing by-election.

But that wasn't the real dishonour casting shame and disgrace on the entire institution. The really dishonourable bit was that Patrick had got into all this bother for just a couple of thousand quid, and not for the promise of an extremely lucrative six figure career, a directorship and a consultancy. We already knew MPs whore themselves to commercial interests, but they're not high class sex workers plying their trade in exclusive hotels, they're dockside rent boys who'll offer a knee trembler up an alley for a tenner. It's not the thought that Westminster politicians sell themselves that's so offensive. It's that they're so bloody cheap.

But what was getting Michael Crick all excited was that the by-election would be held shortly after the European elections and the local elections in England, when it's expected that UKIP will perform strongly and could even become the leading party in terms of vote share in England. Michael thought likely that Nigel Farage, UKIP's bawbag in chief, would stand for election and could become UKIP's first MP, inflating the right wing populist bubble even more and increasing pressure on Davie Cameron to hold an in-out referendum on EU membership.

Torygasm upon torygasm, Michael mused about the possiblity that the Tories might respond by sending in the clowns, and put Boris Johnson forward as candidate. Boris wants Davie's job, because the Tories think that the way to make up for the unpopularity of a posh rich Etonian PM is to choose another rich Etonian who's even posher.

And that's what could have been the most important and exciting by-election of Michael Crick's career. A showdown between a rightwing Thatcherite bawbag and a rightwing Thatcherite clown. One wants to abolish the Scottish parliament and replace it with a glorified Commons committee, the other thinks that a pound of government spending is better spent in Croydon than in Strathclyde.

But by Wednesday morning Nige has announced that he's not a bawbag, he's a crapbag, and he won't be standing in the by-election. It would be a distraction, Nigel said, and he'd look like a carpetbagger. Though why that should worry a man who looks like a spiv wasn't explained.

The real reason of course is that Nige couldn't be sure he'd win, the constituency has a huge Tory majority and UKIP would require an unprecedented swing of over 25% in order to take the seat. And if he stood and lost, he'd have burst his own bubble. Especially since

Labour has no chance of winning and would not have campaigned too hard in order to give the Tory candidate a better chance, whereas the Lib Dems may not have stood at all. UKIP is a major threat to the interests of the established parties, and they'll cheerfully plot together to keep them at bay - which is the only similarity between Nige's inward looking little Englandism and the outward looking Scottish independence movement.

Other Tory commentators had mused that it's too early for Boris to return to Westminster. Boris is waiting for the outcome of the Scottish referendum, if there's a yes vote Davie will come under intense pressure to resign, then the blonde clown can do his Bonnie Prince Boris impression and return like the king over the watter.

But although the bawclown facedown isn't going to happen, the episode is further illustration of both the vast gulf which has opened up between Scottish politics and the politics of England. What place does Scotland have in a Union whose politics are dominated by the Tory party and its mutant UKIP offspring.

Labour doesn't have the answer, Labour voters are deserting Ed's mini band for UKIP in ever increasing numbers. Labour is also forced to tack to the right, or more accurately even further to the right, in order to forestall the loss of its support Nige's band of swivel eyed loons.

Still if nothing else, the weather forecast would be much more interesting if UKIP was in power. We'd have much more to hurl abuse at than a misshapen map. We'd be getting told there was a surge in sodomy in Shropshire leading to heavy showers, and an outbreak of oral sex in overcast Ongar.

But UKIP continues to gain in strength. And that's not a joke.

They tell us they don't want Scotland to become a foreign country. But by their own actions, their own politics, they show us that Scotland already is a foreign country. One they neither care about nor know much about.

Better together with this farago of farce? You've got to be joking. We've got to make our own plans for Nigel, and get away from this.

End of Volume 1

Lightning Source UK Ltd.
Milton Keynes UK
UKOW01f0540101017
310712UK00005B/192/P